THE BUSINESS VALUE OF AGILE SOFTWARE METHODS

MAXIMIZING ROI WITH JUST-IN-TIME PROCESSES AND DOCUMENTATION

THE BUSINESS VALUE OF AGILE SOFTWARE METHODS

MAXIMIZING ROI WITH JUST-IN-TIME PROCESSES AND DOCUMENTATION

Dr. David F. Rico
Dr. Hasan H. Sayani
Dr. Saya Sone

Foreword by Dr. Jeffrey V. Sutherland

Copyright 2009 by J. Ross Publishing

ISBN: 978-1-60427-031-0

Printed and bound in the U.S.A. Printed on acid-free paper
10 9 8 7 6 5 4 3 2 1

Library of Congress Cataloging-in-Publication Data

Rico, David F., 1964–
  The business value of agile software methods: maximizing ROI
with just-in-time processes and documentation / by David F. Rico,
Hasan H. Sayani, and Saya Sone.
     p. cm.
  Includes bibliographical references and index.
  ISBN 978-1-60427-031-0 (hardcover : alk. paper)
  1. Agile software development. 2. Computer software—Development—
Costs.
I. Sayani, Hasan H., 1938- II. Sone, Saya, 1963- III. Title.
  QA76.76.D47R558 2009
  005.1—dc22

                                                        2009032545

Direct all inquiries to J. Ross Publishing, Inc., 5765 N. Andrews Way, Fort Lauderdale, FL 33309.

Phone: (954) 727-9333
Fax: (561) 892-0700
Web: www.jrosspub.com

Dedication

Dr. David F. Rico

This book is dedicated to my wife, Celia, and our four children, David, Serena, Faith, and Christian. May we find the rest and peace we so eagerly desire. This book is also dedicated to my parents, who created a sense of purpose in their children, a relentless desire for learning, and a foundation to pursue our dreams.

Dr. Hasan H. Sayani

This book is dedicated to my students. Their curiosity and thirst for knowledge is truly inspiring! Especially the students at the University of Maryland University College, who, while working full-time and participating in rich family lives, find the time to dedicate to the advancement of their skills and knowledge.

Dr. Saya Sone

This book is dedicated to my children, Sanshiro and Sid, who have sacrificed so many of their formative years to support their mother in this journey. They have inspired their mother to seek a better way of life for her family and have been an immense source of pride, energy, joy, and happiness.

Contents

Acknowledgments .... *xiii*
About the Authors .... *xv*
Foreword .... *xvii*
Preface .... *xix*
Web Added Value™ .... *xxi*

Chapter 1—Introduction to Agile Methods 1
1.1   What Are Agile Methods? 1
1.2   Why Agile Methods Emerged 2
1.3   How Agile Methods Emerged 3
1.4   First Agile Methods 3
1.5   Agile Methods Explosion 4
1.6   Summary 5
1.7   Further Readings 5

Chapter 2—Values of Agile Methods 7
2.1   Major Values of Agile Methods 7
2.2   Customer Collaboration 8
2.3   Individuals and Interactions 9
2.4   Working Software 9
2.5   Responding to Change 10
2.6   Summary 10
2.7   Further Readings 11

Chapter 3—History of Agile Methods 13
3.1   Project Management 13
3.2   Software Methods 14
3.3   Software Standards 15
3.4   Process Improvement 15
3.5   Agile Methods 16
3.6   Summary 17
3.7   Further Readings 17

Chapter 4—Antecedents of Agile Methods **19**
4.1 New Product Development..20
4.2 Systems Engineering..20
4.3 Software Project Management...21
4.4 Software Engineering...21
4.5 Lean Thinking 22
4.6 Summary..23
4.7 Further Readings 23

Chapter 5—Types of Agile Methods... **25**
5.1 Scrum...25
5.2 Extreme Programming..27
5.3 Dynamic Systems Development..27
5.4 Feature Driven Development 30
5.5 Crystal Methods 31
5.6 Summary..32
5.7 Further Readings 33

Chapter 6—Practices of Agile Methods.. **35**
6.1 Onsite Customers...35
6.2 Pair Programming 37
6.3 Test-Driven Development 38
6.4 Refactoring..39
6.5 Release Planning..40
6.6 Summary..41
6.7 Further Readings 41

Chapter 7—Agile Project Management **43**
7.1 Initiating Process Group 44
7.2 Planning Process Group...44
7.3 Executing Process Group..45
7.4 Monitoring Process Group...45
7.5 Closing Process Group 46
7.6 Summary..47
7.7 Further Readings 47

Chapter 8—Agile Software Engineering.. **49**
8.1 Requirements 50
8.2 Architecture 50
8.3 Design 51
8.4 Construction 51
8.5 Testing...52
8.6 Summary..53
8.7 Further Readings 53

Chapter 9—Agile Support Processes **55**
9.1   Documentation 55
9.2   Configuration Management 56
9.3   Quality Assurance..57
9.4   Verification and Validation..57
9.5   Maintenance...58
9.6   Summary...59
9.7   Further Readings...59

Chapter 10—Agile Tools and Technologies **61**
10.1   Workflow Tools...62
10.2   Collaboration Tools...62
10.3   Development Tools..63
10.4   Support Tools 63
10.5   Technologies 64
10.6   Summary..65
10.7   Further Readings 65

Chapter 11—Comparison of Agile Methods **67**
11.1   Practices 67
11.2   Pros and Cons...68
11.3   Flexibility 70
11.4   Risks..71
11.5   Usage...72
11.6   Summary..73
11.7   Further Readings 73

Chapter 12—Agile Metrics and Models **75**
12.1   Traditional Measures..75
12.2   Customer Collaboration 76
12.3   Individuals and Interactions..77
12.4   Working Software 78
12.5   Responding to Change..79
12.6   Summary..80
12.7   Further Readings 81

Chapter 13—Surveys of Agile Methods.. **83**
13.1   Microsoft...84
13.2   UMUC 85
13.3   AmbySoft...86
13.4   IT Agile 87
13.5   Version One..88

13.6   Summary 89
13.7   Further Readings 90

Chapter 14—Costs and Benefits of Agile Methods 91
14.1   Pair Programming 92
14.2   Test-Driven Development 93
14.3   Extreme Programming 94
14.4   Scrum 95
14.5   Agile Methods 96
14.6   Summary 97
14.7   Further Readings 97

Chapter 15—ROI Metrics for Agile Methods 99
15.1   Cost Metric 99
15.2   Benefit Metric 100
15.3   ROI Metric 101
15.4   NPV Metric 102
15.5   Real Options Analysis Metric 102
15.6   Summary 103
15.7   Further Readings 104

Chapter 16—Measures of Agile Methods 105
16.1   Pair Programming 106
16.2   Test-Driven Development 107
16.3   Extreme Programming 108
16.4   Scrum 109
16.5   Agile Methods 110
16.6   Summary 111
16.7   Further Readings 112

Chapter 17—Costs of Agile Methods 113
17.1   Pair Programming 113
17.2   Test-Driven Development 115
17.3   Extreme Programming 116
17.4   Scrum 118
17.5   Agile Methods 118
17.6   Summary 119
17.7   Further Readings 120

Chapter 18—Benefits of Agile Methods 121
18.1   Pair Programming 123
18.2   Test-Driven Development 123

18.3   Extreme Programming...124
18.4   Scrum..125
18.5   Agile Methods 125
18.6   Summary..127
18.7   Further Readings 129

Chapter 19—Return on Investment of Agile Methods 131
19.1   Pair Programming 131
19.2   Test-Driven Development 132
19.3   Extreme Programming...134
19.4   Scrum..136
19.5   Agile Methods 137
19.6   Summary..138
19.7   Further Readings 138

Chapter 20—Net Present Value of Agile Methods 141
20.1   Pair Programming 143
20.2   Test-Driven Development 143
20.3   Extreme Programming...144
20.4   Scrum..146
20.5   Agile Methods 147
20.6   Summary..147
20.7   Further Readings 148

Chapter 21—Real Options Analysis of Agile Methods...................... 149
21.1   Pair Programming 151
21.2   Test-Driven Development 151
21.3   Extreme Programming...152
21.4   Scrum..153
21.5   Agile Methods 155
21.6   Summary..156
21.7   Further Readings 157

Chapter 22—Business Value of Agile Methods 159
22.1   Costs 159
22.2   Benefits...160
22.3   Return on Investment..161
22.4   Net Present Value..163
22.5   Real Options Analysis..164
22.6   Summary..165
22.7   Further Readings 165

Chapter 23—Agile vs. Traditional Methods.......................................167
23.1   Agile vs. Traditional Costs 168
23.2   Agile vs. Traditional Benefits...169
23.3   Agile vs. Traditional ROI 170
23.4   Agile vs. Traditional NPV 171
23.5   Agile vs. Traditional ROA...172
23.6   Summary 173
23.7   Further Readings...173

Chapter 24—Future of Agile Methods 175
24.1   Coaching and Mentoring 175
24.2   Values-Driven Thinking 176
24.3   Hybrid Agile Methods 177
24.4   Complexity and Scalability..177
24.5   Quality and Reliability..178
24.6   Documentation and Maintenance.......................................178
24.7   Virtual Distributed Teams...179
24.8   Technological Flexibility 180
24.9   Agile Metrics and Models 180
24.10   Agile Training and Education 181
24.11   Crossing the Chasm...181
24.12   Summary..182
24.13   Further Readings 183

Appendix.. 185
A.   Pair Programming Formulas...185
B.   Test-Driven Development Formulas...187
C.   Extreme Programming Formulas 188
D.   Scrum Formulas..189
E.   Agile Methods Formulas..190

Bibliography..193
Index..203

Acknowledgments

I want to personally thank Dr. Saya Sone for inspiring this research. She insisted that we marry the concepts of agile methods and return on investment to quantify their business value. I'd also like to thank Dr. Hasan H. Sayani for his patient guidance and leadership over the years and for allowing me to introduce agile methods to the Software Engineering graduate program at the University of Maryland University College. Special thanks to Dr. Jeffrey V. Sutherland who invited me to present my ideas on agile methods at the Hawaii International Conference on System Sciences. Hawaii's Big Island will always have a special place in my heart. I owe a debt of gratitude to the agile methods community, who bore the heat of the day with their seminal research, papers, conferences, textbooks, leadership, and personal guidance, and for welcoming me with open arms.

Dr. David F. Rico

I want to personally thank Mike Cohn for helping to make this book more valuable by reviewing some of our early information, assumptions, and data about the business value of agile methods. In addition, I want to thank my colleagues Doug Mangold, Ed Henze, Pushpal Rangwala, Jennifer Briede, Mike Russell, and Matt Leibel for their encouragement and support of my time in co-authoring this book.

Dr. Saya Sone

About the Authors

Dr. David F. Rico has been a technical leader in support of NASA, DARPA, DISA, SPAWAR, USAF, AFMC, NAVAIR, CECOM, and MICOM for over 25 years. He has led, managed, or participated in over 20 organization change initiatives using agile methods, Lean Six Sigma, ISO 9001, CMMI®, SW-CMM®, Enterprise Architecture, Baldrige, and DoD 5000. He specializes in IT investment analysis, IT project management, and IT-enabled change. He has been an international keynote speaker, published numerous articles, and written or contributed to six textbooks. He holds a BS in computer science, MS in software engineering, and a DM in information systems. He is also a certified PMP and CSM.

Dr. Hasan H. Sayani has been in industry and academia for over 40 years. His interests are information systems, information systems development, life cycle methods and tools, and semantic database management systems. He has taught at the University of Maryland-College Park in the Information Systems Management program. He co-founded a firm that built systems for various commercial and governmental organizations. He has participated in various professional and standardization organizations, including IEEE, ACM, CASE, ANS, CODASYL, DoD, and CALS. He holds a BS, MS, and PhD from the University of Michigan.

Dr. Saya Sone has worked for multiple Fortune 500 companies, such as CSC, BT, and AOL. She has led numerous data center design, software development, marketing, and customer support projects. She has managed a corporate-wide rollout of agile methods and Scrum at a major U.S. electronic commerce firm. Her field of specialty is agile project management. She holds an MA in project management and a DBA in information systems. She is also a certified project management professional, as well as a certified Scrum practitioner.

Foreword

One of the most prevalent questions of our time is "What is the business value of agile methods?" People want to know what, if any, the essential benefits of agile methods are. Why do they want to know this? Well, for several reasons. They want to know if there are any good reasons for using agile methods. If they are asked to use them or ask other people to use agile methods, they need to know the benefits. So, it comes down to the question "What is the business case or business justification for agile methods?" Or simply "What is the return on investment of agile methods?"

But there's a deeper issue that needs to be addressed first. Why use agile methods at all? Why not use non-agile methods, referred to as "traditional methods"? The answer is all too familiar for those of us in the information technology field. Traditional methods are project management, systems engineering, and software engineering. It might be the project management, systems engineering, or software engineering body of knowledge. It could be a process improvement or quality management system standard. "Document" everything is at the heart of traditional methods.

So, why use traditional methods? Traditional methods such as systems and software engineering standards have evolved for a number of reasons. They are meant to help people plan, manage, and execute projects. At the highest level, traditional methods are meant to help engineers develop, operate, and maintain computer systems. On another level, traditional methods are meant to help engineers define customer needs, devise a technical solution, and evaluate computer systems. Traditional methods come down to documenting system development from conception to retirement, which is done to improve quality, productivity, and cycle time.

Agile methods are posited as a better alternative to traditional methods. Traditional methods are accused of focusing on the wrong drivers of business value: contracts, processes, tools, documentation, and project plans. These encompass a linear process of planning, analysis, design, development, and testing, whereas agile methods maximize business value by applying just enough discipline to build systems in smaller pieces.

Agile methods are accused of not supporting the total life cycle of a system—that is, development, operation, and maintenance. Furthermore, they are criticized for not using project management, systems engineering, or software engineering discipline. And they are accused of not recognizing the business value of cradle-to-grave documentation. The theory is that system quality cannot be achieved without a thoroughly documented system life cycle. Proponents of agile methods are said to be undisciplined because they don't produce traditional system and software engineering documentation.

This book directly addresses all of these issues, and it challenges many of the fundamental theories underlying traditional and agile methods. The authors discuss both methods' historical roots, the environment in which they emerged, and the reasons they came to be. Defined are the values and practices of both traditional and agile methods. By placing traditional and agile methods in their proper context (i.e., origin and purpose), the authors posit that agile methods are the evolution of 20th-century management thought rather than its antithesis. Used for creating new products, agile methods are based on values, principles, and discipline. The authors demonstrate that agile methods are right-sized, just-enough, and just-in-time approaches for maximizing business value.

Dr. Jeffrey V. Sutherland

Preface

The purpose of this book is to illustrate the business value of using agile methods to create innovative software products. It provides a comprehensive methodology for estimating the costs and benefits of agile methods using bottom-line dollars and cents. Using cost of quality, total cost of ownership, and total life cycle costs, we estimate return on investment and net present value. For the first time, the use of advanced measures, such as real options for quantifying the business value of agile methods, is simplified.

Agile methods are right-sized, just-enough, and just-in-time ways to manage the development of innovative software products. That is, they are a streamlined and highly efficient way to reduce cycle time and bring new products to market as fast as possible. Because agile methods increase business value by delivering the products customers need to successfully compete in the market, they are inextricably linked to valuation techniques such as return on investment, net present value, and real options.

As agile methods are still a new phenomenon, the agile methods community is immersed in the education, adoption, and culture change process. Therefore, little data exist on how to quantify the business value of agile methods in economic terms, such as return on investment. Thus began our journey on how to identify the costs and benefits of agile methods and how to quantify their business value. We didn't stop until we quantified their value using return on investment, net present value, and real options.

This book is a self-contained reference guide to agile methods, providing a comprehensive introduction, description, and history. It links the creation of agile methods to major disciplines, such as project management, systems engineering, and lean production. We describe the major types of agile methods and the major forms of best practices. For linking the use of agile methods to major industry standards, such as the project management and software engineering bodies of knowledge, we provide a roadmap.

This book disarms explosive issues such as documentation, configuration management, quality assurance, and maintenance. As a rare treat, it introduces a family of metrics and models specially designed for agile methods. We provide one of the only summaries of survey research on the costs and benefits of agile methods. More importantly, we give the first comprehensive compilation of cost and benefit data on agile methods from an analysis of hundreds of research studies.

This book provides a suite of metrics for estimating the business value of agile methods. Based on real-world data, it then introduces the industry's first top-down models for estimating the costs and benefits of agile methods. Since the inception of the Black-Scholes formulas, it illustrates the first simple-to-use parametric models of real options. Finally, this book closes with numerous examples on how to estimate the costs, benefits, return on investment, net present value, and real options of agile methods.

This book is designed for multiple audiences: for those who are new to agile methods and want to learn more; for those who want to deepen their knowledge of agile methods and grow beyond its simple dogma; and for scholars and students of software engineering who want to understand agile methods. More importantly, it is designed to help executives, change leaders, and managers to learn, understand, master, and apply concepts related to the business value of agile methods.

As a simple foundation for understanding the business value of agile methods, this book marks a significant milestone in their history. However, it is only the humble beginning of a longer conversation, journey, and deeper understanding of agile methods.

 Web Added Value™

Free value-added materials available from
the Download Resource Center at www.jrosspub.com

At J. Ross Publishing we are committed to providing today's professional with practical, hands-on tools that enhance the learning experience and give readers an opportunity to apply what they have learned. That is why we offer free ancillary materials available for download on this book and all participating Web Added Value™ publications. These online resources may include interactive versions of material that appears in the book or supplemental templates, worksheets, models, plans, case studies, proposals, spreadsheets and assessment tools, among other things. Whenever you see the WAV™ symbol in any of our publications, it means bonus materials accompany the book and are available from the Web Added Value Download Resource Center at www.jrosspub.com.

Downloads available for The Business Value of Agile Software Methods include:

- **Agile Methods Cost & Benefit Summary Brief**: A briefing designed for the CEO of a leading agile methods consulting firm to successfully win new business even in today's difficult economy.
- **Agile Methods Cost & Benefit Training Brief**: A comprehensive training brief containing an introduction to agile methods, agile deliverables, ROI metrics, ROI methodology, and ROI summary briefed to numerous U.S. government agencies and contractors, Fortune 500 firms, software conferences, professional societies, and small groups.
- **Agile Methods Cost & Benefit Summary White Paper**: One of the first comprehensive studies of the costs and benefits of agile methods published in an international journal (replete with numerous top-down, parametric metrics, models, and measurements).
- **Agile Methods Cost & Benefit Survey Spreadsheet**: One of the first comprehensive databases on the costs and benefits of agile methods derived from an analysis of over 300 scholarly research experiments, case studies, and project reports (replete with graphical reports and bibliographic references).
- **Agile Methods Productivity & Quality Survey Spreadsheet**: A database containing cost and quality measurements from over 29 real-world projects using agile methods for deriving top-down parametric models of the costs and benefits of agile methods.

- **Agile Methods Business Value Calculator Spreadsheet**: The industry's first ROI calculator for estimating the business value of agile methods (including costs, benefits, benefit-to-cost ratio, breakeven point, return on investment, net present value, project risk, and real options).
- **Agile Methods Cost & Benefit Metrics**: A complete family of simple-to-use parametric models for estimating the business value of agile methods (including costs, benefits, benefit-to-cost ratio, return on investment, net present value, and the industry's first parametric forms of real options simplified for executives, managers, and engineers, since the inception of the Black-Scholes formulas over 30 years ago).
- **Agile Methods Business Value Metrics**: One of the first sets of metrics specially designed for use with agile methods (rather than just another adaptation of traditional, industrial-age metrics such as effort and defect density).
- **Agile Methods Policies & Procedures**: A complete set of project management templates for use with agile methods based on Extreme Programming's Release Planning Methodology (designed to extinguish the myth that agile methods do not have any software engineering documentation discipline).

1

Introduction to Agile Methods

Agile methods are an important new paradigm for maximizing the business value of creating new software products. They are part of the fields of innovation, new product development, systems engineering, and software engineering. Agile methods are a contemporary form of concurrent engineering, cross-functional teams, and overlapping development. They are useful for creating software products in both the commercial marketplace as well as the government sector, particularly for rapidly developing innovative product ideas.

Consisting of right-sized, just-enough, and just-in-time processes and documentation for developing software, agile methods have just enough discipline to capture customer needs, plan projects, and develop high-quality software products. Focused on creating software products that satisfy customer needs without unnecessary bureaucracy, they are the perfect tool for maximizing business value by rapidly responding to market needs with innovative solutions. Agile methods are a win-win solution for most stakeholders.

Agile methods bring high-quality, innovative software to market in the fastest and most cost-effective manner, solving issues such as how to: (1) innovate, (2) manage product development, and (3) ensure quality. Rather than a 19th-century, industrial-era manufacturing process, they are a customer-focused way to develop products and an efficient alternative to traditional document-driven process improvement and systems engineering standards.

1.1 What Are Agile Methods?

Agile methods are contemporary approaches for creating new software based on customer collaboration, teamwork, iterative development, and response to change.

Combining communication and interpersonal trust with a flexible management and development framework, they contain just enough process to capture customer needs in the form of user stories and to rapidly create working software. However, the keys to agile methods are rich, high-context communications with customers along with cohesive teamwork.

There are numerous forms of agile methods, such as Extreme Programming, Scrum, Dynamic Systems Development, Feature Driven Development, Crystal Methods, and many more. Open source software is also considered an agile method. Four values are common to all agile methods: (1) customer collaboration, (2) teamwork, (3) iterative development, and (4) adaptability. Each of the major types of agile methods embraces these values in a unique way. However, it is the best elements of each that represent the body of knowledge for agile methods.

For instance, Extreme Programming utilizes the practices of release planning, user stories, pair programming, and much more. Scrum brings us backlogs, sprints, daily standups, and retrospectives. And open source software uses right-sized, just-enough, just-in-time documentation and collaboration. Although proponents of each feel their method is sufficient for software development, it is the basic premise of this book that the best practices among all of the methods represent the essence of agile methods. Furthermore, this book posits the notion that the values of agile methods outweigh the rules and practices of any one agile method. And we are not alone in that viewpoint.

1.2 Why Agile Methods Emerged

Agile methods emerged in the 1990s for a specific reason: to successfully create new software that satisfies customer needs. Agile methods are really the convergence of multiple phenomena: inexpensive computers, powerful and easy-to-use information technologies, and the desire to succeed. Agile methods are also the result of a convergence of technologies: large process improvement models, large software engineering standards, and large methodologies. Although the creators of agile methods tried to use these large models, standards, and methodologies to create new software products, these projects failed time and time again.

This was an auspicious beginning for what we now know as agile methods. When agile methods were born, large software engineering models, standards, and processes were getting even larger. Rapid Application Development, the Software Capability Maturity Model®, and IEEE standards were hitting their stride with more to come. Traditional methods were based on documented project plans, large-requirements documents, and multi-year project life cycles. However, traditional approaches to software development based on manufacturing processes led to minimal project success. Not even the good ones based on earned-value management and quality-control processes, resulting in zero defects seemed to help.

From 1991 to 1998, at least five major types of agile methods emerged to help projects succeed in lieu of the old ones: Crystal Methods, Scrum, Dynamic Systems Development, Feature Driven Development, and Extreme Programming, in that order. It was a quiet counter-revolution to mega-standards such as the Software Capability Maturity Model® and IEEE standards, against which agile methods were pitted.

1.3 How Agile Methods Emerged

At first, the creators of agile methods attempted to use some of the early traditional methods to manage their software projects. However, these were ineffective, projects were failing, and the creators of agile methods weren't obtaining new business, which often led to lawsuits. Thus, the creators of agile methods started with a clean slate, threw away the old methods, and did what was necessary to succeed. One of the first agile methods was Scrum, which was based on product backlogs, sprints, daily standups, and product owners, and which adapted ideas from new product development approaches from the 1980s, such as iterative development and teamwork.

With an odd mix of customer interaction, iterative development, teamwork, and not much more, Scrum projects began to succeed. Scrum opposed the major values of traditional methods: contracts, processes and tools, documentation, and project plans. Project success was a major result of agile methods such as Scrum, because it was created to save failing projects. Success within traditional methods used manufacturing metrics, such as effort, cost, productivity, schedule, quality, and reliability. However, the creators of Scrum valued project success much more, because it translated directly into customer satisfaction.

The creators of Scrum felt that detailed project plans, requirement documents, and methods didn't contribute to successful projects. Instead, they advocated requirements, such as informal features, product backlogs, and sprints, as well as project plans, such as release and sprint plans. They believed in processes, as long as they didn't stand in the way of delivering valuable software in 30-day sprints. However, Scrum's creators felt that documentation led to poor communication and that informal daily standup meetings and sprint reviews were a far better alternative.

1.4 First Agile Methods

Crystal Methods came to light as an offshoot of object-oriented methodologies from the 1980s merged with other agile practices. Created in 1994, Dynamic Systems Development, an offshoot of Rapid Application Development, was classified as an agile method, as was Feature Driven Development, an object-oriented method created in 1997 to save failed projects. Extreme Programming, originating around 1998, was clearly the capstone of the era of the 1990s when agile methods emerged. Extreme Programming was a confluence of Scrum, Participatory Design, Rapid Application Development, and many others.

Extreme Programming was created to save a failed payroll system at the Chrysler Corporation. There is some evidence to show that Scrum may have been used as a basis for the creation of Extreme Programming, which was an amalgamation of practices, including release planning, user stories, test-driven development, refactoring, pair programming, and onsite customer. In 1999, Extreme Programming was introduced to the masses, and the rest, as they say, is history. Although Extreme Programming seemed to enter the scene with a whimper rather than a bang, it soon became the favorite among methodologists.

In 2001, 17 methodologists gathered to discuss agile methods and their new-found success, and to decide the future of agile methods. They defined the Agile Manifesto consisting of four major values: (1) customer collaboration over contract negotiation, (2) individuals and interactions over processes and tools, (3) working software over comprehensive documentation, and (4) responding to change over following a plan. Although these values seem superficial, they represented a fundamental revolution in software engineering. They are not just opinions but engineering principles.

1.5 Agile Methods Explosion

Four key events precipitated the explosion of agile methods: (1) the creation of Scrum; (2) the creation of Extreme Programming; (3) the emergence of Crystal Methods, Dynamic Systems Development, and Feature Driven Development; and (4) the creation of the Agile Manifesto. However, the marquee event had to be the publication of Extreme Programming in 1999. Extreme Programming did three things: it (1) promised project success, (2) introduced 13 simple practices, and (3) was a big departure from traditional process- and document-driven methods.

The international community was yearning for something new, and Extreme Programming was the fulfillment of those basic desires. Since the 1950s, the software community had been applying traditional methods, and it simply couldn't stomach another one. In particular, the Europeans took to Extreme Programming because it was well-suited to their culture of Participatory Design. They started pair programming, enlisting onsite customers, and knocked down the cubicle walls to open up the workspaces.

By 2002, approximately 67% of leading-edge software developers who elected to use methodologies preferred Extreme Programming. European, Canadian, and Middle Eastern universities began researching, teaching, and writing about agile methods. Conferences dedicated to agile methods sprung up overnight, attracting thousands. Hundreds of papers and 75 books emerged on various topics associated with agile methods. Over the years, Scrum has become the most popular agile method, and agile methods are being applied in ways not previously imagined.

1.6 Summary

Agile methods are fundamentally new approaches created in the 1990s for developing software and to save failing software projects. They are based on customer collaboration, teamwork, iterative development, and adaptability to change-values not unique to agile methods but common in the fields of innovation and new product development. In fact, Scrum was based directly on new product development paradigms and served as a basis for other agile methods. Agile methods amount to right-sized, just-enough, and just-in-time processes and documentation for creating new software products.

Agile methods stand in direct opposition to the values of traditional methods, such as contract negotiation, processes and tools, comprehensive documentation, and following a plan. More importantly, agile methods were created to ensure project success rather than simply adherence to industrial age manufacturing measures such as earned value, programming productivity, and defect density. Communication is valued highly within agile methods, whereas documentation is seen as the key to quality and maintainability in traditional methods.

Within the value of individuals and interactions are principles such as teamwork, interpersonal trust, and communication quality. Attributes such as talent, skill, experience, and programming ability are also buried deep within this agile method value. When you add this up, agile methods amount to extremely talented individuals; just-enough, just-in-time communications, processes, and documentation; and frequent software deliveries. This creates a double-loop feedback system, resulting in project success and maximum business value for all stakeholders. Agile methods fulfill what traditional methods simply cannot do.

1.7 Further Readings

Argyris, C. (1976). Single-loop and double-loop models in research on decision making. *Administrative Science Quarterly, 21*(3), 363–375.

Carmel, E., Whitaker, R. D., & George, J. F. (1993). PD and joint application design: A transatlantic comparison. *Communications of the ACM, 36*(4), 40–48.

DeGrace, P., & Stahl, L. H. (1990). *Wicked problems, righteous solutions: A catalogue of modern software engineering paradigms*. Englewood Cliffs, NJ: Prentice Hall.

Gane, C. (1987). *Rapid systems development*. New York, NY: Rapid Systems Development.

Greenbaum, J., & Kyng, M. (1991). *Design at work: Cooperative design of computer systems*. Hillsdale, NJ: Lawrence Erlbaum.

Martin, J. (1991). *Rapid application development*. New York, NY: Macmillan.

Millington, D., & Stapleton, J. (1995). Developing a RAD standard. *IEEE Software, 12*(5), 54–56.

Muller, M. J., & Kuhn, S. (1993). Participatory design. *Communications of the ACM, 36*(6), 24–28.

Wood, J., & Silver, D. (1989). *Joint application design.* New York, NY: John Wiley & Sons.

2

Values of Agile Methods

Agile methods are somewhat unique in that they are based on a set of values and principles. In one sense, agile methods are an outgrowth of the plethora of rapid development methodologies emerging in the 1980s. Some of these software methodologies, notably Rapid Application Development and its successor, Dynamic Systems Development, came replete with their own manifestos, values, and principles. In effect, agile methods are a values-based, or a principles-based, development approach for creating new software products.

Five major types of agile methods emerged in the 1990s: (1) Crystal Methods, (2) Scrum, (3) Dynamic Systems Development, (4) Feature Driven Development, and (5) Extreme Programming. While some were direct spinoffs of rapid and object-oriented methods in the 1980s, others were simply spinoffs of one another. At first glance, the five major types have little in common. In 2001, the creators of agile methods came together to study the commonalities of their approaches and formed the Agile Manifesto.

The Agile Manifesto outlined four major values of agile methods, along with 12 broad principles. What the creators learned in those fateful days in Snowbird, Utah, is that their methods had a lot in common. They also learned something else: that they shared a common disdain for the values of traditional methods (e.g., contracts, processes, tools, documentation, and project plans). Traditional methods became known as plan-driven methods. Agile methods had a better answer which led to project success.

2.1 Major Values of Agile Methods

The four major values of agile methods are: (1) customer collaboration over contract negotiation, (2) individuals and interactions over processes and tools, (3) working software over comprehensive documentation, and (4) responding to change over following a plan. These basic values are repeated again and again in this book. This is no accident. The theme of this book is how to achieve business value (e.g., return on investment) using agile methods. Be prepared to recite the values of agile methods.

First, we're going to tell you what we will discuss in this book. Then, we're going to tell it to you. Finally, we're going to tell you what we told you. That is, there is business value to be obtained from using agile methods. And why not? Isn't a new software product supposed to provide customers with an exciting new capability? That is, without the software product, there is little or no capability. And, with a new software product, there is more capability. Why else would customers pay for such a product? Besides, aren't agile methods supposed to ensure project success every time? If so, then using agile methods creates business value.

Who is the recipient of this so-called business value? Is it the developer? Is it the customer? Well, the answer is both. That is, both the developer (supplier) and customer (buyer) gain business value from the use of agile methods. So, what are these so-called values of agile methods? They are customer collaboration, individuals and interactions, working software, and responding to change. OK, let's slow down a bit. The values of agile methods are communicating with customers, teamwork, iterative development, and flexibility with just-enough process and product.

2.2 Customer Collaboration

The first major value of agile methods is *customer collaboration over contract negotiation*. What does this mean? In a sense, it means asking the customers what they want. It may also mean listening to and interacting with customers to ascertain their needs. How does this add business value? It's quite simple really. Business value is created by asking customers what they want and then giving it to them. Customers get what they need—that is, some sort of business advantage—and developers get paid and secure even more business.

Traditional methods recognize the need to capture customer needs but in an entirely different manner. Generally, the customer or developer must document, in advance, all of the needs. Although that doesn't seem so bad, this assumes that all of the needs can be documented. Next, this assumes the developer can satisfy all of the needs at once. Finally, this assumes the customer will pay for whatever the developer conjures up in the end. There are a lot of assumptions in traditional methods and little human-to-human communication.

How is customer collaboration performed in agile methods? With right-sized, just-enough, and just-in-time interaction. With Scrum, customer needs are captured in the form of features within a product backlog. After some features have been implemented, customer collaboration takes place after 30 days in what is known as a sprint review. Within Extreme Programming, customer needs are captured in the form of user stories. The customer is actually a full-time member of the project and communicates with the developers throughout the project.

2.3 Individuals and Interactions

The second major value of agile methods is *individuals and interactions over processes and tools*. This means developers are empowered to form teams and manage themselves. This means a lot of rich, high-context interpersonal communication between developers. This also means developers are highly competent computer programmers; that is, they like to create computer programs and they're exceptionally good at it. More importantly, this value means developers work together to solve complex problems that cannot be solved by a single person.

Traditional methods recognize the need to form project teams but in an entirely different manner. Traditional methods depend on roles: the project manager, an autocrat who is responsible for decision-making; the analyst, who develops requirements; the architect, who designs; the programmer, who does the coding; and so forth. Traditional methods are akin to a sequential manufacturing process, replete with functional silos. Furthermore, programmers are regarded as having little engineering discipline.

How do individuals perform interactions in agile methods? Within Scrum, developers form self-organizing teams, which are responsible for implementing features in 30-day sprints. They get together daily for 15-minute standup meetings to identify impediments to progress and obtain needed assistance. Within Extreme Programming, developers are responsible for implementing user stories in 14-day iterations. They use pair programming to code software (e.g., teams of two programmers). This adds business value by shedding unneeded administrative tasks and promptly delivering valuable software to the customer.

2.4 Working Software

The third major value of agile methods is *working software over comprehensive documentation*. This means that producing working software is one of the highest priorities within agile methods. All things being equal, this means that all resources are focused on producing operational software in two- to four-week intervals. This is also known as iterative, incremental, evolutionary, and spiral development. The customer is paying for working software, not documentation. Therefore, the way to maximize business value is to create working software. Also, remember that all iterations are carefully engineered.

Traditional methods recognize the need for working software but in an entirely different manner. In traditional methods, detailed project plans, requirements documents, designs, tests, and other documents must be developed first. If there is time, and there often is not, software is implemented, tested, and delivered. The documentation often becomes obsolete by the time working software is created.

Worse yet, customers receive a product that doesn't meet their needs or add any business value.

How is working software produced in agile methods? Within Scrum, developers implement the highest-priority features in the product backlog in 30-day sprints. Every 30 days, developers demonstrate potentially shippable software to their customers. Within Extreme Programming, developers implement the highest-priority user stories in the iteration plans. Thus, every 14 days, developers deliver operational software to their customers. In both cases, acceptance criteria and unit tests are developed, and the software is implemented and evaluated. More importantly, customers pay for and obtain business value in frequent intervals.

2.5 Responding to Change

The fourth major value of agile methods is *responding to change over following a plan*. This means being adaptable to change. This means capturing customer needs, developing software, showing it to customers, and repeating the process until the customer is completely satisfied. This means right-sized, just-enough, and just-in-time process and product to complete the job. This means just enough project planning to implement a few iterations. And it means replanning without a huge investment in documentation as customer needs evolve and change and the path to the best business value becomes clear.

Traditional methods recognize the need for responding to change but in an entirely different manner. In traditional methods, detailed project plans are created to account for every possible contingency. Likewise, every conceivable customer requirement is carefully documented. Rigorous configuration management processes are instituted to minimize change and stabilize the project plan. Unwanted software is often implemented, and the customer is blamed for changing the requirements and plans.

How is responding to change implemented in agile methods? Within Scrum, customers see potentially shippable software every 30 days, provide new features, and reprioritize product backlogs. Within Extreme Programming, customer needs are recorded in user stories, prioritized, and recorded in flexible release plans. The methodology is called release planning and serves as an adaptable project management paradigm. Release planning provides the necessary discipline for software developers and just the right balance of flexibility for customers to adjust their needs to obtain the best possible business value.

2.6 Summary

Although there are many types and kinds of agile methods, there are four major values common to all agile methods: (1) customer collaboration, (2) individuals and interactions (high-performance teams), (3) working software (produced in

14- to 30-day iterations), and (4) responding to change (highly flexible, right-sized, just-enough, and just-in-time management and development discipline to get the job done).

All agile methods, regardless of their individual practices, are values-based paradigms for maximizing business value. Yes, Scrum has product backlogs, daily standups, sprints, and other practices. And, yes, Extreme Programming has user stories, onsite customers, pair programming, refactoring, and test-driven development. But all agile methods are based on similar foundations of customer collaboration, teamwork, iterative development, and flexible yet disciplined processes. Agile methods form a confluence of values, principles, and practices that converge on creating business value with working software.

Within agile methods, customers come first, are always right, and always get what they want. This is true even if they change their minds every 14 to 30 days. Developers use flexible project management processes that are right-sized for agile methods and carry out highly disciplined development practices. Customers are intimately and intricately involved and able to communicate their needs. Developers verify user stories and the customers validate them, which forms a disciplined verification and validation process. All of this combines to maximize efficiency, ensure software quality, and create business value every step of the way.

2.7 Further Readings

Agile Manifesto. (2001). *Manifesto for agile software development*. Retrieved January 1, 2009, from http://www.agilemanifesto.org.

Brown, S. L., & Eisenhardt, K. M. (1997). The art of continuous change: Linking complexity theory and time-paced evolution in relentlessly shifting organizations. *Administrative Science Quarterly, 42*(1), 1–34.

———. (1998). *Competing on the edge: Strategy as structured chaos*. Boston, MA: Harvard Business School Press.

Costanzo, L. A. (2004). Strategic foresight in a high-speed environment. *Futures, 36*(2), 219–235.

Fishbein, M., & Ajzen, I. (1975). *Belief, attitude, intention, and behavior: An introduction to theory and research*. Reading, MA: Addison-Wesley.

Mintzberg, H. (1994). *The rise and fall of strategic planning*. New York, NY: The Free Press.

Moore, J. F. (1996). *The death of competition: Leadership and strategy in the age of business ecosystems*. New York, NY: Harper Business Press.

Tushman, M. L., & O'Reilly, C. A. (1996). Ambidextrous organizations: Managing evolutionary and revolutionary change. *California Management Review, 38*(4), 8–30.

3

History of
Agile Methods

The history of agile methods is a fascinating although not yet a fully explored and understood topic. Some scholars of software methods and practitioners who use software methods are unfamiliar with the history of agile methods. Some individuals feel agile methods are simply the result of programmers who don't want to use traditional methods—that is, programmers who don't want to document their code. Others feel agile methods are a return to fundamentals—that is, people who simply want to program as they did when electronic computers first emerged in the 1940s and 1950s.

Agile methods have a long and storied history. They are a confluence of numerous, seemingly unrelated disciplines. In the most basic dimension, agile methods evolved from structured design, object-oriented design, software reuse, software architecture, and so forth. They also evolved from early user involvement, rapid development, and Participatory Design. But agile methods also evolved from craft industry principles, scientific management, human and organizational behavior, systems theory, innovation, marketing, and even production flexibility.

Agile methods are based on the values of customer collaboration, teamwork, iterative development, and adaptability. Customer collaboration comes from innovation and marketing; teamwork from craft industry ideas such as autonomous work groups; iterative development from experimentation, concept testing, and feedback loops; and adaptability from systems theory, chaos theory, and production flexibility. In essence, agile methods represent the latest evolution of management thought.

3.1 Project Management

Basic project management principles originated from scientific management principles pioneered around 1900. At that time, Gantt charts were created as a rudimentary scheduling tool. Flowcharts also came out of this era, and literally dozens, if not hundreds, of flowchart variations emerged from 1900 to 1950. However, modern project management principles began taking shape in the late 1950s. At that time, the critical path method and the program evaluation review technique emerged. These techniques focused on time-and-motion activities and tasks, and timelines and schedules as a means of tracking project progress.

The 1960s saw the next major evolution in project management in rather quick succession. First, there was the cost/schedule control systems criteria in 1967, the work breakdown structure in 1968, and the formation of the Project Management Institute in 1969. Designed to track the costs and schedules of projects, the cost/schedule control systems criteria eventually became known as earned value management. Work breakdown structures were used to define the total scope of a project in terms of its products and its activities. The Project Management Institute was formed as a professional society for project managers.

In 1984, the Project Management Institute began certifying project managers and in 1987 formed the project management body of knowledge (PMBoK), which includes scope, cost, time, quality, and risk planning. It represents the capstone of Frederick W. Taylor's scientific management principles created in 1900 and is the crowning achievement of scientific management. The PMBoK is the epitome and embodiment of traditional methods. Frederick Taylor was a late-19th-century American who is credited with founding modern production and manufacturing principles, which enabled the United States to become an economic superpower.

3.2 Software Methods

One of the earliest software methods was flowcharts, which themselves originated with scientific management around 1900. Software methods gained a foothold in 1968, with stepwise refinement, structured programming, structured design, and structured analysis. Other key concepts originating from this era were egoless programming, chief programmer teams, walkthroughs, and inspections. Software testing, software quality assurance, software configuration management, and project management came next. By 1980, computer-aided software engineering tools and software environments rounded out this era.

Formal methods emerged as a sort of mathematical undercurrent to the informal techniques of the 1970s. Due to the unquenchable demand for software, the term *software crisis* was coined in 1968, and the term *software engineering* was created as a sword to slay the dragon of the software crisis. Informal methods, such as structured programming, emerged to answer the need for software engineering. However, formal methods arose to thwart the informal ones and formed a mathematical foundation for a structured discipline in software engineering, carrying on into the late 1980s.

Another major countertrend was the discipline of management information systems. This discipline grew out of the late 1950s as a means of enabling managers to coordinate large computer centers. Principles emerging from this discipline included upper management commitment, user involvement, and Participatory Design. Fourth-generation languages, rapid prototyping, Joint Application Design, computer-supported cooperative development, and Rapid Application Development also came from this genre of software methods. Eventually, information systems flexibility would come from the field of management information systems.

3.3 Software Standards

From 1968 to the present, numerous military, civilian, and commercial standards were created as forms of software methods, including specification practices to document customer requirements (MIL-STD-490), reviews and audits to document software life cycle reviews (MIL-STD-1521), software quality assurance to document a system for controlling software quality (MIL-S-52779), and configuration management to document practices for controlling software products and their components (MIL-STD-973).

In the 1980s, software standards started to take shape with comprehensive documentation frameworks for the software life cycle. A popular model within civilian government agencies was the guidelines for documentation of computer programs and automated data systems (FIPS-PUB-38). A popular model within military agencies was defense system software development (DoD-STD-2167). A popular model within the aerospace industry was a software management and assurance program (NASA-SMAP). These frameworks came replete with document templates for requirements, designs, tests, and maintenance.

The software standards of the 1990s served as a capstone of software life cycle documentation standards. The military standard for software development documentation (MIL-STD-498) served as the culmination and end of military software standards. The standard for software life cycle processes reinterpreted military standards for international commercial use (IEEE-12207). Based on the premise that everything must be documented, the software engineering body of knowledge emerged as a crowning achievement of the era of software standards (SWEBoK-2004).

3.4 Process Improvement

In the mid 1980s, software process improvement arose based on the fundamental notion that software development was a process, not an art. Furthermore, software development processes could be defined, documented, measured, and improved to achieve peak performance. In 1984, IBM created the *process grid*, one of the first software process improvement frameworks, which was a direct spinoff of Philip Crosby's maturity grid created in 1979. IBM's process grid evolved into the process maturity framework and eventually the Software Capability Maturity Model® in 1993.

Numerous software process improvement frameworks emerged at an ever increasing rate, including Trillium, BOOTSTRAP, ISO 9001, TickIT, and Hewlett Packard's Software Quality and Productivity Assessment. These also included Hewlett Packard's Quality Maturity System (QMS); Software Productivity Research's Assessment Method; Assess, Analyse, Metricate, and Improve (AMI); and Software Process Reference Model. The capstones of these models were Software Process Improvement and Capability Determination and Capability Maturity Model Integration®.

These models consisted of a built-in taxonomy of software processes. That is, they came replete with every conceivable process and its characteristics. Organizations were charged with comparing their as-is processes to these comprehensive taxonomies. This comparison would result in a list of gaps, which could then be filled with the requisite processes and then standardized across projects and eventually the entire organization. The software processes could be measured and improved to achieve optimal productivity and quality. These models were predicated on the basic notion that all software processes could and should be documented and standardized.

3.5 Agile Methods

One of the early influences on agile methods was the new product development game. Described in the *Harvard Business Journal*, the ideal new product development principles from Japan influenced a great many companies. One of them was IBM's midrange systems division, which based its new development rhythm on it. Another related method at the time was Microsoft's sync-and-stabilize approach. Computer-supported collaboration, Rapid Application Development, and Participatory Design emerged as well—all sharing values of customer involvement, teamwork, iterative development, and adaptability to change.

In 1995, the Internet exploded onto the global scene, and new software methods were created to deal with its technologies. One of the more notable ones was Netscape's judo strategy, followed by Internet time, which was a study of software methods at U.S. Internet firms conducted by the Harvard Business School. Open source software quickly became one of the fundamental building blocks of the Internet. Judo strategy, Internet time, and open source software also shared values of customer involvement, teamwork, iterative development, and adaptability to change.

Scrum then emerged, also based on the new product development game. Scrum adopted daily standup meetings and iterative development. Extreme Programming was created as a confluence of Scrum, Internet time, Participatory Design, object-oriented design, design patterns, and numerous other techniques. Crystal Methods, Dynamic Systems Development, and Feature Driven Development were then identified as agile methods. All of these agile methods shared values of customer involvement, teamwork, iterative development, and adaptability to change.

3.6 Summary

Agile methods are a continuum of ideas from both the craft industry as well as the earliest days of the scientific management era. Agile methods are not a concoction formulated by programmers too lazy to document their processes and products. Instead, agile methods are the pinnacle in the evolution of management thought in the last century. They are closely related to the schools of human behavior, systems theory, innovation, marketing, and production flexibility (mass customization). That is, agile methods are based on theoretical management principles.

Agile methods are also a confluence of principles representing state-of-the-art scientific management principles—project management, software methods, software standards, and software process improvement models. Agile methods do not reject scientific management values, such as contract negotiation, processes, tools, comprehensive documentation, and following plans. Instead, they use right-sized, just-enough, and just-in-time processes and documentation based on theoretical scientific management principles.

If this is all agile methods did, then they would be nothing more than lightweight traditional methods. Instead, agile methods combine customer collaboration, high-performance teams, and iterative development with processes and documentation that are adaptable to change. So, we see three major schools of thought converging to create agile methods: (1) the power of people from the craft industry and human behavior school of management, (2) the power of right-sized processes and documentation from scientific management, and (3) the power of adaptability from organismic biology.

3.7 Further Readings

Couger, J. D. (1973). Evolution of business system analysis techniques. *ACM Computing Surveys, 5*(3), 167–198.

Kinicki, A., & Kreitner, R. (2003). *Organizational behavior: Key concepts, skills, and best practices*. Boston, MA: McGraw-Hill.

Moore, J. W. (1997). *Software engineering standards: A user's roadmap*. Piscataway, NJ: IEEE Computer Society.

Rico, D. F., Sayani, H. H., & Field, R. F. (2008). History of computers, electronic commerce, and agile methods. In M. V. Zelkowitz (ed.), *Advances in computers: Emerging technologies, vol. 73*. San Diego, CA: Elsevier.

Senge, P. M. (1990). *The fifth discipline: The art and practice of the learning organization*. New York, NY: Doubleday.

Shafritz, J. M., & Ott, J. S. (2001). *Classics of organization theory*. New York, NY: Wadsworth Publishing.

Shapiro, S. (1997). Splitting the difference: The historical necessity of synthesis in software engineering. *IEEE Annals of the History of Computing, 19*(1), 20–54.

Wang, Y., & King, G. (2000). *Software engineering processes: Principles and applications*. Boca Raton, FL: CRC Press.

Wren, D. A. (1993). *The evolution of management thought*. Indianapolis, IN: John Wiley & Sons.

4

Antecedents of Agile Methods

Agile methods are directly related to other major product engineering disciplines, including new product development, systems engineering, software project management, software engineering, and lean thinking. Agile methods are simply one in a long line of approaches for developing software. Put another way, agile methods are an approach for creating new software. Can you see the subtle and almost imperceptible distinction? In the first description they are a scientific management method, and in the second they are a way for creating innovative products.

The relationship is no accident for at least three major reasons. The first is because agile methods are directly related to systems engineering, software project management, and software engineering, which were based on scientific management principles created for mass manufacturing purposes. The second major reason is because agile methods are directly related to methods emerging in the late 1980s, which embodied behavioral principles such as high-context communication with customers and between developers.

The third reason is because new product development and agile methods share four basic values for managing innovation: (1) customer collaboration, (2) teamwork, (3) iterative development, and (4) adaptability to change. All four of these values involve human behavior, psychology, and sociology—that is, people talking to people to get the job done. Is this some sort of socialistic manifesto? No, it's a capitalistic one! Let's get the job done, get paid, get repeat business, and earn more.

4.1 New Product Development

New product development methods are direct antecedents of agile methods. Like agile methods, new product development had auspicious beginnings. The earliest forms were linear or sequential product development life cycles. From this we get the modern-day waterfall. Early new product development approaches were classified as push methods of product development—manufacturers who wanted to push their technological wares on the unsuspecting public. A closely related discipline was marketing; why not form a group to analyze market trends before pushing products out of the door? Traditional methods are based on this basic model.

The next major evolution in new product development was pull methods. A representative method from this era was the customer active paradigm—customers requested new products, manufacturers responded, but not before. Integrated product teams, cross-functional teams, simultaneous engineering, overlapping design, and concurrent engineering emerged as stop-gap measures to marry push and pull concepts. However, scientists and engineers eventually realized it wasn't a matter of push or pull, or half-hearted push and pull, but fully integrated push and pull, necessitating entirely new approaches.

The conclusion of research in the 1980s was that it wasn't just a matter of market pull nor of technology push, but was both market push and technology pull, with flexibility in between. Therefore, new product development values emerged—customer collaboration, teamwork, iterative development, and adaptability to change—that served as a foundation for agile methods. However, agile methods elicited criticism instead of praise because they weren't based on scientific management principles alone.

4.2 Systems Engineering

Systems engineering methods are direct predecessors of agile methods, because they are used for developing systems as well. The term *systems engineering* was first coined at Bell Labs in the 1940s and first taught at MIT in the 1950s. Simply stated, systems engineering is a discipline for managing complex projects. A process of defining customer needs, synthesizing a design and technical solution, and validating the solution, systems engineering is a philosophy of reductionism or functional decomposition. That is, define all the problems and subproblems, solve them, and then reintegrate the pieces into a whole.

Preceding systems engineering, from 1940 to 1970, systems analysis was composed of a seven-stage systems life cycle: (1) prestudy, (2) analyze, (3) design, (4) build, (5) test, (6) operate, and (7) maintain. In the 1960s, numerous systems engineering books emerged and, in the 1970s, the U.S. Department of Defense (DoD) systems engineering standards became prevalent. In 1990, a professional systems engineering society was started, which grew to 7,000 members. In the

1990s, commercial systems engineering standards began, and in 2003, the systems engineering body of knowledge emerged.

The systems engineering body of knowledge consists of seven stages: (1) state the problem, (2) investigate alternatives, (3) model the system, (4) integrate, (5) launch the system, (6) assess performance, and (7) reevaluate. Systems engineering is composed of implicit values and comprised of scientists and engineers solving technical problems using mathematical rigor. Although agile methods could accommodate a modicum of just-enough engineering rigor, does systems engineering embody the behavior-based values of agile methods?

4.3 Software Project Management

Because they are used to manage projects, software project management methods are direct antecedents of agile methods. The project management discipline as we know it today emerged in the late 1950s to support large U.S. DoD computer systems. However, project management publications didn't reach the general public until the early 1960s. Project management methods were then applied to mainframe operating systems and other software-only products by the mid 1960s. The first book on software project management appeared in 1967.

By 1966, the program evaluation and review technique was applied in computer centers, and in 1968, the critical path method was applied to software projects. In the late 1960s, the first publications on how to estimate software costs and quality emerged, and by 1970, the first managers were assigned to software projects. Throughout the 1970s, software quality, complexity, defect, and reliability models were applied to software projects, and by the late 1970s and early 1980s, robust software project management systems and numerous textbooks emerged.

From 1985 to 1995, software process improvement frameworks promoted basic software project management techniques such as practices of size, effort, cost, quality, productivity, and schedule estimation and control. In the mid 1990s, a few software project management methods emerged, replete with earned value and quality management systems—everything known about software project management since the 1960s. Although they embraced scientific management values, such as cost efficiency and defect density, they didn't accept the behavioral values of agile methods. By 2002, they were completely overtaken by the popularity of agile methods.

4.4 Software Engineering

Software engineering methods are direct predecessors of agile methods, because they are used for developing software as well. The term *software engineering* was first coined at a NATO conference in 1968 when computers became powerful, software was in high demand, and software projects were difficult to manage. Big software products required thousands of programmers, billions of dollars, and decades to create. Although software was a critical component of 20th-century weapon systems, it was regarded as an art rather than a science. Nearly a decade earlier the term *management information crisis* was also applied to U.S. DoD projects.

Software projects were regarded as tar pits and death marches. Software engineers began attacking the complexity and the art of programming with a barrage of engineering disciplines. These included project management (1966), structured methods (1969), formal methods (1969), life cycles (1970), reviews (1971), object-oriented methods (1972), testing (1975), and tools (1975). Quality assurance (1978), configuration management (1979), rapid development (1982), processes (1985), reuse (1984), architecture (1987), and agile methods (1990s) were also included.

In 2004, all of these disciplines, and many more, were rolled up into the software engineering body of knowledge. It consists of several broad knowledge areas, such as requirements, design, construction, testing, maintenance, configuration management, project management, process, tools and methods, and quality. Its values consist of contracts, processes, tools, documentation, and project plans. However, the software engineering body of knowledge seems to be inconsistent with the values of agile methods such as customer collaboration, teamwork, iterative development, and adaptability. It doesn't embrace values such as communication with customers and developers or flexibility.

4.5 Lean Thinking

Because it is used for product development as well, lean thinking is a direct antecedent of agile methods. The term *lean thinking* was first coined by John Krafcik of MIT in 1988 and appeared in two books in 1991 and 1996. Described as an adaptable production system, which was flexible and free of waste, lean thinking was described as a mode of human behavior, culture, and an attitude rather than one of computer automation. This stood in direct contradiction to the flexible manufacturing system (1979), which itself evolved from computers in manufacturing (1958), direct numerical control (1964), and computer-aided manufacturing (1971), among others.

Of course, John Krafcik didn't invent lean thinking but merely helped popularize it. Lean thinking is more accurately attributed in the 1950s to Taiichi Ohno, who is responsible for creating the Toyota Production System by adapting Ford's just-in-time system. Lean thinking rests on two pillars: (1) just-in-time and (2) mistake proofing. At the heart of lean thinking is the elimination of waste or muda—rework, overproduction, conveyance, waiting, inventory, motion, and overprocessing. Lean thinking and agile methods have numerous ideas in common.

Lean thinking uses a pull system to avoid overproduction. Like agile methods, it is sensitive to customer needs (customer collaboration), depends on highly skilled people working together (teamwork), produces quantities in small batches (iterative development), and is enabled by simple processes (adaptability). Lean thinking spawned ideas such as flexibility and agility, which reached their peak in the mid 1990s when firms were judged on their agility. Agile methods took their namesake from lean-thinking-inspired agility.

4.6 Summary

Agile methods didn't simply drop out of the sky, as some people would have us believe. New product development, systems engineering, software project management, software engineering, and lean thinking are direct antecedents of agile methods. The values of agile methods are an adaptation of these ideas for creating new software products. Although there are many publications on agile methods, few authoritatively link their origins to these ideas. Because agile methods are not merely based on the values of traditional methods alone, they are regarded as inferior to traditional ones.

Agile methods inherit their values from new product development and their right-sized, just-enough, and just-in-time principles from systems engineering, software project management, and software engineering. The elimination of waste comes from lean thinking, as evident in all four values. We can now see that agile methods are a new product development, systems engineering, software project management, software engineering, and a lean production approach for creating software products.

Therefore, you should give agile methods their due when you're involved in new product development, systems engineering, software project management, software engineering, and lean thinking. In fact, since the creators of agile methods went through such great pains to create them, why not give them a try? If you're doing new product development, then agile methods can be used out of the box. If you're using systems engineering, project management, or software engineering, then ask yourself if these are appropriate. And, of course, agile methods are well-suited for lean thinking projects as well, because they are already lean.

4.7 Further Readings

Abran, A., Moore, J. W., Bourque, P., & Dupuis, R. (2004). *Guide to the software engineering body of knowledge*. Los Alamitos, CA: IEEE Computer Society.

Crawford, C. M. (1991). The dual-drive concept of product innovation. *Business Horizons, 34*(3), 32–38.

Dunn, O. E. (1966). Information technology: A management problem. *Proceedings of the Third ACM IEEE Conference on Design Automation, New York, NY,* 5.1–5.29.

INCOSE. (2003). *Guide to the systems engineering body of knowledge* (*G2SEBOK 1.00*). San Diego, CA: Author.

Naur, P., & Randell, B. (1969). Software engineering. *NATO Software Engineering Conference, Garmisch, Germany*, 1–136.

Poolton, J., & Barclay, I. (1998). New product development from past research to future applications. *Industrial Marketing Management, 27*(3), 197–212.

Rogers, E. M. (1962). *Diffusion of innovation.* New York, NY: The Free Press.

Takeuchi, H., & Nonaka, I. (1986). The new product development game. *Harvard Business Review, 64*(1), 137–146.

Von Hippel, E. (1978). Successful industrial products from customer ideas. *Journal of Marketing, 42*(1), 39–49.

Womack, J. P., & Jones, D. T. (1996). *Lean thinking.* New York, NY: Simon & Schuster.

5

Types of Agile Methods

There are many types of agile methods. Some of the earliest agile methods included Rapid Application Development, Participatory Design, judo strategy, sync-and-stabilize, and even Internet time. Five major agile methods are recognized today: Crystal Methods, Scrum, Dynamic Systems Development, Feature Driven Development, and Extreme Programming. Although Scrum and Extreme Programming are the most often used today, true to their namesake, new agile methods are emerging all the time.

Other recognized agile methods include pragmatic programming, agile modeling, adaptive software development, and even the Rational Unified Process. Although Scrum and Extreme Programming seem unimpeachable today, the two dark horses are open source software and lean development, which are yielding a wealth of innovative ideas. Whereas open source software provides right-sized, just-enough, and just-in-time documentation, lean development gives quantitative theoretical support to agile methods.

All of these agile methods present effective frameworks for creating new software products. The values of agile methods—customer collaboration, teamwork, iterative development, and adaptability—are more important than any one of these agile methods and its practices. What does this mean? When using agile methods to create software, one should always reflect on their values. Technology is rapidly evolving and so are agile methods.

5.1 Scrum

Scrum was first created by Jeff Sutherland and others at the Easel Corporation in 1993 (see Figure 5-1). Together with Ken Schwaber, Jeff Sutherland created a formal description of Scrum in 1995. Scrum was created for two basic reasons:

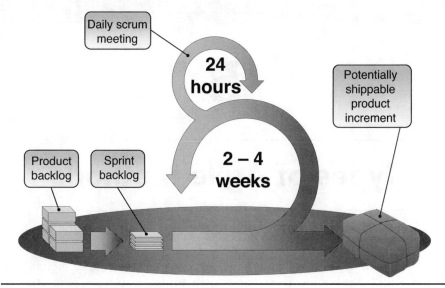

Figure 5-1   Scrum (circa 1993)

(1) existing methods simply did not work and (2) a new method was necessary to ensure project success. Scrum assumes that, because software development is unpredictable, ironclad project plans don't work and, therefore, an adaptable method of software development is necessary. Thus, Scrum was created to help real-world projects get out of first gear and be successful. Scrum's primary goal was project success.

Based on the new product development game, Scrum includes built-in instability, self-organizing teams, subtle control, overlapping phases, multilearning, and organizational learning. The new product development game is Japan's answer to the age-old dilemma of successfully bringing new products to market. From this, we can see the values of agile methods, especially teamwork, iterative development, and adaptability. Of course, the new product development game was adapted to creating software in the mid-1990s. Scrum initially had three broad phases: (1) pre-sprint planning, (2) sprint, and a (3) post-sprint meeting.

Today, Scrum is composed of five major phases: (1) sprint planning meeting, (2) sprint, (3) daily standup meetings, (4) sprint review meetings, and (5) sprint retrospective meetings. Key ideas are its daily standups and retrospectives, which yield rich, interpersonal communication and process improvement. Now the fastest-growing agile method, Scrum is used by 50% of developers who prefer software methods for computer programming. Leading developers combine

Scrum with Extreme Programming practices, which include release planning and user stories as requirements.

5.2 Extreme Programming

Extreme Programming was created around 1996 by Kent Beck and his team of 20 developers at Chrysler, including Ron Jeffries and Martin Fowler (see Figure 5-2). Created to save a failing payroll system project at Chrysler, its practices originally included just-in-time evolution, self-chosen tasks, aggressiveness, model-driven development, and communications. Extreme Programming later grew into 13 practices that included onsite customers, pair programming, test-driven development, and open workspaces. Today, it has over 28 rules and practices for planning, designing, coding, and testing.

Because its origins are unclear and it is a confluence of many disciplines, methods, and practices, Extreme Programming is one of the most enigmatic of the agile methods. Legend says that it is even based on Scrum. Certain influences are clearly evident, such as object-oriented methods, design patterns, rapid application development, and Participatory Design. Some of its practices seem to be add-ons, such as pair programming, and yet others are sophisticated, such as release planning. It also has hints of sync-and-stabilize, judo strategy, and Internet time from Microsoft, Netscape, and Yahoo from the mid 1990s.

Based on the four values of agile methods, Extreme Programming first gained widespread public recognition in 1999. By 2002, over half of all developers who preferred software methods were using Extreme Programming. This was particularly true in Europe, where computer-supported collaboration and Participatory Design were also popular. Today, Extreme Programming is being taken over by Scrum, but its right-sized, just-enough, and just-in-time release planning methodology promises to be a lasting legacy.

5.3 Dynamic Systems Development

Dynamic Systems Development was created in 1993 by a British consortium of 16 academic and industry organizations (see Figure 5-3). Their goal was to create a nonproprietary Rapid Application Development approach. Initially, Dynamic Systems Development consisted of three critical success factors: (1) communication between developers and end users, (2) stable, highly skilled developers, and (3) flexible customer requirements. It also focused on meeting high-priority customer needs, product versus process, and integrated configuration management and testing.

Dynamic Systems Development consists of five major stages: (1) feasibility study, (2) business study, (3) functional model iteration, (4) system design and

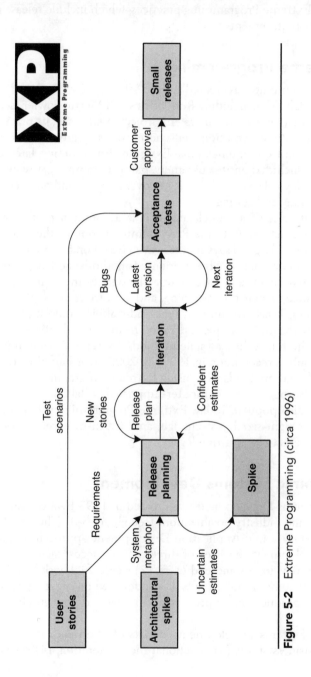

Figure 5-2   Extreme Programming (circa 1996)

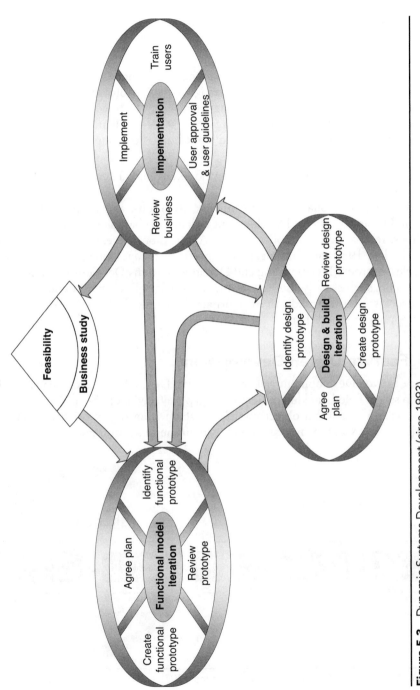

Figure 5-3   Dynamic Systems Development (circa 1993)

build iteration, and (5) implementation. Dynamic Systems Development also has the following 15 practices:

time-boxing	project planning	modeling
daily meetings	quality management	prototyping
requirements prioritization	risk management	testing
project management	estimating	configuration management
escalation management	facilitated workshops	tool support environments

Additionally, Dynamic Systems Development has 12 roles and 23 work products.

With customer collaboration, teamwork, iterations, and adaptability clearly evident, Dynamic Systems Development is definitely based on the values of agile methods. It is a direct spinoff of Rapid Application Development approaches from the late 1980s and has a generous portion of stages, practices, documents, and roles. Extreme Programming and Dynamic Systems Development have a lot in common, such as early user involvement. Although Extreme Programming has assumed a strong foothold in Great Britain, Dynamic Systems Development is still a popular method there.

5.4 Feature Driven Development

Feature Driven Development was created by Jeff De Luca and Peter Coad in 1997 to help save a failed banking project in Singapore (see Figure 5-4). They were attempting to use domain object modeling, which is an object-oriented method, but the project was too large and there were numerous requirements. Peter Coad

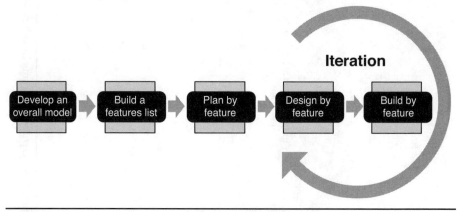

Figure 5-4   Feature Driven Development (circa 1997)

was enlisted to create an evolutionary domain object modeling method. The result was Feature Driven Development, which emphasized iterative development, quality, and working software, as well as a flexible and adaptable project management system and an ease of use by both customers and developers.

Feature Driven Development consists of five broad phases: (1) develop an overall model, (2) build a features list, (3) plan by feature, (4) design by feature, and (5) build by feature. It has roles for project managers, chief architects, development managers, lead programmers, class owners, and domain experts. Its four major practices are object-oriented design, iterative development, inspections, and configuration management. Its deliverables include class diagrams, sequence diagrams, feature sets, and the software products themselves. Its main goal is to frequently produce tangible, high-quality working software.

A key element of Feature Driven Development is a tool, Together Soft's Control Center, for creating diagrams in the Unified Modeling Language. The full list of practices includes domain object modeling, developing by feature, individual class code ownership, feature teams, inspections, configuration management, regular builds, and visibility of progress and results. Feature Driven Development uses the values of agile methods and is a close cousin to Scrum, although not as popular.

5.5 Crystal Methods

Crystal Methods is an object-oriented development method created by Alistair Cockburn at IBM in 1991 (see Figure 5-5). Crystal Methods was created by interviewing real-world software practitioners, rather than following any one of numerous textbooks on object-oriented methods. The interviews uncovered ideas important to the success of software development such as good communication, high morale, and developer access to end users. Projects that followed these practices were successful more often than not, while those that didn't invariably failed. Teamwork, frequent delivery, and customer collaboration were also found to be key characteristics of successful projects.

Crystal Methods is a family of 20 distinct agile methods, which are depicted by a two-dimensional grid. Imagine life, essential money, discretionary money, and comfort on the y-axis and clear, yellow, orange, red, and maroon on the x-axis. Crystal Methods consist of seven broad stages: (1) project cycle, (2) delivery cycle, (3) iteration cycle, (4) integration cycle, (5) week and day, (6) development episode, and (7) reflection about the process. A large agile method, Crystal Methods also consists of seven properties, five strategies, nine techniques, eight roles, and 25 documents.

The latest version of Crystal Methods is a composite of practices from other agile methods. Whereas its information radiators come from Extreme Programming and Scrum, its daily standups, burn charts, and reflection are from Scrum, and side-by-side programming, release plans, and iteration plans derive from

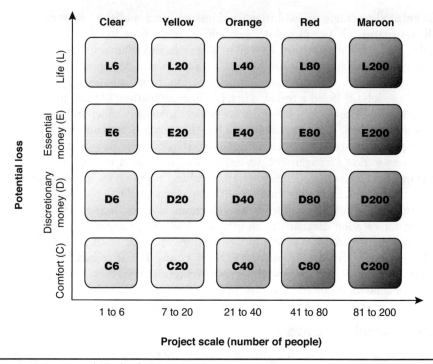

Figure 5-5   Crystal Methods (circa 1991)

Extreme Programming. Although Crystal Methods embraces the values of agile methods, only a small fraction of the software community is using it.

5.6 Summary

There are many types and kinds of agile methods. The major ones are Scrum, Extreme Programming, Dynamic Systems Development, Feature Driven Development, and Crystal Methods. Many more important ones, such as open source software development, lean development, and others, may soon emerge. At the most basic level, they all share something in common—the four basic values of agile methods, but that is where the similarities seem to end.

Agile methods are not just lightweight traditional methods, as some people believe, but are a convergence of principles based on human behavior as well as scientific management. In one dimension, agile methods are about psychology, sociology, and human behavior—for example, interacting and communicating with customers, as well as the other members of the team. In another dimension, agile methods are about processes and documentation—that is, project plans, customer requirements, software designs, and other documents.

In yet another dimension, agile methods are about systems theory, organizational learning, and adaptability to change—easily modifiable without the loss of a large investment. On a scale of high, moderate, and minimal adaptability, Scrum is a highly adaptable agile method, Feature Driven Development and Extreme Programming are moderately adaptable, and Dynamic Systems Development and Crystal Methods are minimally adaptable. All agile methods share common values. They are behavior and process based, setting them apart from their antecedents; they can and should be adaptable; and they are not just lightweight traditional methods.

5.7 Further Readings

Beck, K. (2001). *Extreme Programming: Embrace change*. Upper Saddle River, NJ: Addison-Wesley.

Cockburn, A. (2005). *Crystal clear: A human-powered methodology for small teams*. Upper Saddle River, NJ: Addison-Wesley.

Feller, J., & Fitzgerald, B. (2002). *Understanding open source software development*. London, England: Pearson Education.

Hibbs, C., Jewett, S., & Sullivan, M. (2009). *The art of lean software development*. Sebastopol, CA: O'Reilly Media.

Middleton, P., & Sutton, J. (2005). *Lean software strategies: Proven techniques for managers and developers*. New York, NY: Productivity Press.

Palmer, S. R., & Felsing, J. M. (2002). *A practical guide to Feature Driven Development*. Upper Saddle River, NJ: Prentice Hall.

Pavlicek, R. C. (2000). *Embracing insanity: Open source software development*. Indianapolis, IN: Sams Publishing.

Poppendieck, M., & Poppendieck, T. (2003). *Lean software development: An agile toolkit for software development managers*. Boston, MA: Addison-Wesley.

Schwaber, K., & Beedle, M. (2002). *Agile software development with Scrum*. Upper Saddle River, NJ: Prentice Hall.

Stapleton, J. (2003). *DSDM: Business focused development*. Harlow, England: Pearson Education.

6

Practices of
Agile Methods

There are many types of practices for agile methods. Some of the more salient ones include (1) onsite customers, (2) pair programming, (3) test-driven development, (4) refactoring, and (5) release planning. We focus on these five because they represent the values of agile methods; some of them are greatly misunderstood, and some are key drivers of the business value of agile methods.

Other practices—such as metaphors, backlogs, daily standups, and open workspaces—also represent the values of agile methods and drive business value. We'll talk about those practices within the context of the ones we've identified. For instance, we'll discuss product owners in the context of onsite customers, daily standups and open workspaces in the context of pair programming, and backlogs and sprints in the context of release planning. Two of our goals are to strive for greater integration among the practices of agile methods and to begin describing the technical details of agile methods. In doing so, we hope to establish the context and foundation for the remainder of this textbook.

6.1 Onsite Customers

Onsite customers are end users of the software being created and are part of the development team (see Figure 6-1). The purpose of having an onsite customer is to serve as the source of customer needs (requirements). As a full-time member of the team, the onsite customer has responsibilities—writing user stories, performing functional tests, and evaluating the software throughout development, which is a form of inspection, quality assurance, and verification and validation.

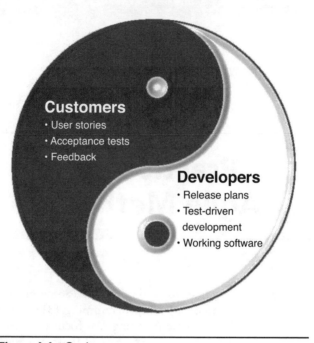

Figure 6-1   Onsite customers

The onsite customer also embodies customer collaboration, which is the first major value of agile methods.

Customer collaboration recognizes the business value of rich, high-context communication with customers. Because developers must communicate with customers, solicit customer needs, and obtain customer feedback, onsite customers are the fulfillment of customer collaboration. This concept evolved from executive involvement (1950s), manager involvement (1960s), customer involvement (1970s), and end-user involvement (1980s). In order to be successful, customers must be involved and committed to the software as it is being created.

Scrum uses the concept of product owners who represent the interests of all key stakeholders and are responsible for creating the product backlog. Developers must obtain feedback from the product owners as well as the customers regarding the software as it is being created. First, there has to be a thorough understanding of the initial customer requirements on the part of the product owners and developers. From there, working software can be released to the market, to customers, and to end users to identify problems and elicit new customer requirements. Because the values of agile methods are more important than the practices, the key to maximizing business value is right-sized, just-enough, and just-in-time customer collaboration.

6.2 Pair Programming

Pair programming consists of two programmers who sit at one computer to implement one or more customer requirements (see Figure 6-2). The concept is that two people can solve a problem faster than one person working alone. Furthermore, two people can produce a higher-quality solution than one. Therefore, pair programming becomes a basic method of quality control. Pair programming embodies teamwork, the second major value of agile methods.

Teamwork recognizes the business value of rich, high-context communication between developers. Developers must communicate to solicit customer needs, create plans, devise technical solutions, and implement them. Pair programming evolved from self-determined groups (1950s), autonomous groups (1960s), self-organizing groups (1970s), and collaborative groups (1980s). To solve highly complex problems, small groups of highly skilled workers must be trusted with a certain amount of autonomy.

Scrum uses the concept of daily standups—teams meet for 15 minutes a day to identify progress, plans, and impediments. Teams are cross-functional groups of developers who are responsible for managing themselves in order to develop software at every sprint. The team analyzes the requirements and determines

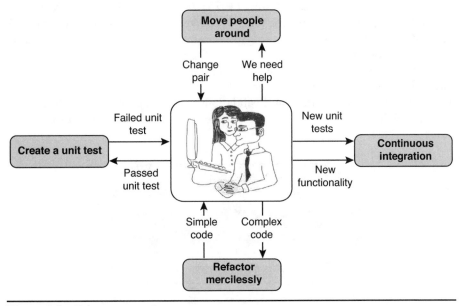

Figure 6-2   Pair programming

what can be done in a 30-day sprint and then implements the requirements. Because the values are more important than individual practices, highly skilled teams must collaborate as much as necessary to get the job done. Therefore, the key to maximizing business value is right-sized, just-enough, and just-in-time teamwork.

6.3 Test-Driven Development

Test-driven development is defined as a process of developing unit tests before programming by using automated frameworks (see Figure 6-3). Used to evaluate a low-level module, procedure, subroutine, or method, it differs from traditional unit testing in that tests are written first and are automated, and it is used for continuous regression testing. Test-driven development is a form of dynamic analysis, quality assurance, and verification and validation. It's not the only form of quality control in agile methods, as some people say. Quality control is built into all of the major practices of agile methods. This includes validation of customer requirements with working software every 14 to 30 days, peer reviews through pair programming, defect prevention through retrospectives, and continuous improvement through iterative development. Test-driven development supports iterative development, which is the third major value of agile methods.

Test-driven development recognizes the business value of making high-quality working software. At every step, developers must solicit customer needs, decompose them into technical tasks, and write automated unit tests. Test-driven development evolved from usage testing (1975), test procedures (1976), regression testing (1976), automated testing (1977), and verification and validation (1982). To ensure requirements are satisfied, software must be evaluated before it is released to customers.

Scrum does not have a practice corresponding to test-driven development but leaves the choice optional. However, it does recognize the need for testing, quality assurance, and verification and validation. Scrum suggests a cross-functional team consisting of testers, if necessary, and even recognizes the need for special

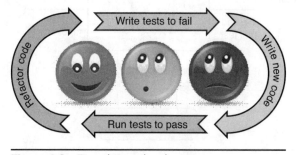

Figure 6-3   Test-driven development

test teams, such as certification teams. Because the values are more important than the individual practices, software teams must evaluate their software to produce the working code. Therefore, the key to maximizing business value is right-sized, just-enough, and just-in-time software testing.

6.4 Refactoring

A process of improving the design of existing code (see Figure 6-4), refactoring is used to remove dead or redundant code, improve code, or simplify code. Programmers accept technical tasks, find a partner, write unit tests, design a technical solution, redesign or refactor the existing code if necessary, and test it. In comparison, traditional methods hold that software needs to be designed, coded, and tested only once. Refactoring is a form of quality assurance and defect prevention. Simplifying a product's design is at the heart of Japan's *Kaizen*, a popular form of total quality management in the 1980s. Refactoring supports iterative development, the third major value of agile methods.

Refactoring recognizes the business value of continuously improving the quality of software. It is like refining gold in the fire to work out the impurities. Developers must gather customer needs, identify technical tasks, write automated unit tests, and continuously refine code quality. Refactoring evolved from structured programming (1969), structured design (1974), and structured analysis (1974). To operate and satisfy software's requirements, the code must be clean and continuously well-structured.

Scrum does not have a practice corresponding to refactoring but leaves the choice of technical practices optional. It does recognize that software must be clean, well-structured, free of errors, and potentially shippable after each 30-day

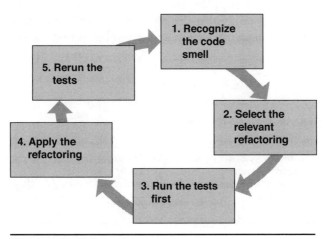

Figure 6-4   Refactoring

sprint. Because the values of agile methods are more important than the individual practices, teams need to produce code that is simple, well-structured, free of defects, and continuously refined from iteration to iteration. Developers know that the key to maximizing business value is right-sized, just-enough, and just-in-time code simplification and restructuring.

6.5 Release Planning

Release planning is the process of deciding which user stories go into a release or iteration to meet business goals (see Figure 6-5). It is a flexible project planning process specially designed for agile methods. User stories—flexible customer requirements specially designed for agile methods—are captured, estimated, decomposed, and ordered. While traditional project plans are meticulous, detailed, and planned out for years, release plans organize activities for a few iterations and are changed as new customer needs emerge. Release plans support adaptability, the fourth major value of agile methods.

Release planning recognizes the business value of delivering working software by adapting to changing customer needs. Developers must gather customer needs, develop a project plan, execute it, and replan if necessary. Release planning evolved from program evaluation and review technique (1966), cost estimation (1968), quality estimation (1972), productivity estimation (1978), and adaptable plans (1984). Project plans must be flexible and adaptive to changing customer needs and market conditions.

Scrum uses the concept of sprint planning meetings. After a product backlog emerges with customer requirements, a sprint backlog is produced for 30-day iterations. Release planning distinguishes between customer needs and technical tasks, and accounts for multiple iterations. The best Scrum projects use release planning in support of sprint planning. The point is to produce flexible project plans. It is important to remember that the values of agile methods are more important than the individual practices. The bottom line is that the key to maximizing business value is right-sized, just-enough, and just-in-time project plans.

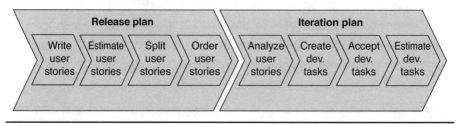

Figure 6-5   Release planning

6.6 Summary

There are many types of practices for agile methods. Onsite customers, pair programming, test-driven development, refactoring, and especially release planning are effective examples. These practices represent the core values of agile methods and are in common use, although they are somewhat misunderstood. For instance, some people believe one isn't being agile if customers are not onsite and pair programming isn't being used or developers are not collocated. What we have shown is that this is not always true.

Agile methods are as misunderstood by the agile methods community as they are by the proponents of traditional methods. Onsite customers and pair programming are nice but not always necessary. We've also unraveled at least two other myths. One is that test-driven development is good for quality control but is not the only means of quality control in agile methods. In fact, practices embodying all four core values of agile methods help build-in quality the first time, serve as a good verification and validation system, and help adapt to changing customer needs. At least one other myth we've uncovered is that refactoring, or continuous software simplification, actually increases software quality, rather than destabilizes the code base, leading to poor software quality, as is commonly thought by proponents of traditional methods. Kaizen has been used by Japanese firms for decades to bring the highest-quality products to the marketplace at the lowest possible cost, by constantly simplifying both a product's design as well as its manufacturing process.

Philip Crosby, the famous American quality management philosopher who popularized the notion of Zero Defects in the 1970s, defined quality as conformance to requirements. Within agile methods, customer requirements are captured using rich, high-context communication. Teams of people collaborate to verify implementation of the requirements; every 14 to 30 days customers validate whether the software satisfies their needs, and projects are replanned to satisfy the customer needs even better. This process results in conformance to requirements that Philip Crosby could not have imagined. The practices of agile methods embody the best ideas handed down over the decades, along with 21st-century behavioral values and principles, to achieve total customer satisfaction and business value.

6.7 Further Readings

Beck, K. (2003). *Test-driven development: By example.* Boston, MA: Addison-Wesley.

Beck, K., & Fowler, M. (2001). *Planning extreme programming.* Upper Saddle River, NJ: Addison-Wesley.

Bittner, K., & Spence, I. (2007). *Managing iterative software development projects.* Boston, MA: Pearson Education.

Cohn, M. (2004). *User stories applied: For agile software development.* Boston, MA: Addison-Wesley.

Duvall, P., Matyas, S., & Glover, A. (2006). *Continuous integration: Improving software quality and reducing risk.* Boston, MA: Addison-Wesley.

Fowler, M. (1999). *Refactoring: Improving the design of existing code.* Boston, MA: Addison-Wesley.

Larman, C. (2004). *Agile and iterative development: A manager's guide.* Boston, MA: Pearson Education.

Lui, K. M., & Chan, K. C. (2008). *Software development rhythms: Harmonizing agile practices for synergy.* Hoboken, NJ: John Wiley & Sons.

Subramaniam, V., & Hunt, A. (2006). *Practices of an agile developer: Working in the real world.* Raleigh, NC: Pragmatic Bookshelf.

Williams, L., & Kessler, R. (2003). *Pair programming illuminated.* Boston, MA: Addison-Wesley.

7

Agile Project Management

Agile project management is the use of customer collaboration, teamwork, iterative development, and adaptability to create new software products, manage the development of software products, and create business value for customers. It is the skillful application of right-sized, just-enough, and just-in-time project management discipline to get the job done—that is, planning a few iterations, developing working software, and then adapting to emerging customer needs and market conditions.

The discipline of agile project management is somewhat of a mystery to proponents of both agile and traditional methods. Some people feel the technical practices of agile methods are undisciplined, and the notion that agile methods use project management discipline may come as somewhat of a surprise. Indeed, there are many books on agile project management. Although many show individuals and organizations how to reinforce the values of agile methods, few describe a means of planning and managing agile projects.

There are several practices for managing agile projects, such as release and sprint planning. Together with other values and practices, release and sprint planning are frameworks for project management. They cover the project management body of knowledge (PMBoK) areas, such as project integration, scope, time, cost, quality, human resources, communications, risk, and procurement management. Agile methods come with a right-sized, just-enough, and just-in-time body of knowledge to manage software projects, develop software, and create business value.

7.1 Initiating Process Group

In the PMBoK, the initiating process group consists of the first set of activities used to start a new project. During initiation, project charters and scope statements are developed. Project charters are formal documents used to authorize new projects, and project scope statements contain summary descriptions of new projects. Within agile methods there are two approaches to the initiating process group: (1) release planning and (2) sprint planning; both have built-in activities that serve the purpose of the initiating process group.

User stories—simple, one-statement customer requirements—are a central component of both release and sprint planning. After a customer writes a user story, developers estimate the effort to complete the user story. Using the estimates, customers split or divide the user stories—an iterative process. Finally, the user stories are sorted by value and risk, initial duration estimates are made, customers select a scope for a project, and a release plan is constructed. The result is a group of user stories that represent customer requirements. This gives the customer and developers a sense of the total scope and charter of the project. Release plans are constructed from the desired user stories, which further delineate the charter and scope of the project. Within agile methods, release and sprint planning are a right-sized, just-enough, and just-in-time initiating process group for maximizing business value.

7.2 Planning Process Group

In the PMBoK, the planning process group consists of the second set of activities used to create a project plan. The planning group, largest of the process groups, contains activities for developing the project plans and the work breakdown structures and for task, cost, quality, human resources, communications, risk, and procurement planning. Within agile methods there are two approaches to address the planning process group: (1) iteration and (2) sprint planning; both have practices to perform the planning process group.

Iteration planning has built-in activities that serve the purpose of the planning process group. Development tasks—defined as one or more technical activities necessary to satisfy a user story—are a central component of iteration planning. Customers may provide an oral or written description of a user story, or they may simply identify its acceptance criteria. After developers iteratively decompose user stories into lower-level development tasks, they are assigned to each task and estimate their duration, and an iteration plan is constructed. Sprint planning has a similar flow, with product backlogs serving as release plans containing customer requirements and sprint backlogs serving as iteration plans and containing development tasks.

From the PMBoK, iteration planning serves the purpose of the planning process group. Together, release and iteration planning cover all 23 of the processes within the initiating and planning process groups. This includes project charters, project plans, work breakdown structures, scope, activity, schedule, cost, quality, human resources, communications, risk, and procurement planning. Iteration planning is a right-sized, just-enough, and just-in-time planning process group for maximizing business value.

7.3 Executing Process Group

In the PMBoK, the executing process group consists of the third set of activities used to execute the project plan. The executing process group has five major categories: (1) project coordination, (2) quality assurance, (3) teams, (4) communications, and (5) subcontracting. It contains activities for directing and managing project execution, performing quality assurance, and acquiring and developing project teams. The executing process group also contains activities for information distribution, requesting seller responses, and selecting sellers. Both iteration and sprint planning have practices to perform the executing process group.

Within agile methods, iteration planning serves as the executing process group. Within Scrum and Extreme Programming, the project team may assign user stories to one or more external groups or suppliers. Acquiring and developing teams are satisfied by pair programming and self-organizing teams. Daily standups serve the purposes of directing and managing project execution and information distribution. Pair programming and self-organizing teams perform quality assurance. To deliver working code in 14- to 30-day intervals, developers are ultimately empowered to perform the executing process group in agile methods.

From the PMBoK, iteration planning serves the purpose of the executing process group. Iteration planning, daily standups, pair programming teams, and self-organizing teams cover the five categories of the executing process group. This includes project coordination, quality assurance, team development, information distribution, and subcontracting. Iteration planning is a right-sized, just-enough, and just-in-time executing process group within agile methods for maximizing business value.

7.4 Monitoring Process Group

In the PMBoK, the monitoring process group consists of the fourth set of activities used to monitor a project's progress. The monitoring process group has three major categories: (1) controlling; (2) managing teams, stakeholders, and subcontractors; and (3) performance reporting. It contains an activity for monitoring and controlling project work and for change, scope, schedule, cost, quality, and risk control. The monitoring process group also has activities for managing teams, stakeholders, and subcontractors. Release, iteration, and sprint planning contain the practices to perform the monitoring process group.

Within agile methods, iteration planning serves as the monitoring process group. The project team is responsible for monitoring and controlling all project work—generally, pair programming and self-organizing teams. They perform change, scope, schedule, cost, quality, risk control, scope verification, quality assurance, and performance reporting. The project teams also manage their team members, stakeholders, and subcontractors. In agile methods, the monitoring process group is a two-layered adaptable process. That is, corrective action takes place at the 14- to 30-day iteration level and then at the release plan level.

From the PMBoK, iteration planning serves the purpose of the monitoring process group. Iteration planning, daily standups, pair programming, and self-organizing teams cover the 12 processes in the monitoring process group. In agile methods, corrective action may result in a new release and iteration plan, whereas in traditional methods, corrective action may erode the integrity of a project plan. Thus, iteration planning is a right-sized, just-enough, and just-in-time monitoring group within agile methods for maximizing business value.

7.5 Closing Process Group

In the PMBoK, the closing process group consists of the fifth set of activities used to deliver a final product to a customer. Interim work products or deliverables and the final products, results, or services are delivered during closing. An interim work product or deliverable may include documentation relevant to operation and maintenance. The final product is what the customer ultimately wants. The closing process group contains two activities: (1) project closure and (2) contract closure. Release, iteration, and sprint planning contain the practices to perform the closing process group.

Within agile methods, iteration planning serves as the closing process group, whereas within traditional methods of closing processes, many projects fail to deliver the specified product or just simply fail. Within agile methods, working software is delivered every 14 to 30 days, satisfying the customer needs. In effect, projects are closed out at the end of all iterations. However, closing processes do not have the same ominous tone as they do in traditional methods. In agile methods, the software actually works. The closing processes take place at the 14- to 30-day iteration level and at the release plan level.

From the PMBoK, iteration planning serves the purpose of the closing process group. Release and iteration plans, as well as all of the values and practices of agile methods, cover the two processes from the closing process group. That is, each iteration or sprint is a complete mini-project that is successfully delivered and closed out every 14 to 30 days on a positive note. Therefore, iteration planning is a right-sized, just-enough, and just-in-time closing group within agile methods for maximizing business value.

7.6 Summary

Agile project management is the application of both traditional and nontraditional project management principles to create software. That is, agile project management involves traditional principles to manage the development of new software products. The PMBoK is the pinnacle of traditional principles, including project integration, scope, time, cost, quality, human resources, communications, risk, and procurement management. However, agile methods use right-sized, just-enough, and just-in-time project management principles.

Agile methods use a series of iterations that are self-contained mini-projects for delivering working software every 14 to 30 days. In that time span, projects using agile methods cover all of the practices found in the PMBoK. They employ all of the basic principles found in its five processes: initiating, planning, executing, monitoring, and closing. While valuable working software is delivered in frequent iterations, much more business value can be achieved by multiple iterations. To adapt to emerging customer needs and market conditions, agile methods projects can be replanned cost-effectively.

This may come as a surprise, but agile methods have project management discipline. They have built-in project management frameworks called release and sprint planning; are a simple, but powerful way to manage integration, scope, time, cost, quality, teamwork, communications, risk, and contracts; and have the appropriate amount of discipline to create new products without using manufacturing-era principles. Both Extreme Programming and Scrum projects now use release planning. Release and sprint planning have right-sized, just-enough, and just-in-time project management discipline for maximizing business value.

7.7 Further Readings

Aguanno, K. (2005). *Managing agile projects*. Lakefield, ON, Canada: Multi-Media Publications.

Augustine, S. (2005). *Managing agile projects*. Upper Saddle River, NJ: Prentice Hall.

Beck, K., & Fowler, M. (2001). *Planning extreme programming*. Upper Saddle River, NJ: Addison-Wesley.

Chin, G. L. (2004). *Agile project management: How to succeed in the face of changing project requirements*. New York, NY: AMACOM.

DeCarlo, D. (2004). *Extreme project management: Using leadership, principles, and tools to deliver value in the face of volatility*. San Francisco, CA: Jossey-Bass.

Highsmith, J. A. (2004). *Agile project management: Creating innovative products*. Boston, MA: Addison-Wesley.

PMBoK. (2004). *A guide to the project management body of knowledge: Third edition (PMBoK Guide)*. Newtown Square, PA: Project Management Institute.

Schwaber, K. (2004). *Agile project management with Scrum*. Redmond, WA: Microsoft Press.

Sliger, M., & Broderick, S. (2008). *The software project manager's bridge to agility*. Boston, MA: Addison-Wesley.

Wysocki, R. K. (2007). *Effective project management: Traditional, adaptive, and extreme*. Indianapolis, IN: Wiley Publishing.

8

Agile Software Engineering

Agile software engineering combines customer collaboration, teamwork, iterative development, and adaptability to develop, operate, and maintain new software products. By applying flexible and adaptable software development practices that are systematic, disciplined, and quantifiable, the agile software engineering discipline is right-sized, just-enough, and just-in-time to get the job done. Agile software engineering gathers customer needs, produces working software, and applies just enough software engineering discipline to satisfy customers.

Whereas the creators of agile methods wanted to differentiate themselves from traditional methods, the supporters of traditional methods reject agile methods as undisciplined. Are agile methods disciplined or undisciplined? Part of the answer lies in the definition of software engineering found in the software engineering body of knowledge, which is *the application of a systematic, disciplined, and quantifiable approach to the development, operation, and maintenance of software.* Taken at face value, it does not exclude the values or practices of agile methods.

The other part of the answer lies in the interpretation of software engineering. This includes documents for customer requirements, project plans, and development, operation, and maintenance. Although it's easy to see that within traditional methods business value comes from documentation, within agile methods business value comes from delivering working software every 14 to 30 days. This doesn't mean skipping development, operation, and maintenance documentation. It means right-sized, just-enough, and just-in-time software engineering discipline to maximize business value.

8.1 Requirements

In the software engineering body of knowledge, software requirements are properties that must be exhibited to solve a problem. It is also a process of eliciting, analyzing, specifying, and validating customer requirements. In traditional methods, software requirements specifications are a major component, documenting the essential functionality, performance, design constraints, and attributes of software and its interfaces. The skillful application of numerous requirements engineering methods, graphical modeling methods, management processes, and traceability tools is regarded as a software requirements discipline.

Agile methods have a form of software requirements called user stories. They are simple, one-sentence statements describing software functions that customers need to add business value. There is a process for writing, estimating, splitting, spiking, sorting, and determining the velocity of user stories. While splitting decomposes user stories into smaller pieces, spiking prototypes a user story to explore its constraints. User stories can be sorted by risk or business value to prioritize their implementation. Customers can then select the scope of a release by choosing from among user stories.

User stories serve the purpose of software requirements from the software engineering body of knowledge. Release and sprint plans from Extreme Programming and Scrum define the process for managing user stories. User stories are then documented on index cards or within one of many automated workflow tools. The most valuable part of user stories is the collaboration with customers and between developers, as well as their simplicity. User stories are right-sized, just-enough, and just-in-time software requirements within agile methods for maximizing business value.

8.2 Architecture

In the software engineering body of knowledge, software architecture is a description of software subsystems and their relationships. It is also a process of specifying, identifying, evaluating, and selecting an architectural style or pattern. In traditional methods, software architecture descriptions are major components, documenting the description, components, requirements, concepts, resources, and rationale. The skillful application of numerous description languages, analysis methods, quality attributes, frameworks, reference models, and domain analysis tools is regarded as a software architecture discipline.

Agile methods have a form of software architecture called system metaphors, which are narratives that customers, managers, and programmers can use to talk about how the software product works. There is a process for developing metaphors. One of the goals of the initial iteration is to have a functional skeleton of the system as a whole. Customers must choose a set of user stories that will force the developers to create the whole architecture. After user stories are selected from the scope of the initial release defined by customers, customers and developers combine them into a simple narrative about how the whole system works.

System metaphors serve the purpose of software architecture from the software engineering body of knowledge. The release planning methodology from Extreme Programming defines the process for managing software architecture. System metaphors may be recorded in a document that is placed where everyone can see it or stored in workflow tools. System metaphors are simple and effective tools for communicating among teams. Within agile methods, system metaphors are right-sized, just-enough, and just-in-time software architecture for maximizing business value.

8.3 Design

In the software engineering body of knowledge, software design is defined as the components, interfaces, and characteristics. It is also a process of defining software structure, analyzing quality, applying design notations, and utilizing software design methods. In traditional methods, software design descriptions are major components, documenting the description, algorithms, data structures, inputs and outputs, relationships, data flow, traceability, rationale, and reuse options. The skillful application of numerous design styles, patterns, tools, notations, and methods is regarded as a software design discipline.

Agile methods have a form of software design called simple design, which is a code design with the fewest number of classes and methods that satisfy all user stories and pass all tests. The process for creating simple designs starts with a unit test to evaluate software methods. After designing and implementing just enough code to get tests running, the process is repeated; that is, create some code and then remove whatever you don't need. The code must communicate everything you intend, lack redundancy, and have a small number of classes. Additionally, it must require only a small initial investment and must result in working software.

Simplicity serves the purpose of software design from the software engineering body of knowledge. Simplicity practices from Extreme Programming define the process for software design. In traditional methods, software design is a document, but within agile methods it is part of coding. Software design considerations may also be documented directly within source code comments where software maintainers are most likely to look. Within agile methods, simplicity is right-sized, just-enough, and just-in-time software design for maximizing business value.

8.4 Construction

In the software engineering body of knowledge, software construction is the process of creating working software. It is also a process of coding, verification, unit testing, integration testing, and debugging. In traditional methods, software construction can also refer to programming style guides, which document in-dentation, spacing, line length, blank line, statement, parenthesis, class, interface, initialization, declaration, naming, and comment rules. The skillful application of numerous style guides, programming languages, editors, debuggers, and static analyzers, for example, is regarded as a software construction discipline.

Agile methods have practices for software construction, such as pair program-ming, refactoring, coding standards, and collective ownership. Pair programming is the use of two people to code all software; refactoring means to simplify or re-structure code on an as-needed basis; coding standards are programming language style guides; and collective ownership means that all programmers are entitled to change the code on an as-needed basis. Programmers accept tasks, estimate tasks, find a partner, create unit tests, use the coding standard, write simple code, and test it. They also attempt to refactor, simplify, or restructure the code.

Pair programming, refactoring, coding standards, and collective ownership serve the purpose of software construction from the software engineering body of knowledge. In traditional methods, software construction is the least important activity. In agile methods, a flexible and adaptable layer of software engineering discipline is placed over software construction, which enables working software to be created in 14- to 30-day iterations. Within agile methods, these practices are right-sized, just-enough, and just-in-time software construction for maximiz-ing business value.

8.5 Testing

In the software engineering body of knowledge, software testing is an activity performed to evaluate software quality. It is also a process of developing test plans, designs, cases, procedures, scripts, and reports. In traditional methods, soft-ware test plans are major components that document the test levels, conditions, progression, data, procedures, coverage, schedules, and environment. The skillful application of numerous test goals, objectives, strategies, types, methods, tech-niques, measures, tools, and levels of effectiveness is regarded as a software testing discipline.

Agile methods have practices for testing, such as test-driven development and continuous integration, which are processes of developing unit tests before cod-ing and integrating all changes into the system baseline to validate them using automated frameworks. Other practices support the process of verification and validation. Customer collaboration is used to capture user stories, which custom-ers verify. As a type of peer review, developers work in teams and software is continuously integrated using hourly or daily operational builds. Adaptable pro-cesses are used to get valuable software into customers' hands in 14- to 30-day iterations. Agile methods serve as means of in-process verification and validation.

Test-driven development and continuous integration serve the purpose of software testing from the software engineering body of knowledge. However, customer collaboration, pair programming, and adaptable processes form a verification and validation life cycle. Defects are prevented as user stories are captured, code is produced and tested, and working software is created in smaller 14- to 30-day iterations. Within agile methods, test-driven development and continuous integration are right-sized, just-enough, and just-in-time testing for maximizing business value.

8.6 Summary

In the software engineering body of knowledge, software engineering is a systematic, disciplined, and quantifiable approach to software development. Likewise, agile methods are a systematic, disciplined, and quantifiable approach to creating new software products. Traditional software engineering methods get their values from scientific management principles dating back to 1900. Agile methods not only get some of their values from scientific management but from the evolution of management thought during the 20th century, including scientific, behavioral, organization, systems, power, culture, change, and chaos theory, and from new product development approaches pioneered in the mid-1980s. Agile methods simply adapted the values of customer collaboration, teamwork, iterative development, and adaptability to change to the creation of new software products for satisfying its customers.

It may come as a surprise to traditionalists, but agile methods are flexible, adaptable, and highly disciplined. Agile methods are brimming with software engineering discipline: release and sprint planning serve as project management frameworks; user stories serve as verifiable requirements; pair programming teams serve as peer review groups (inspections); test-driven development and continuous integration serve as unit, system, integration, regression, and acceptance testing; coding standards insert design information into code comments; and simple designs and refactoring result in small and highly reliable code. Yes, agile methods are right-sized, just-enough, and just-in-time software engineering discipline for maximizing business value.

8.7 Further Readings

Abran, A., Moore, J. W., Bourque, P., & Dupuis, R. (2004). *Guide to the software engineering body of knowledge.* Los Alamitos, CA: IEEE Computer Society.

DoD-STD-2167A. (1988). *Military standard: Defense system software development.* Washington, DC: Space and Naval Warfare Center.

IEEE. (1997). *IEEE standards collection: Software engineering.* New York, NY: Institute of Electrical and Electronics Engineers.

ISO-12207. (1995). *Standard for information technology: Software life cycle processes.* Geneva, Switzerland: International Organization for Standardization.

J-STD-016. (1995). *Trial use standard: Standard for information technology life cycle processes*. New York, NY: Institute of Electrical and Electronics Engineers.

MIL-STD-1521B. (1985). *Military standard: Technical reviews and audits for systems, equipments, and computer software*. Washington, DC: Air Force Systems Command.

MIL-STD-498. (1994). *Military standard: Software development and documentation*. Arlington, VA: Space and Naval Warfare Center.

Pressman, R. S. (2007). *Software engineering: A practitioner's approach*. New York, NY: McGraw-Hill.

Sommerville, I. (2006). *Software engineering*. Reading, MA: Addison-Wesley.

9

Agile Support Processes

Agile support processes are supplementary administrative and technical activities that enable software engineering discipline. Examples include documentation, configuration management, quality assurance, verification and validation, and maintenance. They are used to provide additional value-added products and services or evaluate the results of software engineering activities. Considered essential to creating high-quality software and held to be a key source of discipline in software engineering, the support processes are often performed by separate functional organizations: documentation groups perform technical writing; configuration management performs material management; quality assurance performs process oversight; verification and validation performs product evaluation; and maintenance groups perform product corrections. Support processes came from scientific management principles such as specialization. Late 20th-century methods used cross-functional project teams, and the best methods formed multi-disciplinary engineers. Agile methods are one of these newer methods, and developers perform support processes on a daily basis.

In agile methods, developers use index cards to document customer requirements and commercial tools to perform automated builds. For quality assurance, they use coaching, pair programming, and test-driven development. For verification and validation, developers use onsite customers and small releases. For evolutionary product maintenance, they use agile methods themselves. Agile methods have built-in, right-sized, just-enough, and just-in-time support processes to maximize business value.

9.1 Documentation

Documentation is a process for recording information produced by a software life cycle process or activity. It consists of activities to plan, design, develop, produce, edit, distribute, and maintain software documentation. Many standards have emerged to help develop, operate, and maintain software. MIL-STD-1521 had 41 documents (1976), DoD-STD-2167 had 33 documents (1985), NASA-SMAP had 30 documents (1989), MIL-STD-498 had 47 documents (1994), J-STD-016 had 22 documents (1995), and ISO-12207 had 30 documents (1997).

Agile methods have flexible counterparts to their industrial-era antecedents. Release and sprint plans are used as project plans; user stories serve as customer requirements; metaphors are used for architecture; coding standards support design information for maintenance; test-driven development and continuous integration support test planning; built-in help menus support user operation; collaboration tools and wikis support maintenance; and a variety of right-sized, just-enough, and just-in-time electronic multimedia embody the best elements of traditional documentation.

Although agile methods are accused of lacking documentation discipline, they have release and iteration plans, user stories, metaphors, coding standards, automated tests, electronic help, and online tools for operation and maintenance. Industrial-age documents are one-dimensional and cannot adequately capture tacit knowledge. However, agile methods combine the use of just-in-time electronic documents with rich, high-context collaboration and communication between customers and developers. Thus, agile methods have right-sized, just-enough, and just-in-time documentation for maximizing business value.

9.2 Configuration Management

Configuration management is a process of identifying, tracking, and controlling work products made during software development. Configuration management documents describe how to identify, control, review, and report the status of developing work products. Standards such as MIL-STD-480 (1968), MIL-STD-483 (1970), IEEE-STD-828 (1983), IEEE-STD-1042 (1987), MIL-STD-973 (1992), MIL-STD-2549 (1997), MIL-HDBK-61 (1997), and ISO 10007 (2003) used the basic formula of configuration identification, control, status accounting, and reviews and audits.

Agile methods have flexible and adaptable counterparts to their industrial-era antecedents. They use the concept of continuous integration and use open source tools for configuration management, version control, and build automation. Agile methods enable one-click automated software builds, pull in the latest source code changes, and integrate tests into the build. They also integrate code coverage metrics, manage code branches, support cross-platform integration, and deploy builds to multiple environments. This is an iterative process of developing user stories, unit tests, simple designs, code, daily operational builds, and small releases.

Although agile methods are accused of lacking discipline, they have configuration management far beyond industrial-age standards. Designed to support release and sprint planning, automated workflow tools help create, track, and manage the release plans, user stories, and other artifacts. In traditional methods, configuration management is an organization, plan, process, and filing cabinet. In agile methods, it is an instinctive developer action to produce a working code. Agile methods have right-sized, just-enough, and just-in-time configuration management for maximizing business value.

9.3 Quality Assurance

Quality assurance is a process of ensuring that the software projects are correctly using the activities and work products to create software. Quality assurance documents describe how to evaluate results of activities, work products, reviews, and other support processes. Standards such as MIL-Q-9858 (1959), MIL-STD-109B (1969), MIL-S-52779 (1974), IEEE-STD-730 (1984), IEEE-STD-730.1 (1986), ISO-9001 (1987), and DoD-STD-2168 (1988) specified how to evaluate development activities, work products, reviews and audits, support processes, and suppliers.

Agile methods have flexible and adaptable counterparts to their industrial-era antecedents. Similar to traditional methods, quality assurance in agile methods ensures that release and iteration plans, user stories, acceptance criteria, and development tasks are produced. It enforces coding standards, metaphors, test practices, and customer satisfaction. Quality assurance also ensures that workflow tools and environments are used properly to support release planning, collaboration, and development. Finally, it ensures that continuous integration is performed using version control, configuration management, and automated builds.

Agile methods are accused of lacking quality assurance discipline. In traditional methods, quality assurance is an organization, plan, and process. In comparison, agile methods employ rich, high-context communications and individual interactions to ensure that users are adhering to practices. Furthermore, agile methods emphasize training and certification. Several built-in roles ensure that teams are following agile practices, including certified trainers, coaches, Scrum masters, and product owners. Agile methods have right-sized, just-enough, and just-in-time quality assurance for maximizing business value.

9.4 Verification and Validation

Verification and validation is a process of ensuring all life cycle work products satisfy the requirements, including the final product. Verification and validation documents describe how to evaluate the work products of the analysis, design, code, and test phases. From 1982 to the present time, standards such as IEEE-STD-1012 (1986) and IEEE-STD-1059 (1993), along with numerous textbooks, specified 33 major verification and validation tasks, along with 31 optional tasks, for phases ranging from management through maintenance.

Agile methods have flexible and adaptable counterparts to their industrial-era antecedents. Verification and validation is integrated throughout the software life cycle in agile methods. This is true from both a technical (verification) and customer (validation) point of view. While verification is concerned with the correctness of the interim work products, validation is concerned with the final product. Teams create test cases, simple designs, and code, and then verify what they've built using continuous integration. After customers create user stories, they use acceptance tests to validate what has been built in 14- to 30-day iterations.

Agile methods are accused of lacking verification and validation discipline. In traditional methods, verification and validation is an organization, plan, and process. Developers perform static and dynamic verification of work products on an hourly and daily basis in agile methods. Customers perform acceptance testing to validate the final work products every 14 to 30 days. Rich, high-context communications enable integrated verification and validation. That has not been present in traditional methods. Thus, agile methods have right-sized, just-enough, and just-in-time verification and validation for maximizing business value.

9.5 Maintenance

Maintenance is a process of making repairs, enhancements, or upgrades to a finished software product following its development. Maintenance documents describe how to analyze, design, code, test, and deliver new software revisions. From 1981 to 2009, standards such as IEEE-STD-1219 (1992), ISO-12207 (1997), and ISO-14764 (1999) emerged, along with numerous textbooks. These standards have five stages: (1) problem and modification analysis, (2) modification implementation, (3) maintenance review/acceptance, (4) migration, and (5) software retirement.

Agile methods have flexible and adaptable counterparts to their industrial-era antecedents. There is little difference between traditional and agile methods approaches to maintenance. Agile methods provide an environment for continuous integration and enhancement of working software releases. That is, customers provide a stream of prioritized user stories for new and enhanced features. Developers simply schedule them, decompose them into technical tasks, write tests, and create simple designs. Then they implement the changes (refactoring if necessary), drop them into the baseline, and deliver them in 14- to 30-day iterations without a lot of fanfare. All things being equal, agile methods tend to resemble the traditional software maintenance process more than the traditional software development life cycle, which is process- and documentation-intensive.

Agile methods are accused of lacking maintenance discipline. In traditional methods, maintenance is an organization, plan, and process, but in agile methods there is no distinction between development and maintenance. Time-based iterations are used in agile methods to code a stream of customer-prioritized user stories. Software design decisions are embedded within code comments, automated workflow tools, and the development environment. A variety of multimedia communications are available to end users. Therefore, agile methods have right-sized, just-enough, and just-in-time maintenance for maximizing business value.

9.6 Summary

Support processes are supplementary activities that provide a foundation for discipline in software engineering. They include documentation, configuration management, quality assurance, verification and validation, and maintenance. Support processes provide value-added products and services, such as technical and customer documentation about the product, and they fulfill critical needs, such as helping to manage or evaluate processes and products. This ensures that customer requirements are satisfied and developers produce the highest-quality software products.

If software engineering is systematic, disciplined, and quantifiable, then the support processes are responsible for making it so. Because agile support processes within agile methods are not visible to proponents of traditional methods, they are accused of not having any support processes. However, release plans, user stories, tests, code comments, and a variety of electronic media serve as documentation within agile methods. Configuration management is fully integrated, as evident by daily operational builds and small releases. Quality assurance is enabled by numerous built-in checks and balances, including trainers, coaches, Scrum masters, product owners, and teams.

Verification and validation is built into agile methods. Customers supply user stories and validate them on a frequent basis. Scrum masters are responsible for leading teams to achieve technical excellence. Teams also cross-check one another. Developers test the implementation of all user stories and development tasks by dropping them into the evolving baseline on an hourly, daily, and weekly basis. Because agile methods are flexible and adaptable enough to implement a steady stream of user stories, they need no separate maintenance process. Agile methods have right-sized, just-enough, and just-in-time support processes to maximize business value.

9.7 Further Readings

Berglund, E., & Priestley, M. (2001). Open-source documentation: In search of user-driven, just-in-time writing. *Proceedings of the 19th Annual International Conference on Computer Documentation, Santa Fe, New Mexico, USA,* 132-141.

IEEE-STD-1042. (1987). *IEEE guide to software configuration management.* Piscataway, NJ: IEEE Computer Society.

IEEE-STD-1059. (1993). *IEEE guide for software verification and validation plans.* Piscataway, NJ: IEEE Computer Society.

IEEE-STD-1219. (1992). *IEEE standard for software maintenance*. Piscataway, NJ: IEEE Computer Society.

IEEE-STD-730.1. (1986). *IEEE guide for software quality assurance planning*. Piscataway, NJ: IEEE Computer Society.

ISO-12207. (1995). *International standard for information technology: Software life cycle processes*. Geneva, Switzerland: International Organization for Standardization.

Rueping, A. (2003). *Agile documentation: A pattern guide to producing lightweight documents for software projects*. West Sussex, England: John Wiley & Sons.

Sfetsos, P. (2007). *Agile software development quality assurance*. Hershey, PA: Idea Group.

Unhelkar, B. (2005). *Verification and validation for quality of UML 2.0 models*. Hoboken, NJ: John Wiley & Sons.

10

Agile Tools
and Technologies

There are many tools and technologies to support agile methods, including tools for agile workflow, collaboration, development, and support. They also include agile technologies—information technology that is flexible and adaptable to change. A major value of agile methods is *individuals and interactions over processes and tools*. This means that rich, high-context personal interactions and communications are more important than processes, tools, and technologies.

Many tools provide direct support for agile methods and their values—they enhance individuals and interactions. Agile workflow tools help teams plan, manage, and execute projects using Scrum and Extreme Programming. Agile collaboration tools help teams collaborate with their customers or with each other. Agile development tools help teams code and test their software. Agile support tools help teams build and deliver working software every 14 to 30 days. Agile technologies are flexible and adaptable tools, which enhance productivity, quality, and customer satisfaction.

Two-thirds of the values of agile methods—customer collaboration, teamwork, iterative development, and adaptability—are about flexibility, adaptability to change, and rich, high-context communications and personal interactions. Rather than replace the basic values, agile tools and technology support and enhance them. A traditional project management tool does not a project manager make. Likewise, agile tools and technologies do not an agile method make. Agile methods are an attitude, a behavior, a culture, and a belief system, not tools or technologies.

10.1 Workflow Tools

Agile workflow tools help teams plan, manage, and orchestrate management and technical activity associated with agile methods. In general, these tools automate the process of planning and managing agile projects. Many traditional tools focus on a narrow aspect of project management such as scheduling. Agile workflow tools, however, cover a broader array of management tasks, including release and iteration plans, user stories, development tasks, and unit and acceptance tests. They even help manage a flexible form of earned value management called burn down charts.

There is a balance of commercial and open source workflow tools for agile methods, ranging from sophisticated web-based applications to simple wikis and specialized utilities. Although the majority of the tools provide support for Extreme Programming and Scrum, there is support for other types of agile methods. Two of the most popular tools—Version One and Rally—provide support for both release and iteration planning. They also help project teams track user stories, developer velocity, and burn down rates. However, simple wikis are powerful tools for sharing information and should not be overlooked to offer support to project management.

There are multiple workflow tools to support project management within agile methods. One of the most basic tools is a whiteboard, often called an information radiator. Another major tool is a wiki, which is useful in small, medium, and large distributed settings. A third type of tool is a multi-faceted, web-based workflow tool for coordinating the work of large, often virtually distributed teams, such as Version One and Rally. The latter has facilities to plan projects, execute and enforce activity workflow, and provide a picture of a project's current state. Agile methods use right-sized, just-enough, and just-in-time workflow tools to maximize business value.

10.2 Collaboration Tools

Agile collaboration tools help teams interact, communicate, and share information necessary for implementing user stories. In general, these tools help small teams communicate and collaborate with one another to accomplish their tasks. Many traditional tools focus on a narrow aspect of collaboration, such as a message board, for posting questions and answers, email, or chatting. Agile collaboration tools, however, provide support for a broader array of collaboration tasks, including voice communications, video conferencing, and virtual software design and development.

There are numerous commercial and open source collaboration tools for agile methods, ranging from sophisticated voice and video applications to wikis. Simple, common, and powerful tools, wikis enable teams to communicate user stories, development tasks, and implementation status. Social networking sites enable teams to share personal data, form trust, establish team cohesion, and improve communication. Some important tools support video and voice communications that are necessary so that teams can leverage the skills of an entire team to solve problems, share the workload, and build trust.

There are multiple collaboration tools to support teamwork within agile methods. Simply talking to another person is one of the most powerful means of human communication, and the telephone is one of the most basic tools for this purpose. Another important element in agile methods is interpersonal trust. Sharing personal data with one another helps build trust, as do social networking sites. Additionally, video conferencing is an important tool in agile methods so that one or more people may work together to solve difficult problems. Agile methods use right-sized, just-enough, and just-in-time collaboration tools to maximize business value.

10.3 Development Tools

Agile development tools help teams with design, development, and testing; create working software; and satisfy user stories. In general, these tools help teams with the technical aspects of software development, such as programming and coding. Many traditional tools focus on a narrow aspect of development—editing, compiling, debugging, and making files. Agile development tools, however, provide support for a broader array of development tasks, including graphical interfaces, modeling tools, visual editors, code interpreters, incremental compilation, and reuse libraries.

There are a variety of commercial and open source development tools for agile methods, ranging from sophisticated application development systems to simple support environments. Commercial application development systems provide compilers and interpreters for multiple languages, graphical user interfaces, modeling tools, databases, and a limitless array of features such as Visual Studio. Open source support environments provide simple modeling tools, graphical editors, debuggers, and reusable frameworks such as Eclipse. Commercial tools support proprietary systems, whereas open source tools support multiple platforms.

There are multiple development tools to support the creation of working software in agile methods. One of the most basic tools may be a proprietary or non-proprietary compiler and rudimentary development toolset. The focus of agile methods is to create working software every 14 to 30 days. Because the members of the teams using agile methods must be highly skilled programmers, they need robust development environments, whether commercial or open source, to create complex applications in short order. Agile methods use right-sized, just-enough, and just-in-time development tools to maximize business value.

10.4 Support Tools

Agile support tools help teams build and verify working code every 14 to 30 days by providing support for development activities. In general, these tools help teams with direct technical and administrative support for programming and testing. Whereas traditional tools focus on loosely coupled and disconnected code analysis, testing, and version control tools, agile support tools provide a broader array of integrated and streamlined processes and tools. This includes built-in code analysis, automated unit and system tests, complete build automation, and continuous integration.

There are a variety of commercial and open source support tools for agile methods, ranging from sophisticated build automation tools to simple but well-integrated services. Commercial tools provide a variety of code coverage tools, automated testing frameworks, and configuration management systems for end-to-end build automation. Open source tools also provide building blocks for code coverage analysis, unit testing, and build automation. The importance of support tools for agile methods cannot be overstated. In traditional methods, these functions are completed manually by separate organizations.

In agile methods, multiple support tools provide direct support for the creation of working software. Automated testing frameworks and simple open source utilities are the most commonly used tools. Many teams know the importance of commercial solutions that provide well-integrated code analysis, testing, and build automation. The mantra of agile methods is to produce working code in 14- to 30-day iterations. Developers must be highly skilled in programming as well as in the use of support tools. Agile methods use right-sized, just-enough, and just-in-time support tools to maximize business value.

10.5 Technologies

Agile technologies help teams build working code every 14 to 30 days using flexible and adaptable information technologies. In general, these technologies help teams with high-level support to rapidly compose multimedia applications. Whereas traditional technologies consist of third-generation computer languages or low-level components for manual coding, agile technologies provide a broader array of high-level tools to rapidly compose applications. This includes fourth-generation languages, code generators, use of high-level building blocks, and even turnkey web solutions.

The variety of commercial and open source technologies for agile methods ranges from sophisticated turnkey systems to simple software components. Commercial technologies generally consist of turnkey web solutions requiring minor customization and configuration to satisfy customer needs. Open source technologies consist of composing new applications from high-level web services using simple integration frameworks. Commercial technologies provide web hosting services that must be leased. Open source technologies can be downloaded at little or no cost, but require web hosting services.

There are multiple technologies to help teams develop working software. Commercial tools consist of turnkey solutions, whereas open source tools offer low-cost web services. A major value of agile methods is that they respond to change, which means using flexible and adaptable processes, products, and technologies. The ultimate goal of agile methods is to satisfy customer needs as quickly as possible with minimal overhead. Agile technologies help developers accomplish this instead of having to code applications by hand. Agile methods use right-sized, just-enough, and just-in-time agile technologies to maximize business value.

10.6 Summary

A key lesson handed down in agile methods over the last century is the value of interpersonal communication and collaboration. Nothing is better than a whiteboard to radiate information, such as a release or iteration plan, user story, and task and project status. The challenge is to adapt just enough technology to enhance the performance of teams using agile methods and to avoid reverting to tenuous workflow ideas of the industrial era. Agile workflow and collaboration tools must help teams maintain a delicate balance between behavior and process principles.

Agile development and support tools reached their pinnacle in the early 21st century. Commercial and open source solutions integrate dozens, if not hundreds, of functions into a single development environment. These include graphical editors, modeling tools, compilers, interpreters, code analyzers, test tools, build tools, and numerous others. Commercial and open source tools support development of both front- and back-end systems and fully integrate and automate the roles of disparate functional organizations typically found in traditional methods.

The early 21st century is the era of agile methods and technologies and that includes highly flexible and adaptable technologies that can be used to rapidly compose applications. These include open source software for composing multimedia applications and commercial turnkey solutions for composing finished end-user applications with little or no programming. Agile technologies also obviate the need for modern development and support tools, which represent the best ideas of traditional methods from the 20th century. Agile methods use a variety of right-sized, just-enough, and just-in-time agile tools and technologies to maximize business value.

10.7 Further Readings

Chow, S. W. (2007). *PHP web 2.0 mashup projects: Practical PHP mashups with google maps, flickr, amazon, youtube, msn search, yahoo!* Birmingham, UK: Packt Publishing.

Guckenheimer, S., & Perez, J. J. (2006). *Software engineering with Microsoft visual studio team system.* Upper Saddle River, NJ: Addison-Wesley.

Hemrajani, A. (2006). *Agile Java development with spring, hibernate, and eclipse.* Indianapolis, IN: Sams Publishing.

Hightower, R., Onstine, W., Visan, P., & Payne, D. (2004). *Professional Java tools for extreme programming: Ant, XDoclet, JUnit, Cactus, and Maven.* New York, NY: John Wiley & Sons.

Klocker, C. (2008). *Mashups: A new concept in web application programming.* Saarbrucken, Germany: VDM Verlag.

Kock, N. (2008). *E-collaboration in modern organizations: Initiating and managing distributed projects.* Hershey, PA: Information Science Reference.

Niemeyer, G., & Poteet, J. (2003). *Extreme programming with Ant: Building and deploying Java applications with JSP, EJB, XSLT, XDoclet, and JUnit.* Indianapolis, IN: Sams Publishing.

Salam, A. F., & Stevens, J. R. (2007). *Semantic web technologies and e-business: Toward the integrated virtual organization and business process automation.* Hershey, PA: Idea Group.

Tapscott, D., & Williams, A. D. (2006). *Wikinomics: How mass collaboration changes everything.* London: Penguin.

11

Comparison of
Agile Methods

In addition to the major types of agile methods—Scrum, Extreme Programming, Dynamic Systems Development, Feature Driven Development, and Crystal Methods—there are numerous lower-level practices. These include onsite customers, release planning, test-driven development, refactoring, pair programming, and daily standups. Agile methods also consist of traditional practices, including risk management, configuration management, inspections, object-oriented design, retrospectives, prototyping, and many more.

Scrum has five practices, three roles, and four work products. Feature Driven Development has eight practices, 14 roles (of which six are major), and 16 work products. Extreme Programming has 28 practices (up from an original 13), seven roles, and seven work products. Crystal Methods has 14 practices, 10 roles, and 25 work products, and Dynamic Systems Development has 15 practices, 12 roles, and 23 work products.

Each obtains business value in different ways: Scrum from sprint planning, daily standups, self-organizing teams, and sprint retrospectives; Feature Driven Development from object-oriented design; Extreme Programming from release planning, test-driven development, refactoring, onsite customers, pair programming, and continuous integration; Crystal Methods from its Scrum and Extreme Programming practices; and Dynamic Systems Development by building a system in three broad-sweeping iterations.

11.1 Practices

Agile methods have similar practices for customer collaboration, teamwork, iterative development, and adaptability (see Figure 11-1). Sprint reviews and onsite

Method	Collaboration	Teamwork	Working software	Adaptability
Crystal	• Interaction design	• Daily standups	• Frequent delivery	• Blitz planning
Scrum	• Sprint reviews	• Daily standups	• 30-day sprints	• Sprint planning
DSDM	• User involvement	• Daily meetings	• Iterations	• Feasibility study
FDD	• Domain walkthrough	• Feature teams	• Feature build	• Feature planning
XP	• Onsite customers	• Pair programming	• 14-day iterations	• Release planning

Figure 11-1 Comparison of practices of agile methods

customers are used for customer collaboration, whereas daily standups and pair programming facilitate teamwork. Sprints are used for iterative development, whereas sprint and release planning are used for adaptation. Sprint reviews are preferable to onsite customers, pair programming can be more useful than daily standups, small iterations are better than long sprints, and release planning is more robust than sprint planning.

Agile methods such as Scrum and Extreme Programming have similar practices, whereas others have more traditional practices. For instance, Extreme Programming uses metaphors and a simple design. Feature Driven Development, on the other hand, uses object-oriented design. Extreme Programming has test-driven development, spikes, refactoring, continuous integration, and pair programmers. On the other hand, Dynamic Systems Development uses test-last development, prototypes, three broad development iterations, configuration management, and project managers. Some agile methods have clear leaders, whereas others barely mention them.

Two other practices that stand out are continuous integration and electronic documentation. Best-in-class Extreme Programming teams have perfected the art of continuous integration—tool environments for version control, hourly and daily operational builds, and completely automated integration, system, and regression testing. Open source developers have introduced the notion of just-in-time electronic documentation for design decisions, user guides, and software maintenance documentation. An important point is that right-sized, just-enough, and just-in-time practices are better than an all-encompassing group of every conceivable technique.

11.2 Pros and Cons

There are pros and cons to each of the major types of agile methods (see Figure 11-2). During a sprint, Scrum insulates developers from outside distractions, whereas Extreme Programming has an effective balance of release planning and a

Method	Pro	Con
Crystal	• Scalable family of practices • Collection of agile methods practices • Support for code reviews and inspections	• Amalgamation of agile methods practices • Traditional requirements methodology • Resembles traditional methodology
Scrum	• Adaptable planning framework • Adaptable requirements model • Emphasis on self-organizing teams	• No code reviews or inspections • No comprehensive testing methodology • Few customer interactions and automation
DSDM	• Strong customer involvement • Use of empowered project teams • Some support for iterative development	• Spinoff of Rapid Application Development • Resembles traditional methodologies • Weak iterative development model
FDD	• Semi-adaptable planning framework • Support for iterative development cycles • Support for code reviews and inspections	• Traditional requirements model • Significant up-front architecture and design • Few customer interactions and automation
XP	• Adaptable planning framework • Adaptable requirements model • Comprehensive testing methodology	• No code reviews or inspections • No support for virtual distributed teams • Viewed as a set of rules rather than tools

Figure 11-2   Pros and cons of agile methods

variety of useful practices. Dynamic Systems Development has a product versus a process focus and Feature Driven Development uses inspections for quality control. Crystal Methods has a balanced blend of Scrum and Extreme Programming practices. Additionally, open source software development has a good documentation model.

Agile methods have weaknesses that are difficult to overcome. Scrum has lengthy sprints, a thin planning methodology, use of a product owner instead of a customer, and few practices. Extreme Programming has excessive use of onsite customers, a heavy dependence on testing, and thin documentation. Dynamic Systems Development has too many traditional practices, roles, and work products. Feature Driven Development has significant upfront architecture, object-oriented design, and a thin planning framework. Crystal Methods has a large number of traditional roles and documents and a sheer volume of practices.

One must understand the strengths and weaknesses of agile methods. Some agile methods have few practices, whereas others have numerous ones. However, bigger isn't always better. The essence of agile methods is just enough process, whereas the essence of traditional methods is never enough processes and documentation. However, the issue is not just small versus large number of practices, but the right mix of practices. Seek the right amount of customer interaction, skilled programmers, small releases, and adaptable planning. The key is to strike an effective balance of right-sized, just-enough, and just-in-time practices.

11.3 Flexibility

Agile methods have varying degrees of flexibility (see Figure 11-3). Part of this has to do with the sheer number of practices. Scrum has the fewest number, followed by Feature Driven Development, Dynamic Systems Development, and Crystal Methods. Extreme Programming has twice as many practices as Dynamic Systems Development. Scrum has one-third the total number of practices, roles, and work products as the other four major forms of agile methods. Therefore, from a sheer size perspective, Scrum is the most flexible agile method.

Among agile methods, Extreme Programming's release planning is one of the most flexible and adaptable management frameworks, and Scrum and Extreme Programming have the fewest number of work products. Thus, from a size, planning, and work product perspective, Scrum and Extreme Programming are among the most flexible and adaptable agile methods. Although the roles and work products of Feature Driven Development, Crystal Methods, and Dynamic Systems Development tend to favor traditional methods, Crystal Methods is supposed to be scalable, so it is considered the most flexible and adaptable agile method.

Agile methods have just enough processes and products to get the job done and are generally smaller than traditional methods. However, even agile methods are subject to a steep learning curve, and their practices have to be adopted gradually. In this case, agile methods, such as Scrum and Feature Driven Development, may be the most flexible out of the box, because they are smaller than other agile methods. However, it's not just small size that's important but the flexibility and adaptability of the individual practices. Therefore, right-sized, just-enough, and

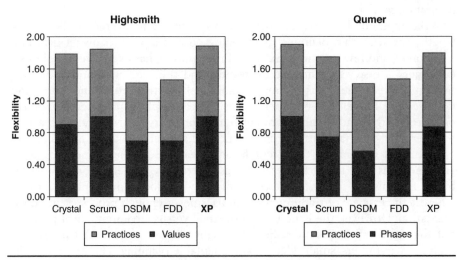

Figure 11-3   Flexibility of agile methods (Highsmith & Qumer)

just-in-time practices that are flexible and adaptable are more important than small-sized agile methods alone.

11.4 Risks

Agile methods have varying degrees of risk, often measured through the lens of traditional methods (see Figure 11-4). That is, the less an agile method is like traditional methods, the more risk it is perceived to have. And, vice versa, the more an agile method is like a traditional method, the less risk it is perceived to have. For instance, because Dynamic Systems Development has many traditional practices, such as project management, configuration management, and documentation, it is perceived to have low risk.

Feature Driven Development is also perceived to have low risk, because it has a high number of traditional practices, roles, and documents. More importantly, it uses software inspections, which are commonly believed to substantially increase software quality. Therefore, Feature Driven Development is perceived to have low risk. Because Crystal Methods also has a high number of practices, roles, and traditional documents, it is perceived to have low risk. Furthermore, Crystal Methods' scalability is reportedly useful for safety-critical software.

Because Extreme Programming also has a high number of practices, roles, and documents, it is perceived to have low risk. Pair programming is believed to be a good substitute for software inspections, and test-driven development is believed to be an effective method of quality control. Because Scrum has the fewest number of practices, roles, and documents, it is perceived to have the highest risk among the major types of agile methods. However, sheer size of a software

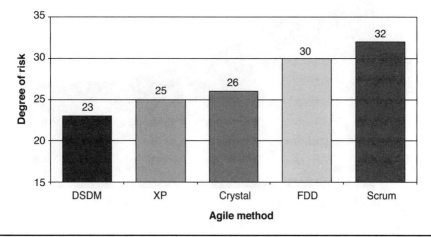

Figure 11-4 Risks of agile methods (Boehm & Turner)

method does not guarantee low risk. Right-sized, just-enough, and just-in-time agile methods may have less risk than large traditional methods.

11.5 Usage

Some agile methods are more widely used than others (see Figure 11-5). From 1999 to 2002, Extreme Programming was one of the most popular agile methods in the world, especially in Scandinavia where Participatory Design and computer-supported cooperative methods were widespread. Today, although Extreme Programming still has a stronghold in certain European countries, Scrum is gaining support in North America. Its small number of practices, roles, and work products makes it one of the most flexible agile methods on the market. Scrum and Extreme Programming hybrids are popular as well.

Just how many projects are using agile methods? Since 2001, various studies have shown that as many as 67% of software developers worldwide use agile methods. However, this doesn't seem to be widely believed, even by proponents of agile methods. That is, traditional methods still have a strong hold in the field of software methods, while there is some resistance to agile methods in the software engineering community.

One explanation of the 67% usage figure may be some unintended bias in the studies. That is, many experienced software methodologists read the literature on agile methods, and it may be these same developers who are participating in the studies. Perhaps 67% of experienced developers who prefer to use software methods have adopted agile methods or at least some practices of agile methods.

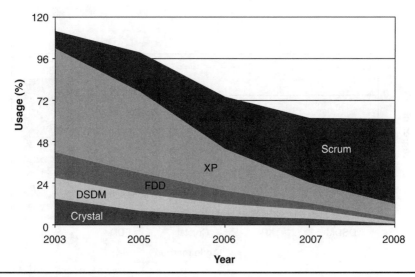

Figure 11-5 Use of agile methods (various sources)

This would partially explain why even the proponents of agile methods may be experiencing some widespread resistance to agile methods. Therefore, right-sized, just-enough, and just-in-time agile methods may be in use by software methodologists.

11.6 Summary

There are many types of agile methods and many individual practices of agile methods. They are not all created equal and have differing strengths, weaknesses, flexibility, risks, and usage. Scrum provides software teams with an environment to succeed, has long sprints and a small number of flexible practices, is considered risky, and is growing in popularity. Extreme Programming has a robust release planning methodology, relies heavily on busy customers, has some flexibility, is considered to be low risk, and seems to be well entrenched worldwide.

The second most flexible agile method, Feature Driven Development, has good quality control and relies on a traditional object-oriented design method, although it does have some risk and its following is unclear. Crystal Methods has a good blend of agile methods practices, a large number of agile and traditional practices, is designed to be scalable, and has only moderate risk. Dynamic Systems Development is product focused, has a large number of practices and low risk but is not flexible, and has a large following in the United Kingdom.

However, we've also shown that agile methods cannot be judged merely upon their size or resemblance to traditional methods but should be judged by the strength of their individual practices as well. For instance, Extreme Programming's release planning methodology is a best-in-class example of a project management framework for agile methods, and it has some key best practices as well. Furthermore, large size doesn't guarantee low risk. In fact, large size may increase risk due to cost and technical challenges associated with adopting a large number of practices. Therefore, right-sized, just-enough, and just-in-time agile methods with adaptable and flexible processes may be best.

11.7 Further Readings

Abrahamsson, P., Salo, O., Ronkainen, J., & Warsta, J. (2002). *Agile software development methods: Review and analysis (478)*. Oulu, Finland: VTT Publications.

Ambler, S. W. (2007). *Agile adoption survey: March 2007*. Retrieved July 23, 2007, from http://www.ambysoft.com/ downloads/surveys/AgileAdoption2007.ppt.

Boehm, B., & Turner, R. (2004). *Balancing agility and discipline: A guide for the perplexed*. Boston, MA: Addison-Wesley.

Coffin, R., & Lane, D. (2006). *A practical guide to seven agile methodologies: Part 1*. Retrieved September 3, 2008, from http://www.devx.com/architect/Article/32761.

Coffin, R., & Lane, D. (2006). *A practical guide to seven agile methodologies: Part 2*. Retrieved September 3, 2008, from http://www.devx.com/architect/Article/32836.

Highsmith, J. A. (2002). *Agile software development ecosystems*. Boston, MA: Addison-Wesley.

Poppendieck, M., & Poppendieck, T. (2007). *Implementing lean software development*. Boston, MA: Addison-Wesley.

Qumer, A., & Henderson-Sellers, B. (2008). An evaluation of the degree of agility in six agile methods. *Information and Software Technology, 50*(4), 280–295.

Sidky, A., Arthur, J., & Bohner, S. (2007). A disciplined approach to adopting agile practices: The agile adoption framework. *Innovations in Systems and Software Engineering, 3*(3), 203–216.

12

Agile Metrics
and Models

There are many choices when it comes to selecting metrics and models for agile methods. To measure the performance of agile methods, traditional or nontraditional metrics and models may be used. Traditional metrics include size, effort, productivity, and quality. Earned value management is a traditional way to measure cost and schedule performance, whereas return on investment and net present value are traditional measures of business value.

Nontraditional methods of measuring agile methods also exist, although much of the literature focuses on traditional metrics. Nontraditional methods include measures to support the values of agile methods—customer collaboration, teamwork, iterative development, and adaptability. Because the four major values of agile methods are more important than the individual practices, it is critical to measure customer collaboration and teamwork, as well as adaptability or response to change.

Developers must collaborate and communicate with customers to capture user stories, whereas development teams must cooperate with one another to implement user stories. Software must also be developed in short time-boxed iterations versus long scope-boxed life cycles. Finally, developers must use an adaptable management framework, such as release planning. Developers have two basic choices when it comes to measuring the performance of agile methods projects: (1) they can fall back on traditional measures or (2) they can use right-sized, just-enough, and just-in-time measures for maximizing business value.

12.1 Traditional Measures

Traditional metrics often measure efficiency in some way, shape, or form (see Figure 12-1). The measurement of size, effort, cost, productivity, schedule, and

75

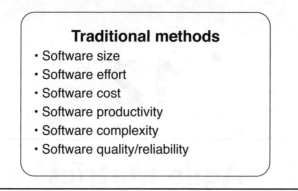

Figure 12-1   Traditional metrics

quality is a hallmark of the industrial era. Traditional measures originated from the early industrial revolution, with its theoretical basis in economics and production. Other traditional measures included reliability, reuse, earned value management, return on investment, and net present value. Specific measures used for benchmarking the performance of traditional methods include size, productivity, and defect density.

A good example is size measurement of a computer program. Another classical example is productivity, a measure of programming speed—that is, lines of code per hour; the more lines per hour the better. Another excellent example is defect density, a measure of how many defects or bugs are present in proportion to software size. Also emerging from this era were reliability measures as a way of determining mean time between software failures. Earned value management, return on investment, and net present value were designed to measure the economic efficiency of a process.

The business value of traditional methods is often quantified using operational manufacturing measures rather than strategic ones—how much, how fast, how bug-free, or how cost-effective. Oftentimes, customers want valuable software in spite of these measures. Whereas traditional methods focus on cost-effective, bug-free source code for small-scale, well-defined problems, agile methods stress successfully creating complex, innovative systems in which requirements aren't known in advance. Measures for creating right-sized, just-enough, and just-in-time business solutions are more important than simple manufacturing-era measures.

12.2 Customer Collaboration

Customer collaboration metrics measure the degree of customer interaction during development (see Figure 12-2), as well as how effectively the programmers interact with the customers to develop software. After all, isn't that the primary

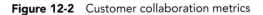

Customer collaboration
- Interaction frequency
- Communication quality
- Relationship strength
- Customer trust
- Customer loyalty
- Customer satisfaction

Figure 12-2   Customer collaboration metrics

purpose of agile methods versus traditional methods? Agile methods are a customer-driven, human-centric approach to developing software. One of the most important success factors in agile methods is how well programmers listen to customers, capture their needs, and respond to them with working software.

In traditional methods, business value often comes from contract negotiation and requirements documents made in a vacuum over a period of years. Some may argue that agile methods have a similar but lighter-weight means of capturing requirements, called user stories. If true, then all we would need to do is train people to create lightweight user stories and measure their quality. But that isn't the end of the story. Because agile methods are a human-centric approach to development, customer collaboration metrics measure how well customers and developers interact, communicate, relate, and if they trust one another. This type of social and psychological phenomenon simply can't be measured by productivity and defect density metrics but belongs to the organizational or human behavior school of management, which has many models that can be used to measure human interaction, communication, relationships, and trust. Or one can simply measure the degree to which frequent, high-quality customer feedback is solicited, received, and incorporated into working software releases.

12.3 Individuals and Interactions

Individual and interaction metrics measure the degree of interaction between software developers (see Figure 12-3). Because agile methods are considered a human-centric way of developing software, this applies to developer interactions, not just interaction with customers. One of the most important factors in agile methods is how well developers interact with one another to capture customer needs and respond to them in frequent intervals with working software. Talented,

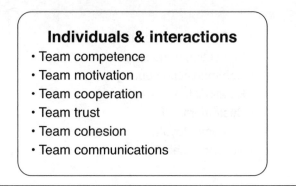

Figure 12-3   Individuals and interactions metrics

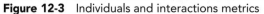

skilled, and motivated programmers must work together in high-performance teams to solve complex software problems.

In traditional methods, business value comes from processes and tools derived from early 20th-century manufacturing paradigms. Some may argue that agile methods have a similar but lighter-weight means of processes and tools, called sprint or release planning. If true, then all we would need to do is train people to create lightweight sprint or release plans and measure their quality. But, because agile methods are a human-centric approach to development, individual and interaction metrics measure how well developers interact, communicate, relate, and if they trust one another. They also measure the talent, skill, and motivation of the developers. These attributes can't be measured with productivity and defect density. Individual and interaction measures belong to the organizational behavior school of management and human capital management, which has many models to measure human interaction, communication, relationships, trust, talent, skill, and motivation. Or one can simply measure the degree to which a small, high-performance team produces frequent working software releases.

12.4 Working Software

Working software metrics measure how well developers create frequent iterations of operational software (see Figure 12-4). Agile methods are a customer-driven, iterative approach to create business value with working software every two to four weeks. One of the most important success factors in agile methods is for developers to create working software for customers to evaluate, as performed in small, time-boxed, frequent, numerous, and operational iterations. That is, the entire agile methods life cycle is executed every two to four weeks.

In traditional methods, business value comes from comprehensive documentation derived from military standards utilized from 1950 to 1990. Some may

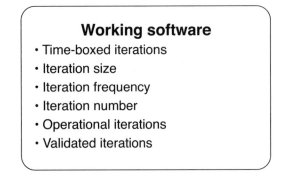

Figure 12-4 Working software metrics

argue that agile methods have a similar but lighter means of documentation, such as user stories, sprint or release plans, coding standards, software tests, and other electronic data. If true, then all we would need to do is train people to create lightweight user stories, plans, code comments, tests, etc. But agile methods are a customer-centric approach for creating small, time-boxed, frequent, numerous, and operational iterations. Programmers must develop user stories every two to four weeks.

Working software metrics measure how well developers create these iterations. Compare these to traditional manufacturing measures of success defined by programmers, such as productivity and defect density. Working software metrics come from marketing, innovation, and new product development fields where customers define success. They also measure user and customer satisfaction, system and project success, and software quality using multi-attribute models. Or one can simply measure the degree to which customers see and evaluate working software every two to fours weeks.

12.5 Responding to Change

Responding to change metrics measure how well developers can adapt to new or changing customer requirements (see Figure 12-5). Because agile methods are a customer-driven, adaptable approach to implement and deliver user stories every two to four weeks, one of the most important success factors in agile methods is for developers to adapt processes and products to new user stories. Developers must have an attitude, culture, aptitude, process, product, and technology that are adaptable to changing situations. Responding to change also involves flexible tools and automation.

In traditional methods, business value comes from following a plan based on the project management disciplines from the 1950s. Some may argue that agile methods have a similar but lighter means of project management, such as sprint

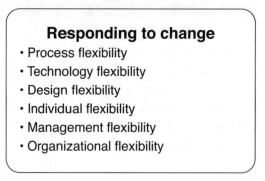

Figure 12-5   Responding to change metrics

or release planning. If true, then all we would need to do is to train people to create a user story, coding task, release plan, and iteration plan. But agile methods are an *adaptive systems-centric* approach to attitude, culture, aptitude, process, product, and technology. Programmers must be willing to adapt their organizations, behaviors, project plans, and products to meet emerging needs.

Responding to change metrics measure how well developer attitude, culture, aptitude, process, product, and technology can adapt to change. Responding to change can't be measured by traditional metrics such as software size, programming productivity, or defect density. Responding to change metrics come from systems dynamics, systems theory, double-loop learning, and adaptive organizations. Such metrics can also be used to measure the simplicity or complexity of organizations, business units, projects, or software source code. Or one can simply measure the flexibility or adaptability of a project management system to adapt to new customer needs.

12.6 Summary

There are many types of major metrics, models, and measures for gauging the performance of agile methods projects. The two broad categories of measures are (1) traditional metrics and (2) models specifically designed to measure values of agile methods. Software measurement is a controversial field. Although it has matured after four decades of research and practice, it is still in its infancy, because software is a synthetic man-made technology with constantly changing properties. Agile methods involve attitudes and behaviors rather than technology.

Traditional metrics are often used to gauge the performance of projects using agile methods. These include effort, productivity, defect density, code complexity, and earned value management. Many studies cite the effort, productivity, defect density, and code complexity measures for traditional versus agile methods.

These studies are either performed at the level of an agile method or one of the numerous practices of agile methods. The best agile methods and practices have programming productivity values at or near the best traditional methods. However, defect density values of agile methods tend to trail their best traditional counterparts.

Agile metrics differ from traditional ones and are designed to mirror the values of agile methods: collaboration, teamwork, iterative development, and adaptability. Collaboration metrics gauge how well customers and developers interact, communicate, relate, and if they trust one another. The same can be said of teamwork metrics. Iterative development metrics gauge how well developers create small, time-boxed, frequent, numerous, and operational iterations. Adaptability metrics gauge how well attitude, culture, aptitude, process, product, and technology can respond to change.

12.7 Further Readings

Barki, H., & Hartwick, J. (1994). Measuring user participation, user involvement, and user attitude. *MIS Quarterly, 18*(1), 59–82.

Conte, S. D., Dunsmore, H. E., & Shen, V. Y. (1986). *Software engineering metrics and models*. Menlo Park, CA: Benjamin Cummings.

Fichman, R. G., Keil, M., & Tiwana, A. (2005). Beyond valuation: Options thinking in IT project management. *California Management Review, 47*(2), 74–96.

Hayes, B. E. (2008). *Measuring customer satisfaction and loyalty: Survey design, use, and statistical analysis*. Milwaukee, WI: ASQ Press.

Hericko, M., & Zivkovic, A. (2008). The size and effort estimates in iterative development. *Information and Software Technology, 50*(7/8), 772–781.

Jones, S. D., & Schilling, D. J. (2000). *Measuring team performance*. New York, NY: Jossey-Bass.

Kan, S. H. (2002). *Metrics and models in software quality engineering*. Reading, MA: Addison-Wesley.

Napier, R., & McDaniel, R. (2006). *Measuring what matters: Simplified tools for aligning teams and their stakeholders*. Mountain View, CA: Davies-Black.

Woodcock, M., & Francis, D. (2008). *Team metrics: Resources for measuring and improving team performance*. Amherst, MA: HRD Press.

13

Surveys of Agile Methods

Numerous individuals, firms, and organizations use survey research to collect important data concerning the use of agile methods. One of the most important tools in social science, surveys are often used to collect data about management trends, such as agile methods. Surveys are a form of quantitative research and are often used to collect attitudinal data. That is, they collect data about people's attitudes toward a particular management phenomenon.

Surveys have been used to measure a variety of factors related to agile methods, including general attitudes about the use of agile methods as well as about the types and practices being used. Surveys are also used to collect key quantitative information, such as the number of people trained to use agile methods and the size of the projects. The amount of time agile methods have been used, years of experience, and organization size and revenues are also important.

The impacts of agile methods on costs, productivity, cycle time, quality, customer satisfaction, and morale are often measured. Whereas agile methods lead to satisfaction of customer needs and successful project completion, key studies such as the Standish Report and pivotal textbooks on agile and iterative development methods have demonstrated that traditional methods lead to cost escalation, poor requirements, poor quality, high maintenance costs, and project cancellation. Therefore, one of the most frequently asked questions is, "Do agile methods lead to project success?" Some surveys focus on agile methods in general, whereas others focus on a specific type. This chapter focuses on general purpose or method-agnostic surveys of agile methods.

13.1 Microsoft

Circa 2006, Microsoft conducted a survey of agile methods among its software developers (see Figure 13-1). This survey is somewhat ironic since Microsoft's own software development practices are often considered the progenitors of agile methods. That is, MIT conducted a study of software development practices from 1993 to 1995 and published the results in the form of a major textbook and in numerous journal articles. Extreme Programming's practices, such as continuous integration, test-driven development, and release planning, came from Microsoft.

Of course, not all Extreme Programming practices or agile methods came directly from Microsoft's much-publicized sync-n-stabilize approach. Nonetheless, in Microsoft's 2006 textbook survey of its own use of agile methods, it sampled 2,800 (10%) of its 28,000 developers and had a response rate of 492 people (17%). About 32% of Microsoft's developers said they used agile methods—or roughly 9,000 of Microsoft's 28,000 developers. This data came as a surprise to the researchers who conducted the survey, because they were unaware of the link between MIT's earlier research, the origin of agile methods, and how widespread agile methods had become. About 5,800 (21%) of Microsoft's developers were estimated to be using Scrum.

The top five practices of agile methods used at Microsoft were team coding standards, continuous integration of code, system metaphors, simple designs, and sustainable pace. This is not surprising, as these practices form the basis of Microsoft's sync-n-stabilize approach popularized by MIT in the mid-1990s prior to the explosion of agile methods. One of the most frequently reported attitudinal

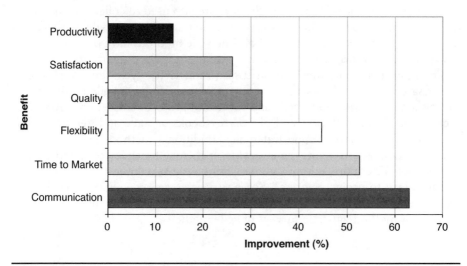

Figure 13-1   Microsoft agile method survey

factors was that agile methods worked well for individuals, teams, and groups, whereas the least frequently reported factor was morale. The two benefits reported the most were improved communication and quick releases, which go hand in hand with sync-n-stabilize.

13.2 UMUC

In 2007, University of Maryland University College (UMUC) conducted a survey of agile methods among software developers (see Figure 13-2). Its purpose was to determine if web developers using agile methods produced higher-quality e-commerce websites. Although the survey's primary contribution was an instrument to measure the use of agile methods independent of any one type or kind, additional data were collected on improvements in cost, quality, cycle time, productivity, and customer satisfaction, and it became one of the broadest cost and benefit surveys ever conducted.

UMUC's survey was conducted in association with *Dr. Dobbs Journal*, a popular software development magazine whose readership consists of leading software developers. UMUC's 2007 survey of agile methods received 250 responses, and a more recent UMUC survey received 350 responses. Although not representative, the surveys do indicate attitudes toward agile methods among worldwide software development professionals, who reflect *Dr. Dobbs'* moderately progressive readership.

Of these developers, 70% were using most practices associated with agile methods, which is a high number, as found in UMUC's 2007 survey. Over 80% of

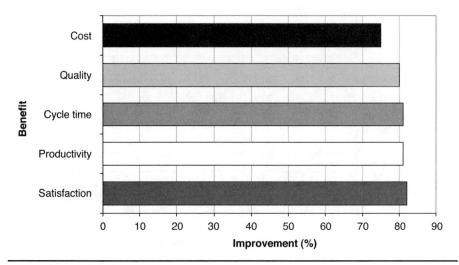

Figure 13-2   UMUC agile method survey

the respondents were from small- to medium-sized firms and had over 10 years of experience. Some of the weakest areas were customer collaboration, flexibility, and adaptability to change. Roughly 25% of the respondents felt confident enough to assert agile methods improved costs, quality, cycle time, productivity, and customer satisfaction. UMUC's study seemed to reaffirm the findings of other major studies, namely that up to 70% of worldwide developers may be using agile methods.

13.3 AmbySoft

Scott Ambler of both IBM and AmbySoft conducts annual surveys of agile methods in conjunction with *Dr. Dobbs Journal* (see Figure 13-3). He has written numerous books on the subject of software development and on agile methods-related topics. Although one of Ambler's first surveys garnered over 4,000 respondents, subsequent surveys average 600 to 700 respondents. One of his primary goals is to measure the rate of adoption: how many people are using agile methods and to what effect?

Ambler's surveys have measured such topics as organization size, knowledge of agile methods, and type of method or practice. He measures the impact of agile methods on productivity, quality, cost, customer satisfaction, and project success. He also focuses on iteration length, team size, number of projects, modeling, and effectiveness. In his first survey, 65% of the respondents came from small organizations, only 10% considered themselves experts, and only 41% had adopted agile methods. Extreme Programming and Feature Driven Development were the most often used methods, and only 10% reported significant benefits.

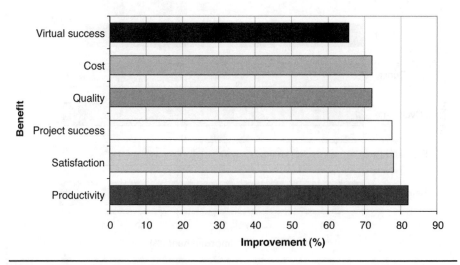

Figure 13-3 AmbySoft agile method survey

In his latest survey, 69% reported having adopted agile methods and that 73% of projects were successful as a result of agile methods. Large improvements in cost, quality, productivity, and customer satisfaction as a result of agile methods leapt from 10% to 20%. Ambler's recent work focuses on the scalability of agile methods. That is, agile methods were believed to only work for small and simple problems, but we're beginning to realize agile methods are ideally suited for large and complex problems. In a rather startling role reversal, we're also starting to realize that traditional methods may be ideally suited for small and simple problems.

13.4 IT Agile

In 2008, two consultants conducted a survey of agile methods in Germany (see Figure 13-4). Since the emergence of Extreme Programming in 1999, agile methods became quite popular in Europe. Europe is somewhat enigmatic when it comes to software methods. On one hand, software methods originating in North America seem to be more widely adopted in Europe than in the U.S. On the other hand, Europeans seems to either dramatically tailor North American software methods or simply create their own, especially in Northern Europe or Scandinavia.

In the 1990s, Participatory Design was a popular method throughout Europe and was similar to Joint Application Design, which emerged in North America during the 1980s and was a precursor to Rapid Application Development. However, Participatory Design and Joint Application Development were starkly different. While Joint Application Development was viewed as having a distinct business or

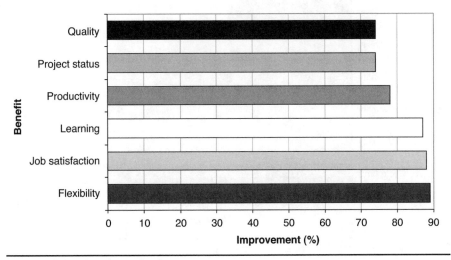

Figure 13-4 IT agile method survey

capitalistic focus (i.e., get the job done on a schedule to maximize profit), Participatory Design was viewed as a means of improving the quality of work life, especially for blue-collar union workers (i.e., socialist focus).

Europe's egalitarian culture and propensity towards Participatory Design may have made Europeans well-suited for agile methods. The 2008 German survey showed that as many as 36% of German software developers were using agile methods, and almost half of Germany's agile developers were using Scrum or Extreme Programming. The surprising statistic is that nearly 80% of those using agile methods reported significant improvements as a result of using them. These included improvements in cost reductions, quality, project success, customer satisfaction, and productivity, among many others, such as flexibility.

13.5 Version One

Version One conducts an annual survey of agile methods, often in conjunction with major conferences (see Figure 13-5). In 2006, 2007, and 2008, it conducted global surveys of agile methods and will most likely continue this trend. Its first survey garnered 722 responses and its second two garnered 1,700 and 3,000 respondents. Version One often measures the effects of agile methods on time-to-market, productivity, quality, costs, and project success, as well as the type of agile methods most often used.

Its 2006 survey reported 80% improvements in time-to-market, productivity, quality, and costs as a result of using agile methods. While 40% of organizations were using Scrum, only 23% were using Extreme Programming. However, 77%

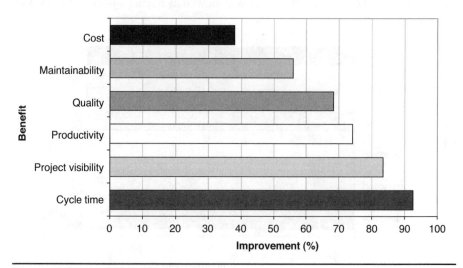

Figure 13-5   Version One agile method survey

were using Scrum and Extreme Programming hybrids. Well over 606 (84%) of the respondents said they were using agile methods. In Version One's 2007 survey, 80% continued to see improvements in time-to-market, productivity, quality, and costs. Almost 37% were using Scrum and only 12% were using Extreme Programming. Only 23% of these respondents said they were using a hybrid of the two.

Version One's 2008 survey focused on length of time agile methods have been in use. It also identified organization size, collocation, and the number of projects using agile methods. Finally, it reported data on factors that affect adoption, barriers to success, practices being used, detailed benefits, and automated tools. The number of Scrum users was up to 50%, whereas Extreme Programming was in dramatic decline, although hybrids held steady at 22%. In some cases, the number of organizations employing the individual practices of agile methods grew 20% from 2007 to 2008. The survey also asked penetrating questions on the cause of project failure.

13.6 Summary

Surveys, especially the annual ones by AmbySoft and Version One, are important research studies for measuring agile methods. These surveys indicate that the number of worldwide developers using agile methods is rising and the size of organizations using agile methods is getting larger. That is, agile methods are no longer confined to extremely small organizations. The surveys also indicate that the number of Scrum users is on the rise and the number of people using the individual practices of agile methods is increasing dramatically.

It is important to note that many of the respondents to these surveys represent the international community. It is difficult to say with certainty how many represent North America or precisely where the respondents are located. More importantly, there may be bias in some of these surveys, because it's difficult to tell how many respondents represent a cross-section of all developers or merely the body of agile methods enthusiasts worldwide. One thing is certain: Only a few large organizations are routinely using agile methods, although more and more large organizations are beginning to adopt them in special circumstances.

Surveys aren't the only type of quantitative measurement being used by researchers. For precise measurements on the costs and benefits of using agile methods, experimental research has been more widely used. However, this chapter was devoted to the study of survey data. Whereas experimental studies tend to focus on a specific type of agile method, surveys tend to examine the use of all agile methods. That is, they are method-agnostic to a certain extent. Also, experimental research focuses on small-scale problems, whereas survey research tries to uncover broad-ranging phenomena and trends with respect to agile methods.

13.7 Further Readings

Abrahamsson, P. (2007). *Speeding up embedded software development: Application of agile processes in complex systems development projects.* Eindhoven, Netherlands: Information Technology for European Advancement.

Ambler, S. W. (2008). *Agile adoption survey.* Retrieved October 17, 2008, from http://www.ambysoft.com.

Begel, A., & Nagappan, N. (2007). Usage and perceptions of agile software development in an industrial context: An exploratory study. *Proceedings of the First International Symposium on Empirical Software Engineering and Measurement, Madrid, Spain,* 255–264.

Behrens, P. (2006). *Agile project management (APM): Tooling survey results.* Louisville, CO: Trail Ridge Consulting.

Digital Focus. (2006). *Agile 2006 survey: Results and analysis.* Herndon, VA: Author.

Johnson, M. (2003). *Agile methodologies: Survey results.* Victoria, Australia: Shine Technologies.

Rico, D. F., Sayani, H. H., Stewart, J. J., & Field, R. F. (2007). A model for measuring agile methods and website quality. *TickIT International, 9*(3), 3–15.

Version One. (2008). *The state of agile development: Third annual survey.* Alpharetta, GA: Author.

Wolf, H., & Roock, A. (2008). Agile becomes mainstream: Results of an online survey. *Object Spektrum, 15*(3), 10–13.

14

Costs and Benefits of Agile Methods

Hundreds of case studies and experiments have been conducted to analyze the effects of agile methods. However, this hasn't always been true. Throughout the 1960s, 1970s, and 1980s, experience reports and opinion papers were the primary means of promoting software methods. During this period, scientists encouraged the community to use systematic research studies to analyze the impacts of software methods. This came to fruition in the 2000s as hundreds of scientists analyzed agile methods.

There are two forms of systematic research studies: (1) qualitative and (2) quantitative methods. Qualitative research often takes the form of interviews and systematic case studies. Quantitative research may take on multiple forms, such as survey research, experiments, or simply correlational studies. Qualitative methods yield rich, high-context descriptive text that often describes an up-close and personal view of agile methods. Experimental research often measures the performance of small student teams.

Agile methods were a controversial topic when they emerged in the late 1990s. Dozens of freshly minted scientists began to apply experimental research to test the mettle of this new phenomenon. Throughout this timeframe, hundreds of studies were conducted to evaluate the effects of agile methods. What resulted was one of the largest collections of scientific studies for any one type of software method. We'll present the results of 78 such studies out of 300. The goal is to begin the process of identifying the effects of agile methods on cost, schedule, productivity, quality, customer satisfaction, and return on investment.

14.1 Pair Programming

Pair programming is one of the most studied practices in the field of agile methods. There are several hundred case studies and experiments on pair programming alone. Because early proponents of pair programming claimed it increased productivity, quality, and cycle time, among other benefits, scientists began to test the validity of these claims in earnest. In general, developers can complete a high-quality computer program faster using pair programming than comparable traditional methods; although one developer takes longer, he or she uses less total effort for the same amount of work.

However, there are numerous qualitative considerations that must also be pondered. For instance, many programmers prefer to work alone, and pair programmers often complain about the social difficulties of working together. On another plane, two programmers can actually solve complex computer programming problems faster when they combine forces. Researchers often suggest pairing up a more experienced programmer with a less experienced one to minimize a clash of egos. To solve hard problems, developers need to set aside their egos and use pair programming on an as-needed basis, rather than all of the time.

We identified 30 studies of pair programming with data on its quantitative benefits (see Figure 14-1). They report an average of 34% cycle-time reductions, 76% productivity improvements, and 69% quality improvements. Eight of these studies had the detailed measurement data necessary to estimate return on investment, which averaged 2300%. That is, for every dollar invested in pair programming, $23 were returned. This comes from a combination of high productivity and higher quality, which reduces the costs of software maintenance. Pair programming is far more efficient than traditional methods.

Category	Low%	Median%	High%	Points
Cost	n/a	n/a	n/a	n/a
Schedule	11	34	70	12
Productivity	14	76	201	5
Quality	10	69	1000	24
Satisfaction	n/a	n/a	n/a	n/a
ROI	542	2303	4893	8
				49

Figure 14-1   Pair programming costs and benefits

14.2 Test-Driven Development

Test-driven development is the second most often studied phenomenon in the field of agile methods, with well over a hundred studies. The use of test-driven development has several implications: All software must be unit tested; the test cases must be written before the code; and the tests should be completely automated. The last implication goes hand in hand with the practice of continuous integration. The notion is that a system should be regression tested after every code change is made.

The idea that all software must be unit tested or that unit tests should be written first is not new. What is new is that computer programmers should do test-driven development as a matter of routine, they should enjoy it, and that it leads directly to project success. North American programmers, especially those in the commercial sector, were notorious for failing to test their code. Therefore, test-driven development came as a bit of a shock to the community and was viewed as a revolutionary new idea in 1999, although testing had been around since the 1950s. However, continuous integration is indeed a revolutionary idea. It still is!

Continuous integration goes hand in hand with agile methods. That is, the creation of working software is the highest priority because it creates the most business value. The basic idea is that programmers get a requirement, write a test, code it, and test it against the whole system every time. This ensures changes are verified and validated and the system is bug-free at minimal cost. In the 20 studies we found on the benefits of test-driven development, productivity improved by an average of 64% and quality improved by 50% (see Figure 14-2). Four of the studies contained the data necessary to estimate a return on investment of 2120%.

Category	Low%	Median%	High%	Points
Cost	n/a	n/a	n/a	n/a
Schedule	n/a	n/a	n/a	n/a
Productivity	18	64	172	6
Quality	16	50	153	16
Satisfaction	n/a	n/a	n/a	n/a
ROI	916	2120	4540	4
				26

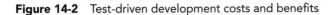

Figure 14-2   Test-driven development costs and benefits

14.3 Extreme Programming

Extreme Programming, created around 1999 and which spread rapidly, was also a much studied agile method. In the mid-1990s, the Internet exploded onto the global scene, and the notion of Internet time became popular. That is, new software products could be developed in a fraction of the time required by traditional methods. Internet software was being developed in 24-hour intervals and instantly downloaded by millions of people. Historically, using traditional methods, a small computer program could take one or two years to develop.

Extreme Programming had a set of revolutionary practices, including release planning, 14-day iterations, pair programming, test-driven development, and continuous integration. It also included simple design, onsite customers, and open workspaces. Scientists evaluated the impact of its practices in earnest, especially pair programming and test-driven development. On the other hand, continuous integration—considered revolutionary—and release planning—also a novel approach to project management—were rarely studied. However, many scientists elected to study Extreme Programming in its entirety.

We identified 17 studies of Extreme Programming with data on its quantitative benefits (see Figure 14-3). Improvements in cost, schedule, productivity, and quality performance averaged 18, 53, 143, and 60%, respectively. Ironically, none of these studies reported data concerning customer satisfaction, although agile methods are supposed to shine in this area. About 13 of the studies had the data necessary to estimate the return on investment of Extreme Programming, which averaged 3546%. Extreme Programming is 16 times faster than the average traditional method and three times faster than the most efficient traditional methods.

Category	Low%	Median%	High%	Points
Cost	10	18	28	5
Schedule	53	53	53	1
Productivity	20	143	384	8
Quality	13	60	89	5
Satisfaction	n/a	n/a	n/a	n/a
ROI	1290	3546	8852	13
				32

Figure 14-3 Extreme Programming costs and benefits

14.4 Scrum

Scrum has grown in popularity in North America, Europe, and Asia. In some instances, over half of the developers who use agile methods use Scrum. This was not always true. From 1999 to 2002, Extreme Programming was the most popular method, although Scrum was created earlier. In this period, nearly 75% of all developers using agile methods preferred to use Extreme Programming and its practices. At the same time, scientists conducted hundreds of studies on Extreme Programming and its practices. Only recently has Scrum overtaken Extreme Programming as the agile method of choice.

As its basic tenets, Scrum has sprint planning, daily standups, 30-day sprints, and sprint retrospectives. Whereas scientists latched onto pair programming and test-driven development as part of Extreme Programming, Scrum has few similar salient practices. However, Scrum has a few key practices worth further study. Like release planning, sprint planning is a powerful alternative to traditional project management and has the power to drive business value. Daily standups are a powerful form of problem solving and teamwork, which drives business value. Also worth studying are 30-day sprints and sprint retrospectives.

We identified five studies of Scrum with quantitative data, which is a fraction of those found for other agile methods (see Figure 14-4). Most of these were case studies, and none was of the experimental variety, which carries more weight among scientists. These studies reported a 305% increase, on average, in productivity and a 267% increase in quality. Four of the studies contained the data necessary to estimate return on investment, which averaged 837%. Scrum is five times faster than older traditional methods and is on a par with the most efficient traditional methods. The amount of Scrum research needs to increase, and will, by virtue of the large number or projects now using it.

Category	Low%	Median%	High%	Points
Cost	n/a	n/a	n/a	n/a
Schedule	n/a	n/a	n/a	n/a
Productivity	29	305	712	4
Quality	30	267	700	3
Satisfaction	n/a	n/a	n/a	n/a
ROI	240	837	1785	4
				11

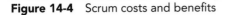

Figure 14-4   Scrum costs and benefits

14.5 Agile Methods

The earliest agile method, Scrum, emerged in the early 1990s as a response to contemporary ideas in new product development from the 1980s. Like Extreme Programming, agile methods emerged in the 1990s on the heels of Microsoft's sync-n-stabilize approach, Netscape's judo strategy, and Yahoo's Internet time. Agile methods, with their insistence on customer collaboration, teamwork, iterative development, and adaptability, polarized the software community. Of concern were their lightweight project management framework, focus on programming, and lightweight documents.

Agile methods were a confluence of several major trends during the 20th century: a focus on customers, teamwork, delivering working software every few weeks, and lightweight project management. These came from the best ideas in computer science, software engineering, and management information systems. None was the result of a rebellion by programmers who were too lazy to create the voluminous documentation required by traditional methods. In fact, maybe people were just too lazy to understand agile methods.

Agile methods are right-sized, just-enough, and just-in-time processes and documentation. Their purpose is to maximize business value by creating working software in frequent intervals. We found 79 studies with quantitative data on the benefits of agile methods (see Figure 14-5). They cited an average of 26% improvement in cost, 71% improvement in schedule, and 122% improvement in productivity performance. Quality improvement averaged 75%, and customer satisfaction improvement averaged 70%. Over 29 of these studies had the data necessary to estimate an average return on investment of 2633%.

Category	Low%	Median%	High%	Points
Cost	10	26	70	9
Schedule	11	71	700	19
Productivity	14	122	712	27
Quality	10	75	1000	53
Satisfaction	70	70	70	1
ROI	240	2633	8852	29
				138

Figure 14-5   Agile methods costs and benefits

14.6 Summary

Few studies of agile methods are devoted to costs and benefits, although there are hundreds of papers and books on this topic. However, we were able to identify more than 79 studies with the data necessary to begin compiling the costs and benefits of agile methods. We are not alone, as other scientists attempt to do the same: that is, piece together the puzzle of literature into a coherent statement of the costs and benefits to render judgment on agile methods.

The study of the costs and benefits of agile methods is a serious undertaking. Thoughtful scientists take many factors into account before considering a single data point. They determine the type of study performed, population of programmers, sample size, and various other factors of statistical purity and power. What we have done here is not a rigorous analysis but only a cursory analysis to provide early feedback to the community on the range of costs and benefits to expect from agile methods.

This is not to say that statistical purity and power are all they're cracked up to be. For instance, we know that teamwork is more important than individuals when solving complex problems. However, scientists from both the traditional and agile methods community do not believe there is sufficient statistical power to justify teamwork in lieu of individuals. Another criticism of agile methods is levied upon test-driven development, whereas best-in-class projects using continuous integration experience improvements in testing efficiency and quality on the order of 100:1 or more. The final verdict on the cost and benefits of agile methods has not been reached. In fact, this journey is just beginning.

14.7 Further Readings

Dyba, T., & Dingsoyr, T. (2008). Empirical studies of agile software development: A systematic review. *Information and Software Technology, 50*(9/10), 833–859.

Dyba, T., Arisholm, E., Sjoberg, D. I., Hannay, J. E., & Shull, F. (2007). Are two heads better than one? On the effectiveness of pair programming. *IEEE Software, 24*(6), 12–15.

Jeffries, R., & Melnik, G. (2007). TDD: The art of fearless programming. *IEEE Software, 24*(3), 24–30.

Kampenes, V., Dyba, T., Hannay, J. E., & Sjoberg, D. I. (2007). A systematic review of effect size in software engineering experiments. *Information and Software Technology, 49*(11/12), 1073–1086.

Kampenes, V., Dyba, T., Hannay, J. E., & Sjoberg, D. I. (2009). A systematic review of quasi-experiments in software engineering. *Information and Software Technology, 51*(1), 71–82.

Rico, D. F. (2008). What is the ROI of agile vs. traditional methods? An analysis of extreme programming, test-driven development, pair programming, and scrum (using real options). *TickIT International, 10*(4), 9–18.

————. (2008). *What is the ROI of agile vs. traditional methods? An analysis of agile methods using real options.* Retrieved June 28, 2008, from http://davidfrico .com/agile-benefits.xls.

————. (2009). *Business value of agile methods: Using return on investment.* Retrieved May 24, 2009, from http://davidfrico.com/rico09b.pdf.

15

ROI Metrics for
Agile Methods

There are numerous types of metrics for measuring the business value of any investment such as agile methods. Virtually any textbook on business value or return on investment (ROI) will have a virtual smorgasbord of metrics, models, and measurements. The philosophy seems to be the more the better. Sometimes these are called key management ratios, and there are textbooks with literally hundreds of key management ratios. Although well-meaning, these textbooks can be overwhelming.

The two most basic inputs into almost any measure of business value are (1) costs and (2) benefits. That is, one must count up all of the costs associated with what one desires to do. Costs generally include training, materials, consulting, development, and maintenance—often called total life cycle costs. There is also a myriad of benefits, such as increased productivity, reduced cycle time, lower development costs, and lower maintenance costs—often referred to as total life cycle benefits.

Once costs and benefits have been identified, which is no easy feat, measures of business value may be selected. ROI is a classical measure for estimating the business value of agile methods, although it is accused of being too optimistic. For that reason, net present value (NPV) is advocated by economics experts, because it takes the time value of money into account. However, real options analysis (ROA) is a better measure of business value, because it takes time, inflation, and risk into consideration. The value of ROA and ROI becomes similar, because NPV dramatically understates benefits.

15.1 Cost Metric

Costs are simply all of the expenses necessary to apply agile methods for creating new software products (see Figure 15-1). These may include expenses for training,

$$\sum_{i=1}^{n} Cost_i$$

Figure 15-1   Cost metric

materials, coaching, mentoring, consulting, tools, development, and maintenance. Training includes fees, travel costs, accommodations, lost work time, and effort associated with performing follow-up exercises. There may be expenses associated with tools to support workflow management as well as software development itself. For example, tools to support sprint or release planning are popular.

The two largest expenses associated with agile methods are the costs associated with software development and maintenance. For software development, the costs are linked with sprint or release planning and sprint or iteration development time, including the costs of tools for programming, collaboration, test-driven development, and continuous integration harnesses. For software maintenance, this may include the effort associated to find and fix bugs, refactoring the code, and regression testing. The costs of agile methods are lower than for traditional methods due to the lack of nonvalue-adding processes and documentation.

The costs of coaching and mentoring to facilitate the use of agile methods are often overlooked. Agile methods aren't intuitive for the worldwide community of novices or even experts immersed in the values of traditional methods but rather require practice to yield the maximum benefit possible. Oftentimes, developers use agile methods incorrectly and then complain of a mysterious, systemic, and organizational malady. Agile methods require coaches and mentors to guide, lead, and gently correct the misapplication of their practices. Without them, projects may revert to traditional methods.

15.2 Benefit Metric

Benefits are simply all of the advantages to be gained from using agile methods to create new software products (see Figure 15-2). Advantages or gains may be tangible or intangible. Traditional methods are reported to have tangible and intangible benefits, often in the form of higher quality or improved morale among programmers. Because agile methods have a rather large impact on both tangible and intangible benefits, one of the challenges is to identify, monetize, and aggregate their benefits to estimate their business value.

$$\sum_{i=1}^{n} Benefit_i$$

Figure 15-2   Benefit metric

Over three-fourths of the values of agile methods are devoted to increasing the intangible benefits, including customer collaboration, teamwork, and adaptability. Customer collaboration and flexibility have a myriad of benefits, including getting accurate requirements, validating them, building the right product, satisfying the customer, and increasing the customer's competitive market position, as well as yours. Teamwork leads to increased communication, trust, cooperation, and execution among developers. This is tantamount to building the product right, otherwise known as verification.

All intangible benefits can be monetized. That is, not only can they be expressed in qualitative terms, but they can be translated into hard economic benefits. For example, satisfied customers garner more revenues and remunerate developers accordingly. Agile methods also have traditional benefits, such as increased productivity due to streamlined processes and products—ranging from 6 to 39 times faster than traditional methods. Agile methods also result in higher quality that lowers maintenance costs and leads to lower overall total life cycle costs. Even the most inefficient agile method saves millions of dollars over traditional methods.

15.3 ROI Metric

ROI is a common way to measure the business value of agile methods for creating new software products (see Figure 15-3). The oldest and most often cited method for valuating or measuring the economic efficiency of agile methods, it takes both the costs and benefits of agile methods into consideration when determining business value. In other words, it doesn't just consider the costs or benefits but evaluates both simultaneously. In its most basic terms, it is a simple ratio of benefits to costs.

In spite of its age, detractors, and weaknesses, ROI brings cost realism into the evaluation of business value. For instance, most people will simply reject the benefits of a new approach such as agile methods if the costs are too high. In the ROI formula, the costs are subtracted before stating the benefits. In other words, ROI is a ratio of benefits to costs, but the benefits are first reduced by the costs.

For example, let's say agile methods return $1,000,000 in benefits. Is the ROI $1,000,000? What if the cost of using agile methods is $100,000? First, we subtract the costs from the benefits, which gives us $900,000. Then we divide the benefits by the costs and multiply the result by 100%, which gives us a value of 900% (e.g., [$1,000,000 − $100,000] ÷ $100,000 × 100% = 900%). By

$$\frac{Benefits - Costs}{Costs} \times 100\%$$

Figure 15-3 ROI metric

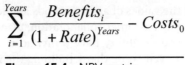

Figure 15-4 NPV metric

subtracting the costs from the benefits, the ROI formula introduces cost realism into the equation; that is, the benefits are not overstated. In spite of its built-in method of checks and balances, its detractors still decry ROI as being out of touch with reality.

15.4 NPV Metric

NPV is a preferred way of measuring the business value of agile methods for creating new software products (see Figure 15-4). It is considered one of the most responsible methods of measuring the economic efficiency of agile methods. There are many similarities between NPV and ROI. First, both formulas use costs and benefits as an input. Second, both formulas subtract the costs before stating the benefits. However, NPV takes two additional inputs—discount rate and time—before making the final valuation.

NPV is based on the time value of money and assumes ROI overstates the benefits. If we say that agile methods will yield benefits of $1,000,000, then someone may ask, "Over what period of time?" Due to inflation and other market conditions, currency may lose its value. That is, $1,000,000 today may not be worth $1,000,000 a few short years from now if not managed wisely. In fact, $1,000,000 may lose 10 to 20% of its value (or more) over a few short years due to unstable market conditions (or simply due to nominal inflation).

For example, if the costs of agile methods are $100,000 at the outset and they return $1,000,000, then the benefits may only be worth $765,895 using NPV, if we use five years and a discount rate of 5% (e.g., Σ [$1,000,000 ÷ 5] ÷ 1.05^5 − $100,000). This would be the equivalent ROI of 766%. Using ROI alone, without time and discount rate, the business value would have been 900%. We can begin to see how NPV introduces more cost realism into the picture than ROI alone. Both have the same noble goal, but NPV is more critical. Actually, it's too critical and more unrealistic than ROI, because it assumes too much market volatility and doesn't reward a strategic delay in the face of too much market or project risk, as other, more sophisticated, valuation measures do.

15.5 Real Options Analysis Metric

ROA is a better way of measuring the business value of agile methods for creating new software products (see Figure 15-5). A contemporary approach for measuring the economic efficiency of agile methods, it is different from either ROI or

$$N(d_1) \times Benefits - N(d_2) \times Costs \times e^{-Rate \times Years}$$

$$d_1 = \frac{\ln(Benefits/Costs) + (Rate + 0.5 \times Risk^2) \times Years}{Risk \times \sqrt{Years}}$$

$$d_2 = d_1 - Risk \times \sqrt{Years}$$

Figure 15-5   ROA metric

NPV in terms of its mathematical design. But it does have similar inputs to both, namely costs and benefits, and has similar inputs to NPV, such as discount rate and time. However, ROA has an additional input that NPV doesn't have: risk.

To a certain extent, ROA is based on the time value of money but also on risk. For instance, let's say an investment is inherently risky, but we go ahead and invest in it anyway. Let's say all of the risk is realized and our investment is lost. Some may say it wasn't wise to invest in it because of its risk. However, let's say we could delay investing in a high-risk venture and instead spend more when the risk subsides. That's ROA, because it models the benefits of strategic delay due to high risk.

Software projects are risky, because requirements are unstable. Using traditional methods is tantamount to investing in a high-risk project. No wonder project failure rates are near 70%. However, let's say we can invest in a project a little at a time and then invest more when the risk subsides. That's an agile method, and ROA is a way to model its business value. If our costs are $100,000 and our benefits are $1,000,000, then our business value is $923,000 using ROA (i.e., 50% risk, five years, and a 5% discount rate). This is the equivalent of 923% using ROI. The ROI is 900% and NPV is 766%. We can see how the effects of agile methods maximize business value.

15.6 Summary

ROI is a way to measure the economic business value of using agile methods for creating new software products. Business value is a broad term referring to both tangible and intangible costs and benefits. An example of a tangible cost may be the expenses associated with training, development, tools, and coaching. An intangible cost may be resistance to organizational change (e.g., transitioning from traditional to agile methods). While a tangible benefit may be increased revenues or decreased operating costs, an intangible benefit may be happier customers.

Using costs and benefits as their basic inputs, ROI, NPV, and ROA are methods to measure the economic business value of agile methods. After adding up all of the economic costs, we must often monetize or translate intangible benefits into tangible ones. When our costs and benefits are known, we can then use ROI,

NPV, and ROA. Hence, we've illustrated how to estimate costs, benefits, ROI, NPV, and ROA.

First, the costs must be quantified, which isn't a common practice. Then, the benefits must also be quantified, and there are two ways to increase benefits: (1) increase revenues and (2) decrease costs (e.g., the cost of quality). Using agile methods decreases costs and increases quality. So we simply estimate the benefits of reduced total life cycle costs by monetizing productivity and quality. ROI is a simple ratio of benefits to costs, NPV is the time value of our benefits, and ROA is the estimated business value of using agile methods to thwart the risk associated with software projects, otherwise known as new product development.

15.7 Further Readings

Biffl, S., Aurum, A., Boehm, B., Erdogmus, H., & Grunbacher, P. (2006). *Value-based software engineering*. Berlin, Germany: Springer-Verlag.

Devaraj, S., & Kohli, R. (2002). *The IT payoff: Measuring the business value of information technology investments*. Upper Saddle River, NJ: Prentice Hall.

El Emam, K. (2005). *The ROI from software quality*. Boca Raton, FL: Taylor and Francis.

Morgan, J. N. (2005). A roadmap of financial measures for IT project ROI. *IT Professional, 7*(1), 52–57.

Reifer, D. J. (2002). *Making the software business case: Improvement by the numbers*. Upper Saddle River, NJ: Addison-Wesley.

Rico, D. F. (2004). *ROI of software process improvement: Metrics for project managers and software engineers*. Boca Raton, FL: J. Ross Publishing.

———. (2008). What is the ROI of agile vs. traditional methods? An analysis of extreme programming, test-driven development, pair programming, and scrum (using real options). *TickIT International, 10*(4), 9–18.

Sikka, V. (2005). *Maximizing ROI on software development*. Boca Raton, FL: CRC Press.

Tockey, S. (2004). *Return on software: Maximizing the return on your software investment*. Boston, MA: Addison-Wesley.

16

Measures of Agile Methods

There are many different forms of measures and measurement data for using agile methods to create new software products. Measures, measurements, and measurement data are a sign that agile methods are well understood and a mature discipline, although it remains to be seen if agile methods have matured. To determine whether agile methods are a mature discipline, basic measures such as size, effort, cost, schedule, and quality suffice.

We were able to locate 29 such studies of agile methods with measurement data collected from more than 839 programmers. The data came from projects using agile methods and practices, such as pair programming, test-driven development, Extreme Programming, and Scrum. It consisted of software effort and quality measurements, which were most often expressed in terms of programming productivity and defect density (e.g., lines of code [LOC] per hour and defects per thousand LOC [KLOC]).

Two important data points can be extracted from effort and quality measures such as these: (1) costs and (2) benefits. That is, we can estimate not only development costs but total life cycle costs using effort and quality. Furthermore, we can compare these total life cycle costs to those of traditional methods. We can also use these data to estimate the benefits of agile methods, especially if the total life cycle costs of agile methods prove to be lower than those of traditional methods. Finally, we can begin the process of estimating the economic business value of agile methods once we've estimated their costs and benefits.

16.1 Pair Programming

Within the Extreme Programming agile method, all software is implemented by two programmers working at the same computer. When agile methods exploded onto the global scene from 1999 to 2002, pair programming became one of the most prevalent practices. Numerous organizations adopted pair programming, and it became one of the most studied phenomena in the field of software engineering research. Curious managers, practitioners, and scientists wanted to know if two heads were better than one. They concluded that two people could code faster than two programmers working separately.

But how fast can two people code using pair programming? Eight studies involving 258 programmers found that pair programming productivity was quite high (see Figure 16-1), ranging from 16 to 87 LOC/hour, with a mean of 33, or 33.4044 LOC/hour, to be exact. What this means is that two programmers could produce 334 LOC in 10 hours, or 3,340 LOC in 100 hours. Compare this to traditional methods that produce one or two LOC per hour. However, these data may have been produced in ideal laboratory conditions and need to be interpreted with caution.

But what is the quality of the software produced by pair programmers? Six studies involving 105 programmers found pair programming quality was quite high, ranging from 0.325 defects/KLOC to 5.85 defects/KLOC, with a mean of 2.355 (see Figure 16-1). What this means is that pair programming teams produce about 24 defects for every 10,000 LOC. This comes to about 2,400 hours

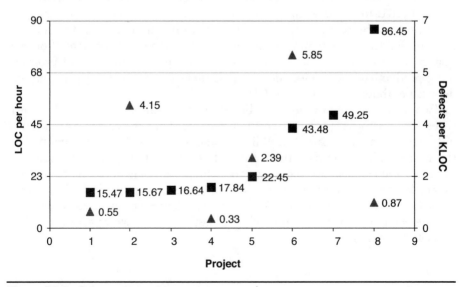

Figure 16-1 Pair programming measurement data

of maintenance if defects cost 100 hours each to repair. We now have the basic measures necessary to estimate the costs and benefits of pair programming.

16.2 Test-Driven Development

Within the Extreme Programming agile method, customers and developers write acceptance and unit tests before programming. Next to pair programming, test-driven development became a prevalent practice when agile methods spread from 1999 to 2002. Numerous organizations also adopted test-driven development, and it became a much studied phenomenon. Computer scientists wanted to know if test-driven development was better than traditional test-last development. They concluded that test-driven development did increase productivity and quality.

But how fast can people code using test-driven development? Two such studies involving 275 programmers found that test-driven development productivity was quite high (see Figure 16-2). In fact, it ranged from 12 to 46 LOC/hour, with a mean of 29, or 29.28 LOC/hour, to be exact. What this means is that programmers could produce 293 LOC in 10 hours, or 2,928 LOC in 100 hours. Compare this to traditional methods that produce one or two LOC/hour. Once again, these data were produced under ideal laboratory conditions and need to be interpreted with caution.

But what is the quality of the software produced by test-driven development? Two studies involving 23 programmers found test-driven development quality

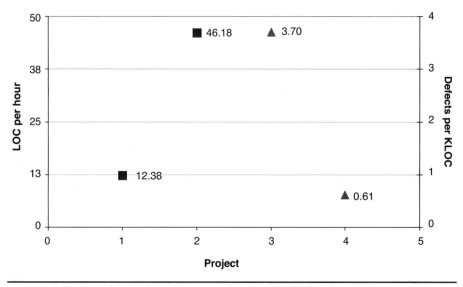

Figure 16-2   Test-driven development measurement data

was quite high, ranging from 0.61 defects/KLOC to 3.7 defects/KLOC, with a mean of 2.155 (see Figure 16-2). What this means is that test-driven development teams produce about 22 defects for every 10,000 LOC. This comes to about 2,200 hours of maintenance if defects cost 100 hours each to repair. We now have the basic measures necessary to estimate the costs and benefits of test-driven development.

16.3 Extreme Programming

Within the Extreme Programming agile method, customers and developers perform release planning and many other practices. From 1999 to 2002, Extreme Programming was responsible for popularizing agile methods. Numerous organizations in almost every country adopted Extreme Programming, and it became one of the most controversial phenomena in software engineering. Computer scientists who wanted to know if Extreme Programming was better than traditional methods concluded that its use increased productivity and quality.

But how fast can developers code using Extreme Programming? Thirteen such studies involving 176 programmers found that Extreme Programming productivity was quite high (see Figure 16-3). In fact, it ranged from 4 to 43 LOC/hour, with a mean of 16, or 16.1575 LOC/hour, to be exact. What this means is that programmers could produce 162 LOC in 10 hours, or 1,616 LOC in 100 hours. Compare this to traditional methods that produce one or two LOC/hour. Once again, these data were produced under ideal laboratory conditions and need to be interpreted with caution.

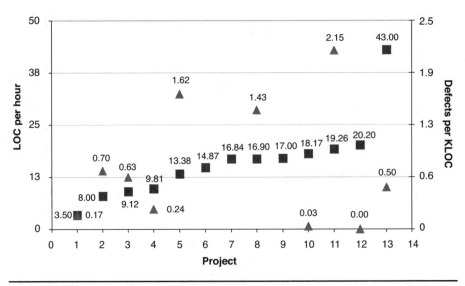

Figure 16-3   Extreme Programming measurement data

But what is the quality of the software produced by Extreme Programming? Ten studies involving 93 programmers found Extreme Programming quality was quite high, ranging from 0.0032 defects/KLOC to 2.145 defects/KLOC, with a mean of 0.7466 (see Figure 16-3). What this means is that Extreme Programming teams produce about eight defects for every 10,000 LOC. This comes to about 800 hours of maintenance if defects cost 100 hours each to repair. We now have the basic measures necessary to estimate the costs and benefits of Extreme Programming.

16.4 Scrum

Within the Scrum agile method, customers and developers perform sprint planning and hold daily standup meetings, among other activities. Although Scrum was one of the first agile methods, it only began growing in popularity from 2002 to 2008. Scrum embraces the values of agile methods, such as customer collaboration, teamwork, iterative development, and flexibility. But these values reflect the soft side of software development, something software engineering scholars are not accustomed to measuring. In spite of this, a few studies have measured Scrum's productivity and quality.

How fast can developers code using Scrum? Three such studies involving 17 programmers found that Scrum productivity was above average, ranging from 5 to 6 LOC/hour, with a mean of 5.4, or 5.4436 LOC/hour, to be exact (see Figure 16-4). What this means is that programmers could produce 54 LOC in 10 hours

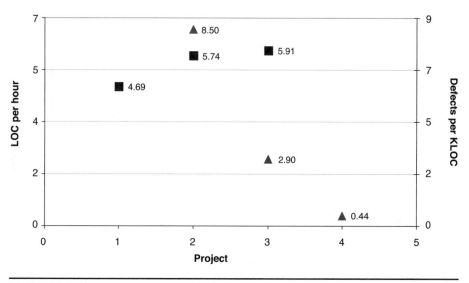

Figure 16-4   Scrum measurement data

or 544 LOC in 100 hours. Compare this to traditional methods that produce one or two LOC/hour. These data may be slightly more accurate than laboratory studies, because they came from studies of actual software development projects.

But what is the quality of the software produced by Scrum teams? Three studies involving 102 programmers found the quality produced by Scrum teams was quite high, ranging from 0.435 defects/KLOC to 8.5 defects/KLOC with a mean of 3.945 (see Figure 16-4). What this means is that Scrum teams produce about 40 defects for every 10,000 LOC. This comes to about 4,000 hours of maintenance if defects cost 100 hours each to repair. We now have the basic measures necessary to estimate the costs and benefits of teams using the Scrum agile method.

16.5 Agile Methods

Within agile methods there is a high degree of customer collaboration, teamwork, iterative development, and flexibility. Although agile methods began emerging in the early 1990s, they only began growing in popularity from 1999 to 2002. Numerous organizations in almost every country adopted agile methods, and they became one of the most controversial phenomena in software engineering. Computer scientists wanted to know if agile methods were better than traditional methods. They concluded that the use of agile methods increased productivity and quality.

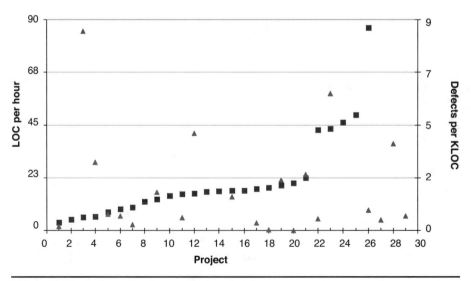

Figure 16-5 Agile methods measurement data

But precisely how fast can developers code using agile methods? Well, 26 such studies involving 726 programmers found that agile methods' productivity was quite high, ranging from 4 to 87 LOC/hour, with a mean of 21, or 21.2374 LOC/hour, to be exact (see Figure 16-5). What this means is that programmers could produce 212 LOC in 10 hours or 2,124 LOC in 100 hours. Compare this to traditional methods that produce one or two LOC/hour. However, many of these data were produced under ideal laboratory conditions and need to be interpreted with caution.

But what is the quality of the software produced by agile methods? Twenty-one studies involving 323 programmers found the quality produced by agile methods teams was quite high, ranging from 0.0032 defects/KLOC to 8.5 defects/KLOC, with a mean of 1.7972 (see Figure 16-5). What this means is that agile methods teams produce about 18 defects for every 10,000 LOC. This comes to about 1,800 hours of maintenance if defects cost 100 hours each to repair. We now have the basic measures necessary to estimate the costs and benefits of teams using agile methods.

16.6 Summary

The effort and cost of agile methods can and should be quantified through a variety of techniques. Bottom-up techniques from release and sprint planning should certainly be used for this purpose. They consist of documenting and estimating user stories and rolling these estimates into release, iteration, and sprint plans. Primarily due to the controversy surrounding agile methods, literally hundreds of studies have been conducted on agile methods and their associated practices. These studies have yielded numerous data points that can be used to construct top-down parametric models to estimate the costs of agile methods.

At least 26 of these studies, involving over 726 programmers, yielded an average productivity of over 21 LOC/hour. This is roughly 10 to 20 times the productivity rate associated with traditional methods. At least 21 of these studies, involving over 323 programmers, yielded an average defect density of about two defects/KLOC. Together, these data can be used to estimate the development and maintenance costs of agile methods—also known as the total life cycle costs. It's important to measure both, because maintenance may represent up to 70% of total life cycle costs.

Business value refers to both tangible and intangible benefits. Agile methods can be used to optimize both soft- and hard-side benefits. From the soft side, agile methods enhance the value of customer relationships—customer trust, communication, and satisfaction. From the hard side, agile methods positively impact the bottom line by enhancing productivity and quality. In doing so, agile methods reduce the total life cycle costs of software development. Total life cycle costs are an important ingredient to another measure of business value—return on investment.

16.7 Further Readings

Abrahamsson, P., Moser, R., Pedrycz, W., Sillitti, A., & Succi, G. (2007). Effort prediction in iterative software development processes: Incremental versus global prediction models. *First International Symposium on Empirical Software Engineering and Measurement (ESEM 2007), Madrid, Spain,* 344–353.

Benediktsson, O., & Dalcher, D. (2005). Estimating size in incremental software development projects. *Journal of Engineering Manufacture, 152*(6), 253–259.

Cohn, M. (2006). *Agile estimating and planning.* Upper Saddle River, NJ: Pearson Education.

Dalcher, D., & Benediktsson, O. (2006). Managing software development project size: Overcoming the effort-boxing constraint. *Project Management Journal, 37*(2), 51–58.

Galorath, D. D., & Evans, M. W. (2006). *Software sizing, estimation, and risk management.* Boca Raton, FL: Auerbach.

Rico, D. F. (2008). What is the ROI of agile vs. traditional methods? An analysis of extreme programming, test-driven development, pair programming, and scrum (using real options). *TickIT International, 10*(4), 9–18.

———. (2008). *What is the ROI of agile vs. traditional methods? An analysis of agile methods using real options.* Retrieved June 28, 2008, from http://davidfrico.com/agile-benefits.xls.

Ton, H. (2007). A strategy for balancing business value and story size. *Proceedings of the Agile 2007 Conference, Washington, District of Columbia, USA,* 279–284.

17

Costs of Agile Methods

The costs of agile methods consist of the expenses in time, labor, materials, and other expenditures to apply them, including training. Agile cost estimation is the process of predicting the effort, or labor hours, required to develop a software system using agile methods. There are a variety of top-down and bottom-up approaches for estimating the costs of using agile methods. One can use top-down parametric models derived from historical data. Some cost models and tools even support limited top-down cost estimation.

One of the simplest and most straightforward ways to estimate the costs of agile methods is bottom-up estimation of user stories. That is, one applies an agile project management framework such as release planning, which is an iterative methodology of writing, estimating, splitting, and ordering user stories. There are minor variations that involve the use of story points, which are a measure of complexity for a given user story. The basic notion is to estimate the size of user stories, prioritize them, and schedule their implementation in a series of releases and iterations.

Top-down models are simple equations or formulas that measure the cost-estimating relationships between size, speed, and effort. For instance, if one built a system at a coding speed of 10 lines of code (LOC) per hour, we can estimate that one could code 1,000 lines of software in 100 hours. With more data points or projects in a cost-estimating database, top-down models of agile estimation may become more reliable.

17.1 Pair Programming

What is the development cost of pair programming? Eight studies involving 258 programmers exhibited productivity ranging from 15.4667 to 86.4502 LOC/hour. Pair programming teams averaged about 33.4044 LOC/hour, and the effort

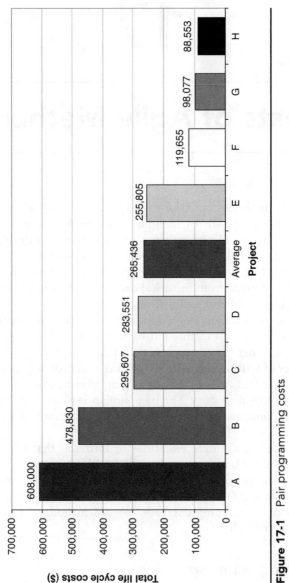

Figure 17-1   Pair programming costs

model may be expressed as LOC $\div$ 33.4044. Using this model, the effort to produce 10,000 LOC comes to 299 hours (e.g., 10,000 $\div$ 33.4044 = 299). Monetized or translated into economic terms, the cost of pair programming is estimated to be $29,936 at $100/hour.

What is the maintenance cost of pair programming? Six studies involving 105 programmers exhibited quality ranging from 0.325 to 5.85 defects/thousand LOC (KLOC). Pair programming teams averaged about 2.355 defects/KLOC, and the effort model may be expressed as 2.355 $\times$ KLOC $\times$ 100. Using this model, the effort to maintain 10,000 LOC comes to 2,355 hours (e.g., 2.355 $\times$ 10 KLOC $\times$ 100 = 2,355). Monetized or translated into economic terms, the maintenance cost of pair programming is estimated to be $235,501 at $100/hour.

However, the complete costs of pair programming must be considered, which is known as the total life cycle cost. Combining the development and maintenance effort, the total life cycle effort model for pair programming may be expressed as LOC $\div$ 33.4044 + 2.355 $\times$ KLOC $\times$ 100. Using this model, the total effort to develop and maintain 10,000 LOC comes to 2,654 (e.g., 10,000 $\div$ 33.4044 + 2.355 $\times$ 10 KLOC $\times$ 100 = 2,654). Monetized or translated into economic terms, the total life cycle cost of pair programming is estimated to be $265,436 at $100/hour (see Figure 17-1).

17.2 Test-Driven Development

What is the development cost of test-driven development? Two studies involving 275 programmers exhibited productivity ranging from 12.38 to 46.18 LOC/hour. Test-driven development teams averaged about 29.28 LOC/hour, and the effort model may be expressed as LOC $\div$ 29.28. Using this model, the effort to produce 10,000 LOC comes to 342 hours (e.g., 10,000 $\div$ 29.28 = 342). Monetized or translated into economic terms, the cost of test-driven development is estimated to be $34,153 at $100/hour.

What is the maintenance cost of test-driven development? Two studies involving 23 programmers exhibited a quality ranging from 0.61 to 3.7 defects/KLOC. Test-driven development teams averaged about 2.155 defects/KLOC, and the effort model may be expressed as 2.155 $\times$ KLOC $\times$ 100. Using this model, the effort to maintain 10,000 LOC comes to about 2,155 hours (e.g., 2.155 $\times$ 10 KLOC $\times$ 100 = 2,155). Monetized or translated into economic terms, the maintenance cost of test-driven development is estimated to be $215,500 at $100/hour.

However, the complete costs of test-driven development must be considered. Combining the development and maintenance effort, the total life cycle effort model for test-driven development may be expressed as LOC $\div$ 29.28 + 2.155 $\times$ KLOC $\times$ 100. Using this model, the total effort to develop and maintain 10,000 LOC comes to 2,497 (e.g., 10,000 $\div$ 29.28 + 2.155 $\times$ 10 KLOC $\times$ 100 = 2,497). Monetized or translated into economic terms, the total life cycle cost of test-driven development is estimated to be $249,653 at $100/hour (see Figure 17-2).

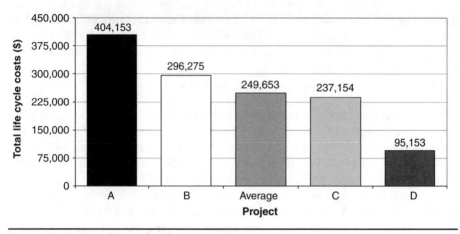

Figure 17-2   Test-driven development costs

17.3 Extreme Programming

What is the development cost of Extreme Programming? Thirteen studies involving 176 programmers exhibited productivity ranging from 3.5 to 43 LOC/hour. Extreme Programming teams averaged about 16.1575 LOC/hour and the effort model may be expressed as LOC ÷ 16.1575. Using this model, the effort to produce 10,000 LOC comes to 619 hours (e.g., 10,000 ÷ 16.1575 = 619). Monetized or translated into economic terms, the cost of Extreme Programming is estimated to be $61,891 at $100/hour.

What is the maintenance cost of Extreme Programming? Ten studies involving 93 programmers exhibited quality ranging from 0.0032 to 2.145 defects/KLOC. Extreme Programming teams averaged about 0.7466 defects/KLOC, and the effort model may be expressed as 0.7466 × KLOC × 100. Using this model, the effort to maintain 10,000 LOC comes to 747 hours (e.g., 0.7466 × 10 KLOC × 100 = 747). Monetized or translated into economic terms, the maintenance cost of Extreme Programming is estimated to be $74,657 at $100/hour.

However, the complete costs of Extreme Programming must be considered. Combining the development and maintenance effort, the total life cycle effort model for Extreme Programming may be expressed as LOC ÷ 16.1575 + 0.7466 × KLOC × 100. Using this model, the total effort to develop and maintain 10,000 LOC comes to 1,366 (e.g., 10,000 ÷ 16.1575 + 0.7466 × 10 KLOC × 100 = 1,366). Monetized or translated into economic terms, the total life cycle cost of Extreme Programming is estimated to be $136,551 at $100/hour (see Figure 17-3).

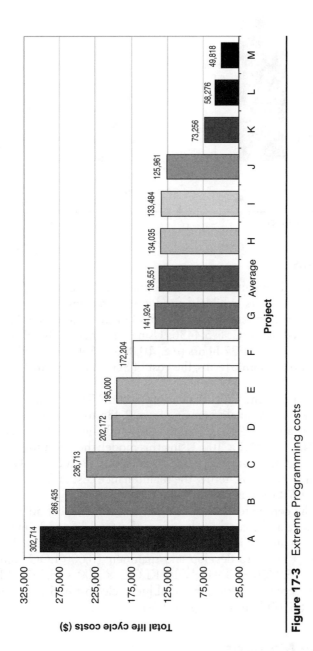

Figure 17-3 Extreme Programming costs

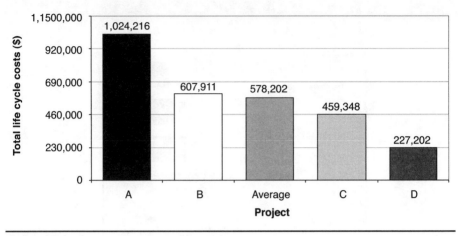

Figure 17-4   Scrum costs

17.4 Scrum

What is the development cost of the Scrum agile method? Three studies involving 17 programmers exhibited productivity ranging from 4.6858 to 5.905 LOC/hour. Scrum teams averaged about 5.4436 LOC/hour, and the effort model may be expressed as LOC ÷ 5.4436. Using this model, the effort to produce 10,000 LOC comes to 1,837 hours (e.g., 10,000 ÷ 5.4436 = 1,837). Monetized or translated into economic terms, the cost of Scrum is estimated to be $183,702 at $100/hour.

What is the maintenance cost of using Scrum? Three studies involving 102 programmers exhibited quality ranging from 0.435 to 8.5 defects/KLOC. Scrum teams averaged about 3.945 defects/KLOC, and the effort model may be expressed as 3.945 × KLOC × 100. Using this model, the effort to maintain 10,000 LOC comes to 3,945 hours (e.g., 3.945 × 10 KLOC × 100 = 3,945). Monetized or translated into economic terms, the maintenance cost of Scrum is estimated to be $394,500 at $100/hour.

However, the complete costs of using Scrum must be considered. Combining the development and maintenance effort, the total life cycle effort model for Scrum may be expressed as LOC ÷ 5.4436 + 3.945 × KLOC × 100. Using this model, the total effort to develop and maintain 10,000 LOC comes to 5,782 (e.g., 10,000 ÷ 5.4436 + 3.945 × 10 KLOC × 100 = 5,782). Monetized or translated into economic terms, the total life cycle cost of Scrum is estimated to be $578,202 at $100/hour (see Figure 17-4).

17.5 Agile Methods

What is the development cost of agile methods? Twenty-six studies involving 726 programmers exhibited productivity ranging from 3.5 to 86.4502 LOC/hour.

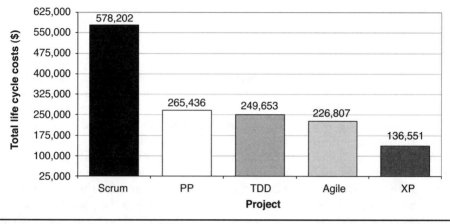

Figure 17-5 Agile methods costs

Agile methods teams averaged about 21.2374 LOC/hour, and the effort model may be expressed as LOC ÷ 21.2374. Using this model, the effort to produce 10,000 LOC comes to 471 hours (e.g., 10,000 ÷ 21.2374 = 471). Monetized or translated into economic terms, the cost of agile methods is estimated to be $47,087 at $100/hour.

What is the maintenance cost of using agile methods? Twenty-one studies involving 323 programmers exhibited quality ranging from 0.0032 to 8.5 defects/KLOC. Agile methods teams averaged about 1.7972 defects/KLOC, and the effort model may be expressed as 1.7972 × KLOC × 100. Using this model, the effort to maintain 10,000 LOC comes to 1,797 hours (e.g., 1.7972 × 10 KLOC × 100 = 1,797). Monetized or translated into economic terms, the maintenance cost of using agile methods for software maintenance is estimated to be $179,718 at $100/hour.

However, the complete costs of using agile methods must be considered. Combining the development and maintenance effort, the total life cycle effort model for using agile methods may be expressed as LOC ÷ 21.2374 + 1.7972 × KLOC × 100. Using this model, the total effort to develop and maintain 10,000 LOC comes to 2,268 (e.g., 10,000 ÷ 21.2374 + 1.7972 × 10 KLOC × 100 = 2,268). Monetized or translated into economic terms, the total life cycle cost of using agile methods is estimated to be $226,807 at $100/hour (see Figure 17-5).

17.6 Summary

Measurements of software effort and quality can be used to determine the economic business value of agile methods, especially if they are expressed in quantitative terms. Rudimentary measures of effort include programming productivity or LOC/hour. Rudimentary measures of quality include defect density or defects/

KLOC. We found 29 studies with measurement data for pair programming, test-driven development, Extreme Programming, and Scrum.

Software effort, or LOC/hour, can be translated into development costs. Software quality, or defects/KLOC, can be translated into maintenance costs. We can then combine development and maintenance costs into what is known as the total life cycle costs of using agile methods. All of these measurements can be compared to similar data from traditional methods (i.e., effort, quality, and total life cycle costs). The benefits of using agile methods can be derived if their overall costs are lower than those of traditional methods, which they are.

Most measures of economic business value use costs and benefits as their basic inputs, including return on investment, net present value, and real options. An intermediate objective is to monetize the basic measures and use them to estimate economic business value. However, our ultimate goal is to begin answering the question, "What is the business value of agile methods?" This chapter established a quantitative basis from which to begin satisfying these objectives and achieve our ultimate goal. We have identified the effort and quality associated with pair programming, test-driven development, Extreme Programming, and Scrum, as well as agile methods.

17.7 Further Readings

Benediktsson, O., & Dalcher, D. (2003). Effort estimation in incremental software development. *Journal of Engineering Manufacture, 150*(6), 351–357.

Benediktsson, O., & Dalcher, D. (2004). New insights into effort estimation for incremental software development projects. *Project Management Journal, 35*(2), 5–12.

Boehm, B. W., Abts, C., Brown, A. W., Chulani, S., Clark, B. K., Horowitz, E., et al. (2000). *Software cost estimation with COCOMO II.* Upper Saddle River, NJ: Prentice Hall.

Jones, C. (2007). *Estimating software costs: Bringing realism to estimating.* New York, NY: McGraw-Hill.

McGibbon, T. (1997). *Modern empirical cost and schedule estimation.* Rome, NY: Air Force Research Laboratory/Information Directorate, Data and Analysis Center for Software (DACS).

Mendes, E. (2008). *Cost estimation techniques for web projects.* Hershey, PA: IGI Publishing.

Pow-Sang, J. A., & Jolay-Vasquez, E. (2006). An approach of a technique for effort estimation of iterations in software projects. *Proceedings of the 13th Asia Pacific Software Engineering Conference (APSEC 2006), Bangalore, India,* 367–376.

Rico, D. F. (2008). What is the ROI of agile vs. traditional methods? An analysis of extreme programming, test-driven development, pair programming, and scrum (using real options). *TickIT International, 10*(4), 9–18.

18

Benefits of
Agile Methods

The benefits of agile methods consist of tangible and intangible advantages. Communication quality is an example of an intangible benefit and revenues and profits are examples of tangible ones. Agile methods yield many intangible benefits, such as customer satisfaction, teamwork, sustainability, and market responsiveness. However, we're going to focus on the tangible economic benefits of agile methods. There are two ways to improve the economic posture of organizations: (1) increase revenue through advertising or developing a product that satisfies a market need and (2) reduce development and maintenance costs.

Agile methods were created to increase revenues and profits. This is done by collaboration and interaction, listening to customers, and capturing their needs in flexible user stories. After business value is attributed to each of the user stories, the stories with the highest business value are implemented. If market conditions change, business value is reassessed and new user stories are developed and dynamically reprioritized. This way all resources are continuously focused on creating business value and maximizing return on investment.

Agile methods are also an efficient means of development, yield few defects, and have low maintenance costs. By reducing software development costs, agile methods are a means of increasing business value. This is also known as cost of quality, total cost of ownership, and total life cycle costs. For instance, let's say it costs 100 hours to repair a defect during maintenance. If agile methods result in one defect and traditional methods result in 10 defects, then agile methods save 900 hours.

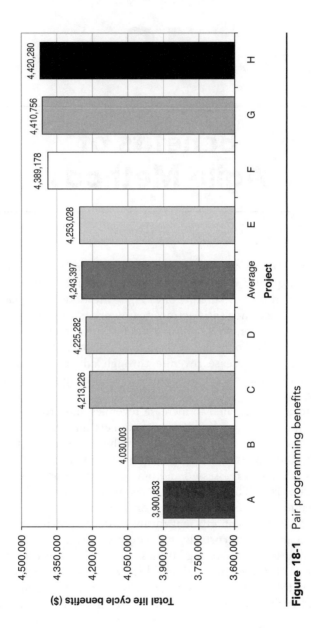

Figure 18-1   Pair programming benefits

18.1 Pair Programming

Pair programming is two highly skilled computer programmers sitting side by side solving difficult programming problems. Its benefits come from two main sources. The first benefit is reduced software development costs due to increased productivity and increased cost efficiency. In pair programming, because the developers are talented and highly skilled, they're naturally going to solve problems faster. Because it has no heavy project plans, software documentation, and non-value-adding functional groups, pair programming has little process overhead.

The second source of benefits is fewer defects, lower software maintenance, and lower total life cycle costs. That is, teams work together as a two-person continuous software inspection or peer review process. Because there are always two sets of eyes on the source code at all times, pair programming teams introduce fewer defects than teams using traditional methods. Extremely low cost and higher quality form a powerful combination to lower total life cycle costs far beyond those of even the most efficient traditional methods.

Compared to pair programming, traditional methods have more people, processes, and documents, which cost more. They also result in more defects than pair programming, which raises total life cycle costs. Traditional methods average less than one line of code (LOC) per hour, or 0.8507 to be exact. Furthermore, traditional methods average 33.3333 defects per thousand lines of code (KLOC). Therefore, the total life cycle cost of traditional methods is LOC ÷ 0.8507 + 33.3333 × KLOC × 100. The total life cycle cost model for pair programming is LOC ÷ 33.4044 + 2.355 × KLOC × 100 (see Figure 18-1). The benefits of pair programming are the difference between the total life cycle costs of traditional methods and pair programming.

18.2 Test-Driven Development

Test-driven development consists of customers and developers who write acceptance and unit tests to validate all user stories and modules. Its benefits come from two main sources. The first is reduced software development costs due to increased testing productivity and cost efficiency. Because test-driven development is completely automated, it's going to help developers perform testing faster. Also, test-driven development has little overhead; that is, it has no heavy test plans, testing documentation, and nonvalue-adding functional groups.

The second source of benefits is fewer defects, lower maintenance, and lower total life cycle costs. Test-driven development goes hand-in-hand with continuous integration; all unit, component, integration, system, and regression tests are completely automated and rerun at frequent intervals. Therefore, test-driven development results in fewer defects than teams using traditional methods. Extremely low cost and higher quality form a powerful combination to lower total life cycle costs far beyond those of even the most efficient traditional methods.

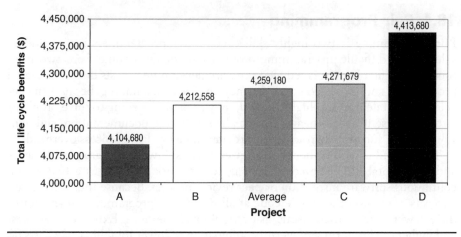

Figure 18-2   Test-driven development benefits

Compared to test-driven development, traditional methods have a heavier process, which costs more. They also result in more defects, which raise total life cycle costs. Traditional methods average less than one LOC/hour, or 0.8507 to be exact. Furthermore, traditional methods average 33.3333 defects/KLOC. Therefore, the total life cycle cost of traditional methods is LOC ÷ 0.8507 + 33.3333 × KLOC × 100. The total life cycle cost model for test-driven development is LOC ÷ 29.28 + 2.155 × KLOC × 100 (see Figure 18-2). The benefits of test-driven development are the difference between the total life cycle costs of traditional methods and test-driven development.

18.3 Extreme Programming

Extreme Programming is an agile method that covers customer interaction, teamwork, iterative development, and adaptability. Its benefits come from two main sources. The first benefit is reduced software development costs due to increased productivity and increased cost efficiency. Extreme Programming uses lightweight project planning, onsite customers, two-week iterations, and pair programming teams. Because it has no heavy project plans, software documentation, and non-value-adding functional groups, Extreme Programming has little process overhead.

The second source of benefits is fewer defects, lower maintenance, and lower total life cycle costs. Extreme Programming uses onsite customers for efficient communication and pair programming to quickly produce high-quality code. It also uses test-driven development for validation and flexible project plans. Therefore, Extreme Programming results in fewer defects than teams using traditional methods. Extremely low cost and higher quality form a powerful combination to lower total life cycle costs far beyond those of even the most efficient traditional methods.

Compared to Extreme Programming, traditional methods are much larger, cost more, and result in more defects, which raise total life cycle costs. Traditional methods average less than one LOC/hour, or 0.8507 to be exact. Furthermore, traditional methods average 33.3333 defects/KLOC. Therefore, the total life cycle cost of traditional methods is LOC ÷ 0.8507 + 33.3333 × KLOC × 100. The total life cycle cost model for Extreme Programming is LOC ÷ 16.1575 + 0.7466 × KLOC × 100 (see Figure 18-3). The benefits of Extreme Programming are the difference between the total life cycle costs of traditional methods and Extreme Programming.

18.4 Scrum

Scrum is an agile method that involves customer collaboration, teamwork, iterative development, and adaptability to change. Its benefits come from two main sources. The first benefit is reduced software development costs due to increased productivity and increased cost efficiency. Scrum uses lightweight sprint planning similar to release planning, product owners who serve as a customer proxy, 30-day sprints, and self-organizing teams. Because it has no heavy project plans, software documentation, and nonvalue-adding functional groups, Scrum has little process overhead.

The second source of benefits is fewer defects, lower software maintenance, and lower total life cycle costs. Because Scrum uses product owners for efficient communication, self-organizing teams, daily standups to quickly resolve problems, and sprint planning as an adaptable and flexible project planning framework, it results in fewer defects than teams using traditional methods. Extremely low cost and higher quality form a powerful combination to lower total life cycle costs far beyond those of even the most efficient traditional methods.

Compared to Scrum, traditional methods have more people, processes, and documents, which cost more and result in more defects than Scrum and which raise total life cycle costs. Traditional methods average less than one LOC/hour, or 0.8507 to be exact. Furthermore, traditional methods average 33.3333 defects/KLOC. Therefore, the total life cycle cost of traditional methods is LOC ÷ 0.8507 + 33.3333 × KLOC × 100. The total life cycle cost model for Scrum is LOC ÷ 5.4436 + 3.945 × KLOC × 100 (see Figure 18-4). The benefits of Scrum are the difference between the total life cycle costs of traditional methods and Scrum.

18.5 Agile Methods

Agile methods are development approaches based on customer collaboration, teamwork, iterative development, and adaptability. Agile methods' benefits come from two main sources. The first benefit is reduced development costs due to increased productivity and cost efficiency. Agile methods use lightweight project

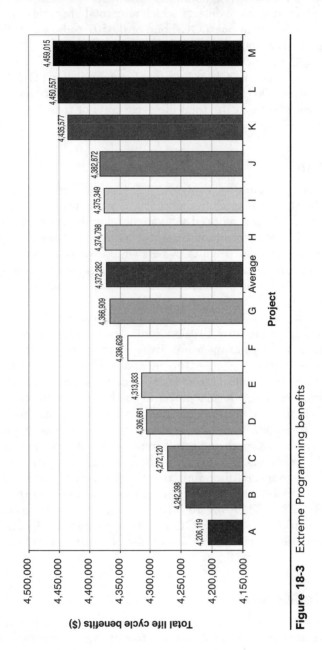

Figure 18-3   Extreme Programming benefits

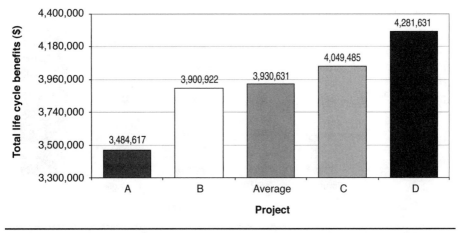

Figure 18-4 Scrum benefits

planning, intensive customer interaction, frequent software releases, and high-performance teams. Because they have no heavy project plans, software documentation, and nonvalue-adding functional groups, agile methods have little process overhead.

The second source of benefits is few defects, low software maintenance, and lower total life cycle costs. Agile methods use customer interaction to efficiently capture the needs and lightweight project management. To obtain fast customer feedback, they use productive teams, continuous integration, and small releases. Therefore, agile methods result in fewer defects than teams using traditional methods. Extremely low cost and higher quality form a powerful combination to lower total life cycle costs far beyond those of even the most efficient traditional methods.

Compared to agile methods, traditional methods have more people, processes, and documents, which cost more, and result in more defects than agile methods, which raise total life cycle costs. Traditional methods average less than one LOC/hour, or 0.8507 to be exact. Furthermore, traditional methods average 33.3333 defects/KLOC. Therefore, the total life cycle cost of traditional methods is LOC ÷ 0.8507 + 33.3333 × KLOC × 100. The total life cycle cost model for agile methods is LOC ÷ 21.2374 + 1.7972 × KLOC × 100 (see Figure 18-5). The benefits of agile methods are the difference between the total life cycle costs of traditional methods and agile methods.

18.6 Summary

Agile methods have many intangible and tangible benefits. Their intangible benefits set them apart from traditional methods and stem from the four major values

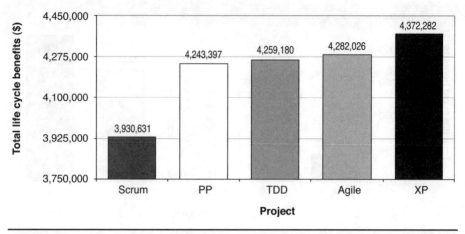

Figure 18-5   Agile methods benefits

of agile methods: customer collaboration, teamwork, iterative development, and adaptability. Customer collaboration leads to enhanced communication, strong relationships, more trust, and higher customer satisfaction. High-performance teams involve highly skilled programmers, better cooperation, communication quality, and problem solving. Adaptability helps firms respond to changing market conditions.

Agile methods also have many tangible benefits. These stem from efficient customer communication; small, highly productive teams; automated testing; and lightweight processes and documents. All of these factors combine to make agile methods more productive to use than traditional methods. Due to greater productivity and efficient defect removal, agile methods result in lower maintenance and total life cycle costs. On average, agile methods are about 25 times more efficient than traditional methods. The benefits of agile methods can be easily expressed using top-down cost and quality metrics, models, and measurements.

However, if that was all, then agile methods would be no more than a highly efficient software development method. But agile methods are so much more. Because they have many more intangible benefits than traditional methods have, agile methods result in greater business value. That is, return on investment can be directly tied to customer needs, and implementation of those needs can result in business value in immediate two- to four-week iterations. Also, agile methods use lightweight project management frameworks that are adaptable to changing market conditions. All of these combine to maximize the business value of agile methods.

18.7 Further Readings

Campanella, J. (1999). *Principles of quality costs: Principles, implementation, and use*. Milwaukee, WI: Quality Press.

Dyba, T., Arisholm, E., Sjoberg, D. I., Hannay, J. E., & Shull, F. (2007). Are two heads better than one? On the effectiveness of pair programming. *IEEE Software, 24*(6), 12–15.

In, H. P., Baik, J., Kim, S., Yang, Y., & Boehm, B. (2006). A quality-based cost estimation model for the product line life cycle. *Communications of the ACM, 49*(12), 85–88.

Jeffries, R., & Melnik, G. (2007). TDD: The art of fearless programming. *IEEE Software, 24*(3), 24–30.

McCann, B. (2007). The relative cost of interchanging, adding, or dropping quality practices. *Crosstalk, 20*(6), 25–28.

Rico, D. F. (2000). *Using cost benefit analyses to develop software process improvement (SPI) strategies*. Rome, NY: Air Force Research Laboratory—Information Directorate, Data and Analysis Center for Software.

———. (2005). Practical metrics and models for return on investment. *TickIT International, 7*(2), 10–16.

———. (2008). What is the ROI of agile vs. traditional methods? An analysis of extreme programming, test-driven development, pair programming, and scrum (using real options). *TickIT International, 10*(4), 9–18.

Van Solingen, R. A. (2004). Measuring the ROI of software process improvement. *IEEE Software, 21*(3), 32–38.

19

Return on Investment of Agile Methods

The return on investment (ROI) of agile methods refers to the economic business value of using nontraditional methods to create new software products. An accounting valuation method, ROI measures the efficiency of an investment or a number of competing investments. Although ROI is a simple ratio of benefits to costs, expressed as a percentage, costs are first subtracted from the benefits. For instance, if one invests $1 and gets $10 in return, then the ROI is 900%; that is, $((10 - 1) \div 1) \times 100\%$. Because ROI is extremely simple to understand, it is a popular measure.

The basic idea behind ROI is that the benefits of an investment must be larger than its costs. If the benefits of an investment are large, then the ROI is also large. If agile methods have ROI, then their benefits must be larger than their costs. Are the benefits of agile methods larger than their costs? The answer is *yes*! Because the costs of agile methods are much smaller and their benefits much larger than those of traditional methods, agile methods have ROI—and a significant one at that.

Because agile methods are fast and efficient, their costs are minimal. They also result in fewer defects, so their maintenance costs are low as well. Traditional methods have large costs stemming from documentation and communication deficiencies between customers and developers. Traditional methods also result in more defects. When this is added together, the total life cycle costs of traditional methods are substantial. Because agile methods' costs are lower than traditional methods, they have a greater ROI.

19.1 Pair Programming

The ROI of pair programming is significant, because it has lower costs, fewer defects, and lower total life cycle costs than traditional methods. Pair programming involves two highly skilled people working together to program high-quality software as quickly as possible. This is naturally going to result in higher productivity, higher quality, and lower total life cycle costs than traditional methods, which involve large teams producing voluminous documentation and more defects. Together, these development and maintenance costs combine to raise the total life cycle costs of traditional methods.

Pair programming teams code quickly and produce few defects, averaging 33.4044 lines of code (LOC) per hour and 2.355 defects per thousand LOC (KLOC). Therefore, the total life cycle costs of pair programming may be expressed as LOC ÷ 33.4044 + 2.355 × KLOC × 100. Traditional method teams program slowly and produce many defects, averaging 0.8507 LOC/hour and 33.3333 defects/KLOC. Therefore, the total life cycle costs of traditional methods may be expressed as LOC ÷ 0.8507 + 33.3333 × KLOC × 100.

The total life cycle cost of producing 10,000 LOC is about 2,654 hours using pair programming, compared to 45,088 hours using traditional methods. The benefits of pair programming are 45,088 − 2,654 or 42,434 hours. So, the ROI of pair programming is (42,434 − 2,654) ÷ 2,654 × 100%, or 1499% (see Figure 19-1). This assumes teams can sustain a pace of 33.4044 LOC/hour and that defects are 100 times more expensive to find in maintenance than development. If so, then pair programming is about 15 times more cost-effective than traditional methods after costs are subtracted.

19.2 Test-Driven Development

The ROI of test-driven development is significant, because it has lower costs, fewer defects, and lower total life cycle costs than traditional methods. Test-driven development involves complete automation of unit and system-level testing to uncover operational defects. This is naturally going to result in higher productivity, higher quality, and lower total life cycle costs than traditional methods, which involve large teams producing voluminous documentation and more defects. Together, these development and maintenance costs combine to raise the total life cycle costs of using traditional methods.

Test-driven development teams program quickly and produce few defects, averaging 29.28 LOC/hour and 2.155 defects/KLOC. Therefore, the total life cycle costs of test-driven development may be expressed as LOC ÷ 29.28 + 2.155 × KLOC × 100. Traditional method teams program slowly and produce many defects, averaging 0.8507 LOC/hour and 33.3333 defects/KLOC. Therefore, the total life cycle costs of traditional methods may be expressed as LOC ÷ 0.8507 + 33.3333 × KLOC × 100.

The total life cycle cost of producing 10,000 LOC is about 2,497 hours using test-driven development, compared to 45,088 hours using traditional methods. The benefits of test-driven development are 45,088 − 2,497, or 42,592 hours. The ROI of test-driven development is (42,592 − 2,497) ÷ 2,497 × 100%, or

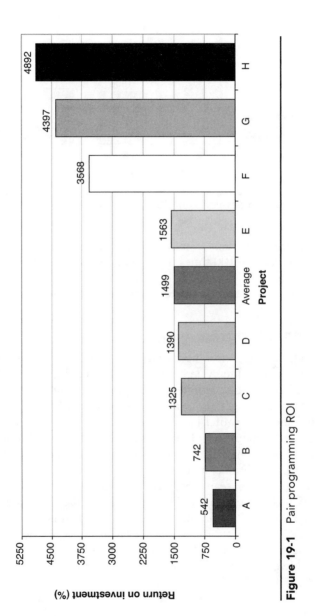

Figure 19-1 Pair programming ROI

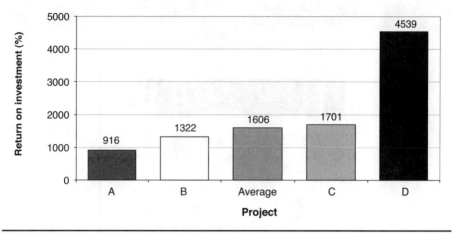

Figure 19-2   Test-driven development ROI

1606% (see Figure 19-2). This assumes teams can sustain a pace of 29.28 LOC/hour and that defects are 100 times more expensive to find in maintenance than development. If so, then test-driven development is about 16 times more cost-effective than traditional methods after costs are subtracted.

19.3 Extreme Programming

The ROI of Extreme Programming is significant, because it has lower costs, fewer defects, and lower total life cycle costs than traditional methods. Extreme Programming involves onsite customers, pair programming, test-driven development, and release planning. This is naturally going to result in higher productivity, higher quality, and lower total life cycle costs than traditional methods, which involve large teams producing voluminous documentation and more defects. Together, these development and maintenance costs combine to raise the total life cycle costs of using traditional methods.

Extreme Programming teams program quickly and produce few defects, averaging 16.1575 LOC/hour and 0.7466 defects/KLOC. Therefore, the total life cycle costs of Extreme Programming may be expressed as LOC ÷ 16.1575 + 0.7466 × KLOC × 100. Traditional methods teams program slowly and produce many defects, averaging 0.8507 LOC/hour and 33.3333 defects/KLOC. Therefore, the total life cycle costs of traditional methods may be expressed as LOC ÷ 0.8507 + 33.3333 × KLOC × 100.

The total life cycle cost of producing 10,000 LOC is about 1,366 hours using Extreme Programming compared to 45,088 hours using traditional methods. The benefits of Extreme Programming are 45,088 − 1,366, or 43,723 hours. The ROI of Extreme Programming is (43,723 − 1,366) ÷ 1,366 × 100%, or 3102% (see Figure 19-3). This assumes teams can sustain a pace of 16.1575 LOC/hour and

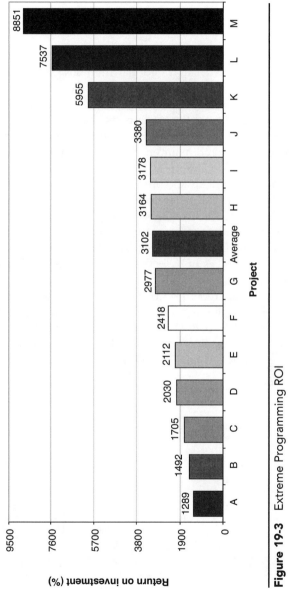

Figure 19-3 Extreme Programming ROI

that defects are 100 times more expensive to find in maintenance than development. If so, then Extreme Programming is about 31 times more cost-effective than traditional methods after costs are subtracted.

19.4 Scrum

The ROI of Scrum is significant, because it has lower costs, fewer defects, and lower total life cycle costs than traditional methods. Scrum involves product owners interacting with self-organizing teams, 30-day sprints, and a lightweight sprint planning framework. This is naturally going to result in higher productivity, higher quality, and lower total life cycle costs than traditional methods, which involve large teams producing voluminous documentation and more defects. Together, these development and maintenance costs combine to raise the total life cycle costs of using traditional methods.

Scrum teams program quickly and produce few defects, averaging 5.4436 LOC/hour and 3.945 defects/KLOC. Therefore, the total life cycle costs of Scrum may be expressed as LOC ÷ 5.4436 + 3.945 × KLOC × 100. Traditional methods teams program slowly and produce many defects, averaging 0.8507 LOC/hour and 33.3333 defects/KLOC. Therefore, the total life cycle costs of traditional methods may be expressed as LOC ÷ 0.8507 + 33.3333 × KLOC × 100.

The total life cycle cost of producing 10,000 lines of code using Scrum is about 5,782 hours compared to 45,088 hours using traditional methods. The benefits of Scrum as an agile method are 45,088 − 5,782, or 39,306 hours. The ROI of Scrum is (39,306 − 5,782) ÷ 5,782 × 100%, or 580% (see Figure 19-4). This assumes teams can sustain a pace of 5.4436 LOC/hour and that defects are 100 times more expensive to find in maintenance than development. If so, then

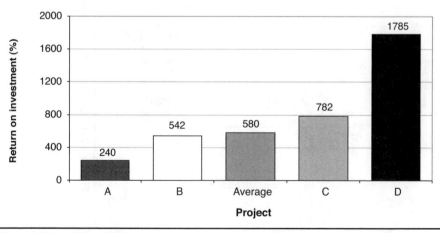

Figure 19-4   Scrum ROI

the Scrum agile method is about six times more cost-effective than traditional methods after costs are subtracted.

19.5 Agile Methods

The ROI of agile methods is significant, because they have lower costs, fewer defects, and lower total life cycle costs than traditional methods. Agile methods involve customer collaboration, teamwork, iterative development, and flexible or adaptable processes and products. This is naturally going to result in higher productivity, higher quality, and lower total life cycle costs than traditional methods, which involve large teams producing voluminous documentation and more defects. Together, these development and maintenance costs combine to raise the total life cycle costs of traditional methods.

Agile methods teams program quickly and produce few defects, averaging 21.2374 LOC/hour and 1.7972 defects/KLOC. Therefore, the total life cycle costs of agile methods may be expressed as LOC ÷ 21.2374 + 1.7972 × KLOC × 100. Traditional methods teams program slowly and produce many defects, averaging 0.8507 LOC/hour and 33.3333 defects/KLOC. Therefore, the total life cycle costs of traditional methods may be expressed as LOC ÷ 0.8507 + 33.3333 × KLOC × 100.

The total life cycle cost of producing 10,000 LOC is about 2,268 hours using agile methods compared to 45,088 hours using traditional methods. The benefits of agile methods are 45,088 − 2,268, or 42,820 hours. The ROI of agile methods is (42,820 − 2,268) ÷ 2,268 × 100%, or 1788% (see Figure 19-5). This assumes agile methods teams can sustain a pace of 21.2374 LOC/hour and that defects are 100 times more expensive to find in maintenance than development. If so,

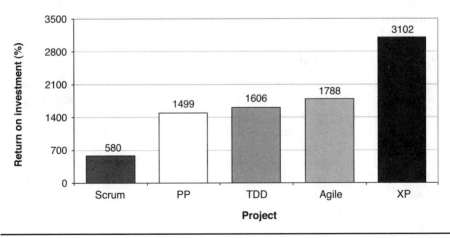

Figure 19-5   Agile methods ROI

then agile methods are about 18 times more cost-effective than traditional methods after costs are subtracted.

19.6 Summary

Agile methods not only have measurable ROI but a significantly larger ROI than traditional methods. The ROI of agile methods is substantial because their benefits are larger than their costs. Agile methods are fundamentally different than traditional methods, because they involve customer collaboration, teamwork, iterative development, and adaptability. Customer collaboration is more effective than documentation; teamwork is more effective than functional groups; iterative development is a more effective process; and adaptability is more effective than project plans.

Agile methods yield a brisk pace of 21.2374 LOC/hour and a highly efficient 1.7972 defects/KLOC. Combined, this yields only 2,268 hours in total life cycle costs. On the other hand, traditional methods yield about 0.8507 LOC/hour and 33.3333 defects/KLOC. This requires approximately 45,088 hours in total life cycle costs. When you subtract the difference, agile methods yield a savings of 42,820 hours for an ROI of 1788%. Therefore, agile methods are 18 times more cost-effective than traditional methods.

Estimating the ROI of agile methods is based on the cost of quality, total cost of ownership, and total life cycle costs. Agile methods are much more than an efficient means of creating innovative software products with few software defects; they are specifically designed to increase tangible and intangible business value for customers every 14 to 30 days. Developers cooperate to improve the economic postures of their customers. After each user story is specially designed to improve revenues or profits for the customer, agile methods are employed to quickly and efficiently develop software to realize these benefits. Agile methods are designed to minimize risk and maximize ROI.

19.7 Further Readings

Rico, D. F. (2001). Cost and benefit analysis: Choosing a SPI method for maximum ROI. *2001 Joint Euroforum/Dutch Software Process Improvement Network Conference, Utrecht, Netherlands.*

———. (2002). How to Estimate ROI for Inspections, PSP, TSP, SW-CMM, ISO 9001, and CMMI. *Software Tech News, 5*(4), 23–31.

———. (2002). Software process improvement: Modeling return on investment (ROI). *2002 Software Engineering Institute (SEI) Software Engineering Process Group Conference, Phoenix, Arizona.*

———. (2002). The return on investment in quality. *TickIT International, 4*(4), 13–18.

————. (2004). *ROI of software process improvement: Metrics for project managers and software engineers.* Boca Raton, FL: J. Ross Publishing.

————. (2005). Practical metrics and models for return on investment. *TickIT International, 7*(2), 10–16.

————. (2008). *What is the ROI of agile vs. traditional methods? An analysis of agile methods using real options.* Retrieved June 28, 2008, from http://davidfrico.com/agile-benefits.xls.

————. (2008). What is the ROI of agile vs. traditional methods? An analysis of extreme programming, test-driven development, pair programming, and scrum (using real options). *TickIT International, 10*(4), 9–18.

20

Net Present Value
of Agile Methods

The net present value (NPV) of agile methods refers to the discounted economic business value of nontraditional methods for creating software. In this case, discount means to reduce in value or otherwise devalue, lessen, cancel, or lower the expected benefits of agile methods over time. There are two ways of increasing the profits of a firm, project, or organization: (1) increase its revenues or (2) decrease its costs. We use the cost of quality, total cost of ownership, and total life cycle cost approach for increasing benefits by decreasing costs.

Maintenance is estimated to cost as much as 70% of a project's total resources to fix defects and nonconformances to requirements. Agile methods cost much less up front than traditional methods and often eliminate or minimize high maintenance costs. Hence, we've described a *spend a little now and save a lot later* way to think about the economic business value of agile methods. Although we could use a simple benefit-to-cost-ratio formula or even a return on investment (ROI) formula to estimate the business value of agile methods, economists recognize the weakness of these approaches.

ROI overstates business value, because benefits are projected far out into the future when economic forces come into play. If not invested wisely, money decreases in value over time due to inflation. Thus, a formula for estimating the time value of benefits is necessary. One popular method is NPV, which discounts a series of cash flows or the discounted difference between costs and benefits. In agile methods, because the costs are incurred first and the benefits are received later, we'll discount the benefit flows and then subtract the initial investment.

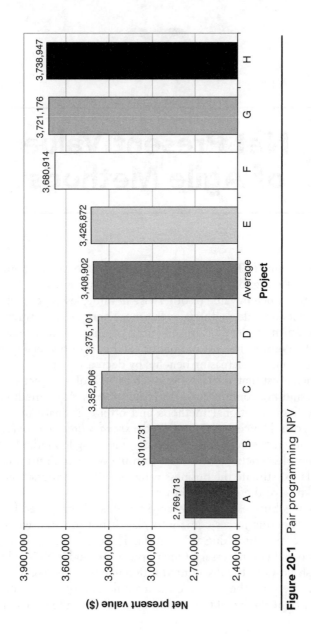

Figure 20-1   Pair programming NPV

20.1 Pair Programming

The NPV of pair programming is substantial, because pair progamming has fewer defects and lower total life cycle costs than traditional methods. However, people who use traditional methods can't understand why pair programming teams, which involve either two coding experts or two moderately good programmers with value to add, are so productive.

Pair programming teams average 33.4044 lines of code (LOC) per hour and produce 2.355 defects per thousand lines of code (KLOC). The total life cycle cost model for pair programming is LOC ÷ 33.4044 + 2.355 × KLOC × 100. Traditional methods average 0.8507 LOC/hour and produce 33.3333 defects/ KLOC. Thus, the total life cycle cost model for traditional methods is LOC ÷ 0.8507 + 33.3333 × KLOC × 100. Therefore, the total life cycle costs of pair programming and traditional methods are 2,654 and 45,088 hours, respectively.

Based on these models, the pair programming benefits are 45,088 − 2,654, or 42,434 hours. The nondiscounted benefits at $100 per hour are $4,243,397. However, the pair programming NPV is Σ (42,434 ÷ 5) ÷ 1.05^5 − 2,654 × $100, or $3,408,902 (see Figure 20-1). Therefore, a realistic estimate of pair programming benefits is $834,495 less than the nondiscounted benefits. Using NPV, pair programming is 13 times more cost-effective than traditional methods. NPV yields a more conservative estimate of pair programming benefits than ROI, which shows that the economic business value of pair programming is high even when discounted.

20.2 Test-Driven Development

The NPV of test-driven development is substantial, because the automation of end-to-end testing, which also involves continuous integration, has fewer defects and has lower total life cycle costs than traditional methods. People who use traditional methods can't understand why test-driven development teams, which are highly productive, collocated teams tirelessly driving out defects, are so productive.

Test-driven development teams average 29.28 LOC/hour and produce 2.155 defects/KLOC. The total life cycle cost model for test-driven development is LOC ÷ 29.28 + 2.155 × KLOC × 100. Traditional methods average 0.8507 LOC/hour and produce 33.3333 defects/KLOC. Thus, the total life cycle cost model for traditional methods is LOC ÷ 0.8507 + 33.3333 × KLOC × 100. Therefore, the total life cycle costs of test-driven development and traditional methods are 2,497 and 45,088 hours, respectively.

The test-driven development benefits are 45,088 − 2,497, or 42,592 hours based on these models. The nondiscounted benefits at $100 per hour are $4,259,180. However, the test-driven development NPV is Σ (42,592 ÷ 5) ÷ 1.05^5 − 2,497 × $100, or $3,438,351 (see Figure 20-2). Therefore, a realistic estimate of test-driven development benefits is $820,829 less than the nondiscounted benefits. Using NPV, test-driven development is 14 times more cost-effective than traditional

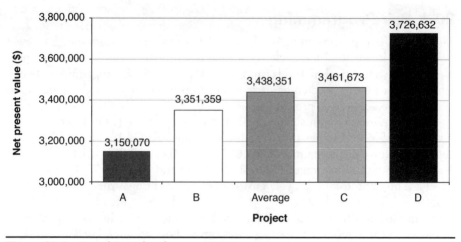

Figure 20-2   Test-driven development NPV

methods. NPV yields a more conservative estimate of the test-driven development benefits than ROI, which shows that the economic business value of test-driven development is high even when discounted.

20.3 Extreme Programming

The NPV of Extreme Programming is substantial, because Extreme Programming has fewer defects and lower total life cycle costs than traditional methods. It uses pair programming, test-driven development, continuous integration, refactoring, and other practices. People who use traditional methods can't understand why Extreme Programming teams, consisting of highly skilled programmers who mercilessly test their software, are so productive.

Extreme Programming teams average 16.1575 LOC/hour and produce 0.7466 defects/KLOC. The total life cycle cost model is LOC ÷ 16.1575 + 0.7466 × KLOC × 100. Traditional methods average 0.8507 LOC/hour and produce 33.3333 defects per/KLOC. Thus, the total life cycle cost model for traditional methods is LOC × 0.8507 + 33.3333 × KLOC × 100. Therefore, the total life cycle costs of Extreme Programming and traditional methods are 1,366 and 45,088 hours, respectively.

Based on these models, the Extreme Programming benefits are 45,088 − 1,366, or 43,723 hours. The nondiscounted benefits at $100 per hour are $4,372,282. However, the Extreme Programming NPV is Σ (43,723 ÷ 5) ÷ 1.05^5 − 1,366 × $100, or $3,649,388 (see Figure 20-3). Therefore, a realistic estimate of Extreme Programming benefits is $722,894 less than the nondiscounted benefits. Using NPV, Extreme Programming is 27 times more cost-effective than traditional methods. NPV yields a more conservative estimate of the Extreme Programming

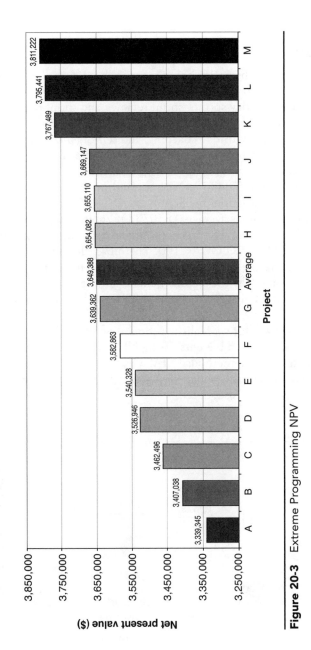

Figure 20-3 Extreme Programming NPV

benefits than ROI, which shows that the economic business value of Extreme Programming is high even when discounted.

20.4 Scrum

The NPV of Scrum is substantial, because Scrum has fewer defects and lower total life cycle costs than traditional methods. Scrum uses lightweight sprint planning, daily standups, 30-day sprints, sprint reviews, and sprint retrospectives. This agile method involves product owners who serve as customer proxies, Scrum masters who perform day-to-day coaching, and self-organizing teams that gather daily to solve the most pressing problems. Those who use traditional methods can't understand why Scrum teams are so productive.

Scrum teams average 5.4436 LOC/hour and produce 3.945 defects/KLOC. The total life cycle cost model for Scrum is LOC ÷ 5.4436 + 3.945 × KLOC × 100. Traditional methods average 0.8507 LOC/hour and produce 33.3333 defects/KLOC. Thus, the total life cycle cost model for traditional methods is LOC ÷ 0.8507 + 33.3333 × KLOC × 100. Therefore, the total life cycle costs of Scrum and traditional methods are 5,782 and 45,088 hours, respectively.

Based on these models, the Scrum benefits are 45,088 − 5,782, or 39,306 hours. The nondiscounted Scrum benefits at $100 per hour are $3,930,631. However, the Scrum NPV is Σ (39,306 ÷ 5) ÷ 1.05^5 − 5,782 × $100, or $2,825,313 (see Figure 20-4). Therefore, a realistic estimate of Scrum benefits is $1,105,318 less than the nondiscounted benefits. Using NPV, Scrum is five times more cost-effective than traditional methods. NPV yields a more conservative estimate of Scrum benefits than ROI, which shows that the economic business value of Scrum is high even when discounted.

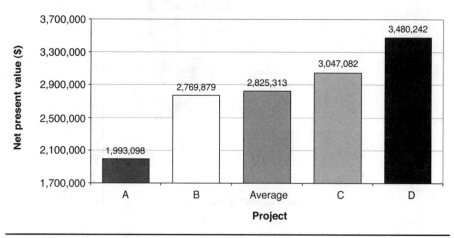

Figure 20-4   Scrum NPV

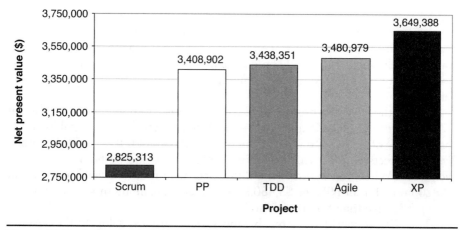

Figure 20-5 Agile methods NPV

20.5 Agile Methods

The NPV of agile methods is substantial, because agile methods have fewer defects and lower total life cycle costs than traditional methods. Agile methods involve close customer interaction, small high-performance teams, and risk-reducing iterations. They also use processes, documents, and technologies that are adaptable to dynamically changing market needs. People who use traditional methods and some agile methods that do not include practices such as pair programming and test-driven development wonder why agile methods teams are so productive.

Agile methods teams average 21.2374 LOC/hour and produce 1.7972 defects/KLOC. The total life cycle cost model for agile methods is LOC ÷ 21.2374 + 1.7972 × KLOC × 100. Traditional methods average 0.8507 LOC/hour and produce 33.3333 defects/KLOC. Therefore, the total life cycle costs for traditional methods are LOC ÷ 0.8507 + 33.3333 × KLOC × 100. The total life cycle costs of agile methods and traditional methods are 2,268 and 45,088 hours, respectively.

Based on these models, agile methods benefits are 45,088 − 2,268, or 42,820 hours. The nondiscounted benefits at $100 per hour are $4,282,026. However, the agile methods NPV is Σ (42,820 ÷ 5) ÷ 1.05^5 − 2,268 × $100, or $3,480,979 (see Figure 20-5). Therefore, a realistic estimate of agile methods benefits is $801,047 less than the nondiscounted benefits. Using NPV, agile methods are 15 times more cost-effective than traditional methods. NPV yields a more conservative estimate of agile methods benefits than ROI, which shows that the economic business value of agile methods is high even when discounted.

20.6 Summary

Agile methods continue to exhibit impressive benefits far beyond traditional methods, even when discounted using NPV. The NPV of using agile methods is significant, because agile methods' costs are minimal and their economic benefits are significant. Agile methods involve customer interaction to capture customer needs and small, high-performance teams to get the job done. They also use iterative development to spread the cost and risk of programming over multiple working software releases. But agile methods aren't just fast, cost-effective, and defect-free.

Agile methods yield a brisk pace of 21.2374 LOC/hour and a highly efficient 1.7972 defects/KLOC. Combined, this yields only 2,268 hours in total life cycle costs. On the other hand, traditional methods yield about 0.8507 LOC/hour and 33.3333 defects/KLOC, which require approximately 45,088 hours in total life cycle costs. When you subtract the difference, agile methods yield a savings of 42,820 hours for an NPV of $3,480,979. Therefore, agile methods are 15 times more productive than traditional methods.

While NPV is considered a reliable measure of business value, ROI overstates business value, because it does not consider the time value of money. If projects are long, benefits minimal, market conditions volatile, and cash flows vacillating, ROI is misleading. If costs and benefits are equal or differentiated by a small amount, then ROI may not actually exist. As a valuation methodology to expose costs and benefits to realistic market conditions, NPV is used for sensitivity analysis to negate the effects of weak benefits. Because our analysis shows that agile methods have low costs and large benefits, agile methods are 15 times more effective than traditional methods under the discriminating lens of NPV.

20.7 Further Readings

Allman, K. A. (2007). *Modeling structured finance cash flows with Microsoft Excel: A step-by-step guide*. Hoboken, NJ: John Wiley & Sons.

Bragg, S. M. (2007). *Business ratios and formulas: A comprehensive guide*. Hoboken, NJ: John Wiley & Sons.

Kruschwitz, L., & Loeffler, A. (2006). *Discounted cash flow: A theory of the valuation of firms*. West Sussex, England: John Wiley & Sons.

Ramsden, P. (1998). *The essentials of management ratios*. Brookfield, VT: Gower.

Rico, D. F. (2008). What is the ROI of agile vs. traditional methods? An analysis of extreme programming, test-driven development, pair programming, and scrum (using real options). *TickIT International, 10*(4), 9–18.

Siegel, J. G., Shim, J. K., & Hartman, S. W. (1997). *Schaum's quick guide to business formulas: 201 decision-making tools for business, finance, and accounting students*. New York, NY: McGraw-Hill.

Tham, J., & Velez-Pareja, I. (2004). *Principles of cash flow valuation: An integrated market-based approach*. London, England: Elsevier.

Walsh, C. (2009). *Key management ratios: The clearest guide to the critical numbers that drive your business*. Indianapolis, IN: Pearson Education.

21

Real Options Analysis
of Agile Methods

The real options analysis (ROA) of agile methods is the economic business value gained because of decreased risk and increased adaptability to change. Creating new software products is a complex and risk-prone activity, because customer needs cannot be defined in advance. Agile methods are based on new product development principles and have built-in practices to manage risk and respond to change. Remember, agile methods are based on the values of customer collaboration, teamwork, iterative development, and adaptability.

Customer collaboration uses close and frequent interactions with stakeholders to continuously capture and respond to their needs. By using teamwork, small groups of highly skilled people work together to solve complex development issues rapidly. Iterative development is used to chip away at uncertainty, risk, and complexity by creating a stream of working software releases. By using adaptability, flexible people, plans, documents, practices, designs, and technology to respond to changing customer needs, agile methods are optimized to manage risk and flexibility.

Although return on investment (ROI) overstates economic business value, the net present value (NPV) is realistic because it exposes benefits to forces such as time and inflation. ROA also accounts for time and inflation but also includes market or project risk. Because software development is inherently risky, a model such as ROA is more appropriate for agile methods. ROA negates the erosive effects of time, to which NPV is sensitive. Agile methods not only negate the effects of using NPV but the original costs as well. Therefore, agile methods maximize economic business value by spreading risk and flexibility over multiple iterations.

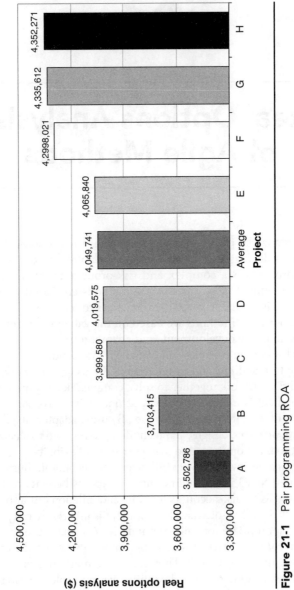

Figure 21-1 Pair programming ROA

21.1 Pair Programming

The ROA of pair programming is significant, because pair programming has fewer defects and lower total life cycle costs than traditional methods. The risk of pair programming is low because the teams, which code at a high rate of speed and produce few defects, spread the risk of creating software over time. By implementing user stories as they emerge, pair programming teams adapt to changing market conditions. Responding to change, coding rapidly, committing few errors, and spreading risk over time negate the erosive effects of volatile market conditions.

The total life cycle cost model for traditional methods is lines of code (LOC) ÷ 0.8507 + 33.3333 × a thousand lines of code (KLOC) × 100. The total life cycle cost model for pair programming is LOC ÷ 33.4044 + 2.355 × KLOC × 100. Therefore, pair programming benefits are 45,088 − 2,654, or 42,434 hours. Pair programming ROI is (42,434 − 2,654) ÷ 2,654 × 100%, or 1499%. Pair programming NPV is Σ (42,434 ÷ 5) ÷ 1.05^5 − 2,654 × \$100, or \$3,408,902. Pair programming benefits are \$834,495 less than the nondiscounted benefits and 13 times better than traditional methods.

However, pair programming ROA is *NORMSDIST* (2.692) × \$4,243,397 − *NORMSDIST* (1.098) × \$265,436 × *EXP* (−5% × 5) or \$4,049,741 (see Figure 21-1). Therefore, risk-adjusted benefits are \$640,839 more than NPV and \$193,656 less than the nondiscounted benefits. Using ROA, pair programming is 15 times more cost-effective than traditional methods. ROA yields less conservative pair programming benefits than NPV. That is, pair programming negates the erosive effects of inflation by spreading risk over time. This shows that the economic business value of pair programming remains high and does not erode over time, as do traditional methods.

21.2 Test-Driven Development

The ROA of test-driven development is significant, because test-driven development has fewer defects and lower total life cycle costs than traditional methods. Test-driven development along with continuous integration completely automates the testing process. It also enables programmers to quickly implement emerging user stories, construct what-if scenarios, identify and eliminate defects, and spread risk over time. Responding to change, coding and testing rapidly, eliminating errors, and spreading risk over time negate the erosive effects of volatile market conditions.

The total life cycle cost model for traditional methods is LOC ÷ 0.8507 + 33.3333 × KLOC × 100. The total life cycle cost model for test-driven development is LOC ÷ 29.28 + 2.155 × KLOC × 100. Thus, test-driven development benefits are 45,088 − 2,497 or 42,592 hours. Test-driven development ROI is (42,592 − 2,497) ÷ 2,497 × 100%, or 1606%. Test-driven development NPV is Σ (42,592 ÷ 5) ÷ 1.05^5 − 2,497 × \$100, or \$3,438,351. Test-driven development benefits are \$820,829 less than the nondiscounted benefits and 14 times better than traditional methods.

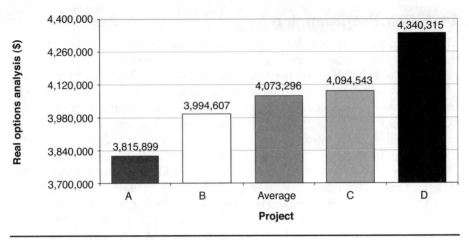

Figure 21-2   Test-driven development ROA

Test-driven development ROA is *NORMSDIST* (2.792) × $4,259,180 − *NORMSDIST* (1.274) × $249,653 × *EXP* (−5% × 5), or $4,073,296 (see Figure 21-2). Therefore, the risk-adjusted benefits are $634,945 more than NPV and $185,884 less than the nondiscounted benefits. Using ROA, test-driven development is 16 times more cost-effective than traditional methods. ROA yields less conservative test-driven development benefits than NPV. That is, test-driven development negates the erosive effects of inflation by spreading risk over time. This shows that the economic business value of test-driven development remains high and does not erode over time, as do traditional methods.

21.3 Extreme Programming

The ROA of Extreme Programming is significant, because Extreme Programming has fewer defects and lower total life cycle costs than traditional methods. Extreme Programming teams use pair programming, test-driven development, and other practices to increase productivity and quality. More importantly, Extreme Programming teams use release planning to adapt to changing market conditions and iterative development to spread risk over time. Responding to change, coding and testing rapidly, eliminating errors, and spreading risk over time negate the erosive effects of volatile market conditions.

The total life cycle cost model for traditional methods is LOC ÷ 0.8507 + 33.3333 × KLOC × 100. The Extreme Programming total life cycle cost model is LOC ÷ 16.1575 + 0.7466 × KLOC × 100. Therefore, Extreme Programming benefits are 45,088 − 1,366, or 43,723 hours. Extreme Programming ROI is (43,723 − 1,366) ÷ 1,366 × 100%, or 3102%. Extreme Programming NPV is

Σ (43,723 ÷ 5) ÷ 1.05^5 − 1,366 × \$100, or \$3,649,388. Extreme Programming benefits are \$722,894 less than the nondiscounted benefits and 27 times better than traditional methods.

However, Extreme Programming ROA is *NORMSDIST* (8.077) × \$4,372,282 − *NORMSDIST* (7.603) × \$136,551 × *EXP* (−5% × 5), or \$4,265,936 (see Figure 21-3). Therefore, risk-adjusted benefits are \$616,548 more than NPV and \$106,346 less than the nondiscounted benefits. Using ROA, Extreme Programming is 31 times more cost-effective than traditional methods. ROA yields less conservative Extreme Programming benefits than NPV. That is, Extreme Programming negates the erosive effects of inflation by spreading risk over time. This shows that the economic business value of Extreme Programming remains high and does not erode over time, as do traditional methods.

21.4 Scrum

The ROA of Scrum is significant, because Scrum has fewer defects and lower total life cycle costs than traditional methods. Scrum uses self-organizing teams, daily standups, and sprint retrospectives to code rapidly and make numerous improvements. More importantly, Scrum teams use sprint planning and sprint review meetings to adapt to changing market conditions and 30-day sprints to spread risk over time. Product owners and Scrum masters communicate customer needs, facilitate Scrum teams, and help remove impediments. Responding to change, working together, coding rapidly, solving problems, and spreading risk over time negate the erosive effects of volatile market conditions.

The total life cycle cost model for traditional methods is LOC ÷ 0.8507 + 33.3333 × KLOC × 100. The Scrum total life cycle cost model is LOC ÷ 5.4436 + 3.945 × KLOC × 100. Therefore, Scrum benefits are 45,088 − 5,782, or 39,306 hours. Scrum ROI is (39,306 − 5,782) ÷ 5,782 × 100%, or 580%. Scrum NPV is Σ (39,306 ÷ 5) ÷ 1.05^5 − 5,782 × \$100, or \$2,825,313. Scrum benefits are \$1,105,318 less than the nondiscounted benefits and five times better than traditional methods.

However, Scrum ROA is *NORMSDIST* (2.087) × \$3,930,631 − *NORMSDIST* (−0.149) × \$578,202 × *EXP* (−5% × 5), or \$3,659,651 (see Figure 21-4). Therefore, risk-adjusted Scrum benefits are \$834,337 more than NPV and \$270,980 less than nondiscounted benefits. Using ROA, Scrum is six times more cost-effective than traditional methods. ROA yields less conservative Scrum benefits than NPV. That is, Scrum negates the erosive effects of inflation by spreading risk over time. This shows that the economic business value of Scrum remains high and does not erode over time, as do traditional methods.

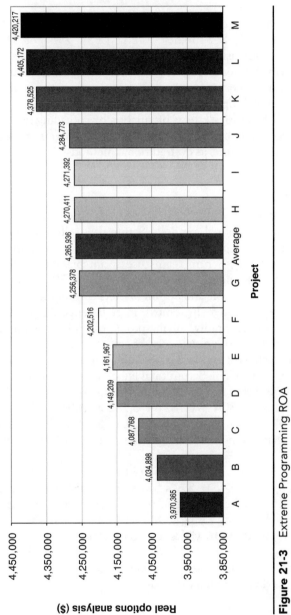

Figure 21-3 Extreme Programming ROA

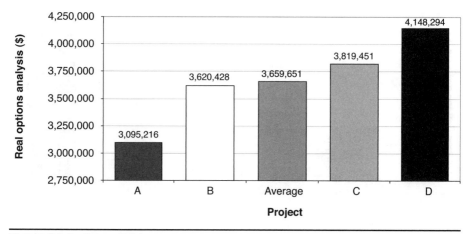

Figure 21-4   Scrum ROA

21.5 Agile Methods

The ROA of agile methods is significant, because agile methods have fewer defects and lower total life cycle costs than traditional methods. Small, highly skilled, and highly motivated agile methods teams collaborate with customers to identify their requirements and rapidly create new software products. Agile methods also use iterative development to spread risk over time and use flexible processes and products to adapt to continuously changing and evolving market conditions. Responding to change, working productively, and spreading risk over time combine to negate the erosive effects of volatile market conditions.

The total life cycle cost model for traditional methods is LOC ÷ 0.8507 + 33.3333 × KLOC × 100. The total life cycle cost model for agile methods is LOC ÷ 21.2374 + 1.7972 × KLOC × 100. Therefore, agile methods benefits are 45,088 − 2,268, or 42,820 hours. Agile methods ROI is (42,820 − 2,268) ÷ 2,268 × 100%, or 1788%. Agile methods NPV is Σ (42,820 ÷ 5) ÷ 1.05^5 − 2,268 × $100, or $3,480,979. Agile methods benefits are $801,047 less than the nondiscounted benefits and 15 times better than traditional methods.

However, agile methods ROA is *NORMSDIST* (2.985) × $4,282,026 − *NORMSDIST* (1.592) × $226,807 × *EXP* (−5% × 5), or $4,109,154 (see Figure 21-5). Therefore, risk-adjusted agile methods benefits are $628,175 more than NPV and $172,872 less than the nondiscounted benefits. Using ROA, agile methods are 18 times more cost-effective than traditional methods. ROA yields less conservative agile methods benefits than NPV. That is, agile methods negate the erosive effects of inflation by spreading risk over time. The business value of agile methods remains high and doesn't erode over time, as do traditional methods.

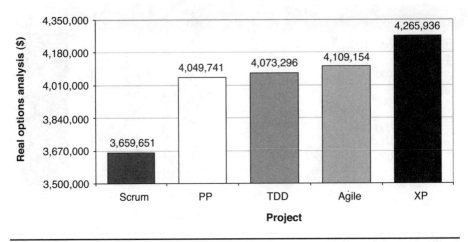

Figure 21-5   Agile methods ROA

21.6 Summary

Agile methods' business value is best expressed using valuation measures such as ROA that consider time, inflation, risk, and change. The ROA of using agile methods is substantial, because agile methods have low costs, high productivity, few defects, and low maintenance. Agile methods use iterative development to spread risk over time and flexible management to adapt to changing market conditions. The business value of agile methods may be as much as 90% higher than NPV using ROA under extreme market conditions, including high inflation, risk, change, and amount of time.

Measures such as ROI do not account for the time value of money and may overstate the benefits of agile methods. Although NPV accounts for the time value of money by discounting benefits due to inflation and is considered more reliable than ROI, it does not measure flexibility or adaptability to change and the minimization of a project's risk by using iterative development. If benefits are low, market conditions are volatile, or projects are long, NPV can actually underestimate benefits. Furthermore, NPV cannot be used to measure the risks of creating new software products, also known as new product development.

ROA is a better method for estimating the benefits of agile methods than NPV. Designed to model the effects of time, inflation, risk, and changing market conditions, ROA is most sensitive to inflation but not to the same degree as NPV. Time is the enemy of NPV, which diminishes benefits too rapidly and may inexplicably negate them altogether. The individual parameters of ROA such as time, discount rate, and risk aren't as sensitive to change as those found in NPV. However, ROA sustains the value of benefits over time and may actually negate the costs themselves. ROA shows that agile methods do indeed maximize business value.

21.7 Further Readings

Benaroch, M. (2002). Managing information technology investment risk: A real options perspective. *Journal of Management Information Systems, 19*(2), 43–84.

Erdogmus, H. (2002). Valuation of learning options in software development under private and market risk. *The Engineering Economist, 47*(3), 308–353.

———. (2005). The economic impact of learning and flexibility on process decisions. *IEEE Software, 22*(6), 76–83.

Erdogmus, H., & Favaro, J. (2003). Keep your options open: Extreme programming and the economics of flexibility. In M. Marchesi, G. Succi, J. D. Wells, & L. Williams (Eds.), *Extreme programming perspectives* (pp. 503–552). New York, NY: Addison-Wesley.

Fichman, R. G. (2004). Real options and IT platform adoption: Implications for theory and practice. *Information Systems Research, 15*(2), 132–154.

Fichman, R. G., Keil, M., & Tiwana, A. (2005). Beyond valuation: Options thinking in IT project management. *California Management Review, 47*(2), 74–96.

Kodukula, P. (2006). *Project valuation using real options*. Fort Lauderdale, FL: J. Ross Publishing.

Rico, D. F. (2008). What is the ROI of agile vs. traditional methods? An analysis of extreme programming, test-driven development, pair programming, and scrum (using real options). *TickIT International, 10*(4), 9–18.

22

Business Value of
Agile Methods

The business value of agile methods is impressive. The costs of agile methods are low, because the overhead associated with using them is minimal. Agile methods teams are highly skilled, talented, motivated, and productive, often producing defect-free code. But the most important features of agile methods are adaptive project management frameworks and iterative development, which are used to respond to changing market conditions and spread project risks over time.

Agile methods teams have high programming productivity levels that lead to low software development costs. The benefits of agile methods are significant, because they have lower costs, fewer defects, and lower total life cycle costs than traditional methods. Regardless of the valuation method utilized—return on investment (ROI), net present value (NPV), or real options analysis (ROA)—agile methods have more business value than traditional methods.

From a cost perspective, agile methods are approximately 25 times more productive to use than traditional methods. From a quality perspective, agile methods have approximately 19 times higher quality than traditional methods. From a total life cycle cost perspective, agile methods are approximately 20 times cheaper to use than traditional methods. The ROI of agile methods is approximately 19 times greater than traditional methods, whereas NPV reduces the ROI of agile methods by approximately 20%. However, ROA reduces the ROI of agile methods by only 4% and is even better under volatile project conditions.

22.1 Costs

The costs of agile methods are lower than the costs of traditional methods, because agile methods involve customer collaboration, teamwork, iterative development,

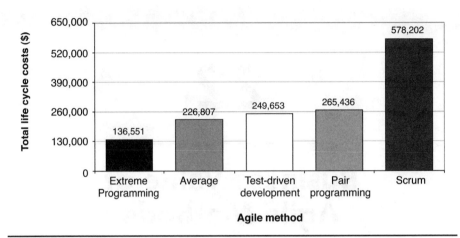

Figure 22-1   Costs of agile methods

and adaptability. It's simply more cost effective to capture user needs by interacting with customers more frequently. Agile methods also rely on small teams of highly skilled programmers who code faster than those using traditional methods and who place a greater emphasis on producing working software in frequent iterations. Also, agile methods use small, lightweight, and highly adaptable processes, products, and technologies.

Extreme Programming teams produce 16.1575 lines of code (LOC) per hour and only 0.7466 defects per thousand lines of code (KLOC). Agile methods teams produce 21.2374 LOC/hour and only 1.7972 defects/KLOC. Test-driven development teams produce 29.28 LOC/hour and only 2.155 defects/KLOC. Pair programming teams produce 33.4044 LOC/hour and only 2.355 defects/KLOC. Scrum teams produce 5.4436 LOC/hour and only 3.945 defects/KLOC.

For a 10-KLOC system, this comes out to a total life cycle cost of 1,366, 2,268, 2,497, 2,654, and 5,782 hours, respectively (see Figure 22-1). Using standard cost-estimating models, traditional methods teams code at a rate of 0.8507 LOC/hour and produce up to 33.3333 defects/KLOC if they use standard testing practices. Using a cost of quality approach, traditional methods have a total life cycle cost of up to 45,088 hours for a 10-KLOC system. Based on this formulation, agile methods are up to 19 times less expensive than traditional methods. From a cost perspective, it is apparent that agile methods are right-sized, just-enough, and just-in-time approaches for maximizing business value.

22.2 Benefits

The benefits of agile methods are greater than the benefits of traditional methods. This holds true from two unique perspectives. As we've indicated, there are two

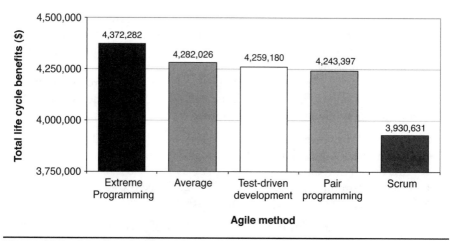

Figure 22-2   Benefits of agile methods

fundamental means of creating business value for a product, project, company, and organization: (1) increase revenue and (2) decrease costs. Although agile methods are designed to increase revenue, they also decrease costs because they are fast and efficient.

We use cost of quality to estimate the business value of agile methods by decreasing costs. The total life cycle cost model for different agile methods and practices follows:

♦ Extreme Programming: $LOC \div 16.1575 + 0.7466 \times KLOC \times 100$
♦ Agile methods: $LOC \div 21.2374 + 1.7972 \times KLOC \times 100$
♦ Test-driven development: $LOC \div 29.28 + 2.155 \times KLOC \times 100$
♦ Pair programming: $LOC \div 33.4044 + 2.355 \times KLOC \times 100$
♦ Scrum: $LOC \div 5.4436 + 3.945 \times KLOC \times 100$.

For a 10-KLOC system, this comes out to a total life cycle cost of 1,366, 2,268, 2,497, 2,654, and 5,782 hours, respectively. The total life cycle cost of traditional methods is $LOC \div 0.8507 + 33.3333 \times KLOC \times 100$. Therefore, the total life cycle cost of traditional methods is 45,088 hours for a 10-KLOC system. When we subtract the costs of agile methods from traditional ones, the benefits of agile methods are 43,723, 42,820, 42,592, 42,434, and 39,306 hours, respectively (see Figure 22-2). The benefit-to-cost ratio is 32:1, 19:1, 17:1, 16:1, and 7:1, respectively. For every dollar spent on agile methods, approximately 19 are returned. The benefits of agile methods are impressive, even under the scrutiny of ROI, NPV, and ROA.

22.3 Return on Investment

The ROI of agile methods is substantial due to the differential between the total life cycle costs of agile and traditional methods. Agile methods are less expensive and more efficient to use than traditional methods. They reduce costs by interacting with customers more frequently, cooperatively working faster, and spending more time building working operational software. Also, teams dramatically reduce operating costs by using lightweight and adaptable processes and products.

The total life cycle costs and benefits of using agile methods are the inputs into the ROI formula: that is, (Benefits − Costs) ÷ Costs × 100%. The ROI model for different agile methods and practices follows:

- Extreme Programming: (43,723 − 1,366) ÷ 1,366 × 100%
- Agile methods: (42,820 − 2,268) ÷ 2,268 × 100%
- Test-driven development: (42,592 − 2,497) ÷ 2,497 × 100%
- Pair programming: (42,434 − 2,654) ÷ 2,654 × 100%
- Scrum: (39,306 − 5,782) ÷ 5,782 × 100%

For a 10-KLOC system, this comes out to an ROI of 3,102%, 1,788%, 1,606%, 1,499%, and 580%, respectively (see Figure 22-3). Extreme Programming, agile methods, test-driven development, pair programming, and Scrum have an ROI of 31:1, 18.1, 16:1, 15:1, and 6:1, respectively. ROI is sort of sensitivity analysis, because the costs are subtracted from the benefits before they are used. If the benefits were weak or negligible, ROI could be critical. However, that is not the case with agile methods. The differential between the costs and benefits is so significant that the ROI is significant. Using the cost of quality approach to economic analysis, the ROI of using agile methods is significant.

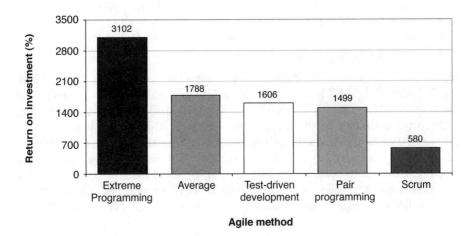

Figure 22-3   ROI of agile methods

22.4 Net Present Value

The NPV of agile methods is substantial due to the differential between the total life cycle costs of agile and traditional methods. Less expensive and more efficient to use than traditional methods, agile methods use a variety of techniques to achieve superior cost and quality, including a lightweight, adaptable project management framework of either sprint or release planning; fast-moving, self-organizing pair programming teams; and test-driven development or continuous integration. They deliver working software in 30-day sprints or 14-day iterations.

The total life cycle costs and benefits of agile methods are the inputs into the NPV formula: that is, Σ (Benefits $\div$ Years) $\div$ $(1 + \text{Rate})^{\text{Years}} - $ Costs $\times$ \$100. The NPV model for different agile methods and practices follows:

- Extreme Programming: Σ (43,723 $\div$ 5) $\div$ 1.05^5 $-$ 1,366 $\times$ \$100
- Agile methods: Σ (42,820 $\div$ 5) $\div$ 1.05^5 $-$ 2,268 $\times$ \$100
- Test-driven development: Σ (42,592 $\div$ 5) $\div$ 1.05^5 $-$ 2,497 $\times$ \$100
- Pair programming: Σ (42,434 $\div$ 5) $\div$ 1.05^5 $-$ 2,654 $\times$ \$100
- Scrum: Σ (39,306 $\div$ 5) $\div$ 1.05^5 $-$ 5,782 $\times$ \$100.

For a 10-KLOC system, this comes to an NPV of \$3,649,388, \$3,480,979, \$3,438,351, \$3,408,902, and \$2,825,313, respectively (see Figure 22-4). Extreme Programming, agile methods, test-driven development, pair programming, and Scrum have an NPV of 27:1, 15:1, 14:1, 13:1, and 5:1, respectively. NPV is sort of sensitivity analysis, because the benefits are discounted using the time value of money. If the benefits were weak or negligible, NPV could be critical. However, that is not the case with agile methods. The difference between costs

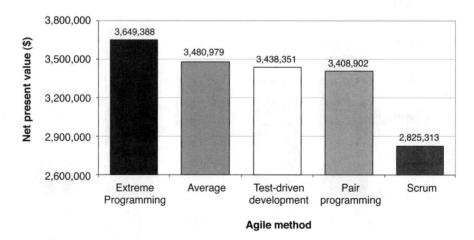

Figure 22-4 NPV of agile methods

and benefits is so substantial that the NPV is substantial. Using the cost of quality approach to economic analysis, the NPV of using agile methods is significant.

22.5 Real Options Analysis

The ROA of agile methods is significant due to the differential between the total life cycle costs of agile and traditional methods. Although NPV sharply discounts benefits based on the time value of money, ROA actually increases with time, inflation, and risk factors. Agile methods have unique tools not found in traditional methods. To respond to changing market conditions, they combine customer collaboration and adaptive planning and use iterative development to spread risk over time. Therefore, ROA is an excellent method of modeling the business value of agile methods.

The total life cycle costs and benefits of agile methods are the inputs into the ROA formula: that is, $NORMSDIST(d_1) \times Benefits - NORMSDIST(d_2) \times Costs \times e^{-Rate \times Years}$. The ROA model for different agile methods and practices follows:

- Extreme Programming: $NORMSDIST(8.077) \times \$4,372,282 - NORMSDIST(7.603) \times \$136,551 \times e^{-5\% \times 5}$
- Agile methods: $NORMSDIST(2.985) \times \$4,282,026 - NORMSDIST(1.592) \times \$226,807 \times e^{-5\% \times 5}$
- Test-driven development: $NORMSDIST(2.792) \times \$4,259,180 - NORMSDIST(1.274) \times \$249,653 \times e^{-5\% \times 5}$
- Pair programming: $NORMSDIST(2.692) \times \$4,243,397 - NORMSDIST(1.098) \times \$265,436 \times e^{-5\% \times 5}$
- Scrum: $NORMSDIST(2.087) \times \$3,930,631 - NORMSDIST(-0.149) \times \$578,202 \times e^{-5\% \times 5}$

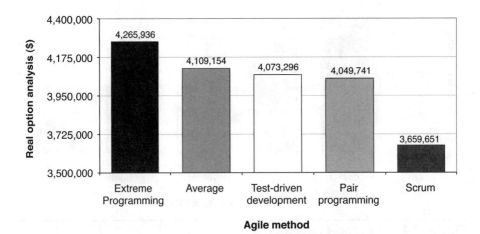

Figure 22-5   ROA of agile methods

For a 10-KLOC system, the ROA is $4,265,936, $4,109,154, $4,073,296, $4,049,741, and $3,659,651, respectively (see Figure 22-5). Extreme Programming, agile methods, test-driven development, pair programming, and Scrum have an ROA of 31:1, 18:1, 16:1, 15:1, and 6:1, respectively. ROA models the business value of spreading risk over time, whereas NPV heavily penalizes benefits over time. That is, ROA penalizes benefits by an average of only 4%, whereas NPV penalizes them by 20%. Furthermore, ROA continues to rise with risk, time, and inflation. Using the cost of quality approach to economic analysis, the ROA of using agile methods is significant and remains so with time, risk, and inflation.

22.6 Summary

Agile methods are new product development patterns for creating innovative software. As contemporary systems and software engineering approaches, agile methods utilize customer collaboration, teamwork, iterative development, and adaptability. Furthermore, they are disciplined, systematic, and effective. Frequent customer interactions and high-performance teams are more cost- and time-efficient than contracts and documentation used in traditional methods. Frequent working software releases put business value at center stage, and flexibility is ideal for changing market conditions.

Teams using agile methods are fast, efficient, and productive, and development costs are 25 times less than for traditional methods. Furthermore, agile teams produce nearly defect-free software that lowers maintenance and total life cycle costs by 20 times. Both ROI and NPV are significant, because of the vast difference between the total life cycle costs of agile and traditional methods. However, the ROA of agile methods is particularly significant, because it maintains or increases the benefits due to time, risk, and inflation. Thus, agile methods have significant economic business value.

Cost of quality isn't the only way to estimate business value. There are at least two more dimensions of tangible and intangible benefits. Not all requirements, iterations, or lines of code are created equal. Within agile methods, each customer need is prioritized based on business value, and each release impacts the bottom line. In yet another dimension, agile methods create intangible business value. They are useful for building strong relationships with customers and between developers, which translate into even more productivity, cost efficiency, and product quality. Therefore, agile methods are right-sized, just-enough, and just-in-time processes and documentation for maximizing business value.

22.7 Further Readings

Harris, D. S., Herron, D., & Iwanicki, S. (2008). *The business value of IT: Managing risks, optimizing performance, and measuring results*. Boca Raton, FL: Taylor and Francis.

McGibbon, T., Ferens, D., & Vienneau, R. L. (2007). *A business case for software process improvement: Measuring the ROI from software engineering and management*. Griffiss AFB, NY: DACS.

Molokken-Ostvold, K., & Jorgensen, M. (2005). A comparison of software project overruns: Flexible versus sequential development models. *IEEE Transactions on Software Engineering, 31*(5), 754–766.

Rico, D. F. (2004). *ROI of software process improvement: Metrics for project managers and software engineers*. Boca Raton, FL: J. Ross Publishing.

———. (2005). Practical metrics and models for return on investment. *TickIT International, 7*(2), 10–16.

———. (2008). What is the ROI of agile vs. traditional methods? An analysis of extreme programming, test-driven development, pair programming, and scrum (using real options). *TickIT International, 10*(4), 9–18.

Shriver, R. (2009). Measurable value with agile. *Overload, 6*(1), 4–12.

Van Solingen, R. A., & Rico, D. F. (2006). Calculating software process improvement's return on investment. In M. V. Zelkowitz (Ed.), *Advances in computers: Quality software development, Vol. 66* (pp. 1–41). San Diego, CA: Elsevier

23

Agile vs. Traditional Methods

The business value of agile methods is impressive when compared to that of traditional methods. The primary drivers of economic business value are costs and benefits. This is true whether return on investment (ROI), net present value (NPV), or real options analysis (ROA) is used to estimate business value. The key to maximizing the business value of any method is low costs and high benefits, be it agile or traditional. This is especially true for valuation based on the cost of quality, total cost of ownership, and total life cycle cost.

Agile methods have both intangible and tangible business value. Examples of intangible business value are improved customer communication, trust, and satisfaction as well as interaction, cooperation, and teamwork between developers. However, even intangible benefits such as these can be monetized and translated into economic terms. Agile methods are particularly well designed to maximize both the intangible and tangible forms of business value, particularly customer satisfaction, at the least possible cost.

The goal of traditional methods is to achieve system quality at any cost, which is a noble goal on the surface. Since the 1950s, traditional methods were an amalgamation of policies, standards, processes, procedures, documentation, tools, and metrics. The philosophy of traditional methods seems to be the more the better! That is, system quality is believed to be a function of large processes. However, traditional methods reached their point of diminishing returns decades ago, adversely affecting their value proposition. That is, their costs are too high and their benefits too low.

23.1 Agile vs. Traditional Costs

The costs of agile methods are significantly low compared to those of traditional methods. This is due to several factors. Teams using agile methods interact with customers more frequently, which obviates the need for voluminous documentation. Conversely, traditional methods use documents as a proxy for communication with customers and between developers. That is, traditional methods produce large volumes of expensive documents rather than meeting with customers to discuss actual business needs. Traditional methods are also based on excessive processes.

Agile methods are based on right-sized, just-enough, and just-in-time processes and documentation. Instead of inefficient documentation, they are based on frequent communications and they use a lightweight and highly adaptable project management framework called sprint or release planning. Agile methods produce user stories instead of requirements specifications, which take years to produce and will become instantly obsolete when the first line of code is produced. Also, all agile methods processes and documentation are right sized to produce validated working software in 14- to 30-day sprints or iterations.

Agile methods are 100% to 700% less expensive than the largest traditional methods optimized for quality (see Figure 23-1). A popular myth is that agile methods are for simple systems and traditional methods are for large and complex systems. This has been shown to be untrue in practice. For decades, the failure rates of projects using traditional methods have been around 70%. This myth also reveals a lack of familiarity with the fundamentals of new product development. Agile methods are designed to adapt to large and complex systems with

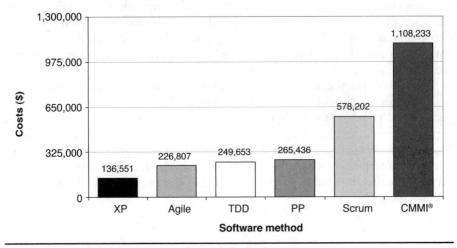

Figure 23-1   Costs of agile vs. traditional methods

volatile requirements. For software, that is nearly every project. Even the most efficient traditional methods would fail at scale, complexity, or volatility.

23.2 Agile vs. Traditional Benefits

The benefits of agile methods are substantial compared to those of traditional methods. This is due to several factors. Teams using agile methods produce higher-quality products than those using traditional methods. Not only do agile teams, in a timely manner, make products that their customers ask for and need, but they produce few defects. Agile methods have a confluence of forces working in their favor: (1) a pull force designed to respond to customer or market needs and (2) a push force designed to make products quickly.

Agile methods have right-sized, just-enough, and just-in-time processes and documentation for high-quality software. A major philosophy of large traditional methods is that numerous processes and documentation are necessary to produce high-quality systems. Although some believe that agile methods result in low-quality software, an analysis of actual, real-world projects using agile methods shatters this myth. That is, agile methods have proven to result in software at levels of quality beyond those of the best traditional methods and at a fraction of their cost.

The benefits of agile methods range from 30 to 45% above those of the largest traditional methods (see Figure 23-2). Agile methods have a series of built-in checks and balances, forming a completely integrated verification and validation system. After customers express requirements in close communication, user stories are created and acceptance criteria written. A simple design is formed, the

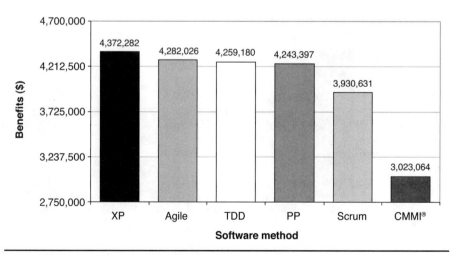

Figure 23-2   Benefits of agile vs. traditional methods

code is refactored and documented, and changes are instantly tested against the whole system. Customers, coaches, mentors, and teams verify and validate everything continuously. Software is released every 14 to 30 days for customers to approve, resulting in only the best software.

23.3 Agile vs. Traditional ROI

Agile methods' ROI is impressive compared to that of traditional methods. This can be attributed to two major factors: (1) low costs and (2) high benefits. ROI measures the efficiency of an investment. That is, to a large extent it measures the ratio of benefits to costs. If an investment's benefits are high and its costs are low, ROI is high. If benefits are less than the costs, then ROI may be fractional. If benefits are only slightly larger, then ROI may be in single or double digits.

Teams using agile methods produce the equivalent software of traditional methods at a fraction of the cost. The benefits of using agile methods are significant, due to the high levels of software quality. High benefits and low costs form a powerful ratio of benefits to costs—extremely high ROI. Agile methods have right-sized, just-enough, and just-in-time processes and documents to result in high benefits and low costs. On the other hand, traditional methods attempt to achieve high system quality at the greatest possible cost and marginal benefits.

Agile methods' ROI is 2 to 17 times greater than that of large traditional methods (see Figure 23-3). They have the discipline necessary to create new software products, including a disciplined project management framework and requirements management process. Agile methods consist of metaphors for architecture, simple designs, and the most exhaustive testing regime of any software method,

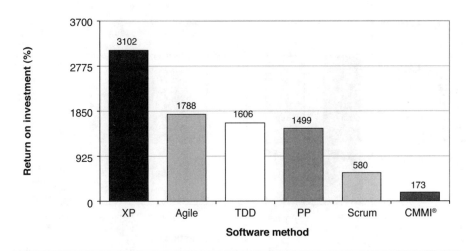

Figure 23-3 ROI of agile vs. traditional methods

whether agile or traditional. They come replete with a comprehensive verification and validation framework. Agile methods can be used to produce higher-quality software at a fraction of the cost of traditional methods—thus their superior return on investment.

23.4 Agile vs. Traditional NPV

The NPV of agile methods is greater than that of traditional methods. This is largely due to the magnitude of the benefits associated with agile methods. NPV is particularly sensitive to time and inflation and, in fact, is sure to erode the economic business value of agile methods if the costs are too high or the benefits are too low. However, the exact opposite is true. The costs of agile methods are low and their benefits are high enough to exhibit an impressive NPV.

Designed to be a reality check, NPV assumes ROI is unrealistic. Although ROI is also a reality check, costs are first subtracted from the benefits in its formula. It is designed to put the benefits of an investment to the test so they are not overstated. NPV takes it one step further by discounting benefits based on the rate of inflation. It too subtracts the costs but not before severely devaluing the benefits. NPV is designed to put an even harsher reality check on the benefits.

The NPV of agile methods is almost twice as large as that of traditional methods (see Figure 23-4). More importantly, the economic business value of agile methods averages nearly $3,500,000 using NPV. NPV is unusually harsh, perhaps more so than necessary. But even under this primitive mid-20th-century valuation method, the business value of agile methods remains impressively high. Once again, this is due to a superior benefit to cost ratio, primarily enabled by

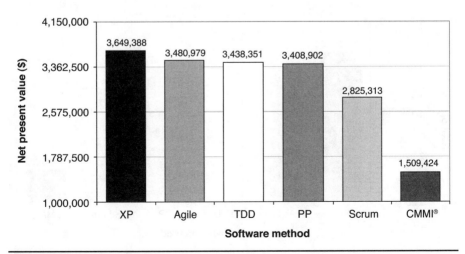

Figure 23-4 NPV of agile vs. traditional methods

extremely low costs and high benefits as a result of high quality. Keep in mind that total life cycle costs—both development and maintenance—were used in this analysis.

23.5 Agile vs. Traditional ROA

Agile methods' ROA is significantly larger than that of traditional methods. This is due to the large differential between their benefits. The benefits of agile methods are great due to their economic efficiencies and high quality. Like NPV, ROA is based on the time value of money, although it also takes risk into account. But there are many differences between these valuation methods. ROA is not as erosive as NPV and rewards methods designed to mitigate risk, such as agile methods.

ROA sustains the economic value of an investment over time, whereas NPV is designed to undermine it. ROA and NPV are based on two different sets of operating principles. NPV is designed to erode benefits to the point of marginalization. In doing so, it aims to undermine the effects of ROI, which are believed to be overstated. On the other hand, ROA sustains the business value of an investment, especially if it is designed to mitigate risk. This is true of agile methods.

The ROA of agile methods is 40 to 60% greater than for traditional methods (see Figure 23-5). Approaches designed to spread risk over time such as agile methods sustain their business value, whereas approaches such as traditional methods that absorb risk all at one time are better modeled by NPV, which erodes their benefits faster. Agile methods have a variety of built-in features to help mitigate risks. Sprint and release planning are adaptable to changing market

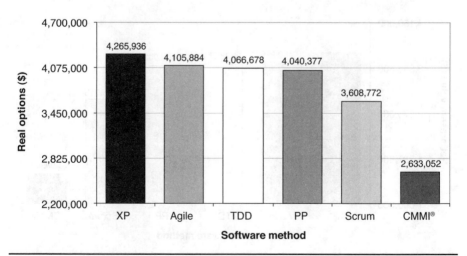

Figure 23-5   ROA of agile vs. traditional methods

conditions; user stories, simple designs, and code comments minimize the investments in documentation; and iterative development is designed to spread risk over time rather than absorb it all at once, as in traditional methods.

23.6 Summary

Agile methods were created for the purpose of creating business value, including both the intangible and tangible forms. On one hand, agile methods are optimized for customer interaction. That is, they are designed to maximize communication with customers to obtain their needs, implement high-quality solutions, and increase market value. Of course, agile methods also have to increase internal communication as well. Therefore, developers have to communicate and cooperate with one another to get the job done.

Agile methods also increase economic business value. Most major forms of valuation methods use costs and benefits as their basic inputs. If the costs of an investment are low and its benefits high, then the business value will be significant. This has proven so for agile methods because of their right-sized, just-enough, and just-in-time processes and documentation. In other words, they are lean, which results in the most cost-efficient process for capturing customer needs and translating them into extremely high-quality solutions at breakneck speed.

Economic efficiency and high quality form a powerful business value proposition. Agile methods' costs are low and their quality is high enough to exhibit excellent economic efficiency using most valuation methods. This is true for ROI, NPV, and ROA. Each of these approaches is designed to subject the benefits of an investment to the test. ROI ensures benefits are adjusted downward, NPV ensures benefits are discounted, and ROA ensures benefits are subjected to market risk. Agile methods not only stand the test of cost adjustment, time, inflation, and risk, but do it better than traditional methods.

23.7 Further Readings

Agrawal, M., & Chari, K. (2007). Software effort, quality, and cycle time: A study of CMM level 5 projects. *IEEE Transactions on Software Engineering, 33*(3), 145-156.

Galin, D., & Avrahami, M. (2006). Are CMM program investments beneficial? Analyzing past studies. *IEEE Software, 23*(6), 81–87.

Rico, D. F. (2004). *ROI of software process improvement: Metrics for project managers and software engineers.* Boca Raton, FL: J. Ross Publishing.

———. (2005). Practical metrics and models for return on investment. *TickIT International, 7*(2), 10–16.

———. (2008). *What is the ROI of agile vs. traditional methods? An analysis of agile methods using real options.* Retrieved June 28, 2008, from http://davidfrico .com/agile-benefits.xls.

————. (2008). What is the ROI of agile vs. traditional methods? An analysis of Extreme Programming, test-driven development, pair programming, and Scrum (using real options). *TickIT International, 10*(4), 9–18.

Subramanian, G. H., Jiang, J. J., & Klein, G. (2007). Software quality and IS project performance improvements from software development process maturity and IS implementation strategies. *Journal of Systems and Software, 80*(4), 616–627.

Van Solingen, R. A., & Rico, D. F. (2006). Calculating software process improvement's return on investment. In M. V. Zelkowitz (Ed.), *Advances in computers: Quality software development, Vol. 66* (pp. 1–41). San Diego, CA: Elsevier.

24

Future of Agile Methods

Agile methods, as we know them today, have only been in the public conscious-
ness for a little more than a decade. Even though they didn't have a $100 million
per year research institute promoting them, as did traditional methods, they enjoy widespread popularity. Between 1999 and 2002, agile methods spread across
the globe by word of mouth at a time when traditional methods reached their
peak of popularity.

However, many questions and doubts still linger about agile methods. Not everyone has heard of agile methods, and many who have remain skeptical and un-
informed. Part of the challenge is to link the emergence of agile methods to the
history and evolution of 20th-century management thought. Another challenge
is to link agile methods to concepts in project management, systems engineering,
and software engineering and to newer disciplines that have yet to fully evolve,
such as lean thinking and concepts in new product development.

Agile methods are not an excuse to hack at breakneck speed to make a quick
buck. Instead, they are a disciplined new product development process that is
optimized for efficiency, speed, and quality. This book is not the final word on the
business value of agile methods. We have applied a few 20th-century approaches,
such as the cost of quality, total cost of ownership, and total life cycle cost, to
quantify the benefits of agile methods. Now we must move on to the greater
task of demonstrating how agile methods may be used to optimize revenues and
profits.

24.1 Coaching and Mentoring

Compared to traditional methods, agile methods are simple, but they are not
easy. It's just as easy to fail at using agile methods as it is with traditional methods.
Large and complex traditional methods require millions of dollars and sometimes

decades to institutionalize. Although agile methods do not require such a significant investment in capital expenditures and large amounts of time to get going, they do require a lot of practice. Agile methods are a double-edged sword. On one hand they may be simple to get going, but they may be challenging to get right for many teams.

Agile methods are based on collaborating with customers, teamwork, iterative development, and adaptability. Only one of these values has to do with technical practices. The other three are concerned with intangible factors such as building relationships with customers, interacting with developers, and having a flexible attitude. Perhaps this is why agile methods seem simple on the surface yet challenging in practice. Maybe developers are quick to adapt their technical practices while failing to grasp their sociological, psychological, and behavioral principles.

This is where coaches and mentors come into play. Gone are the days when project managers are necessary to promulgate the Tayloristic values and principles of traditional methods. Agile methods require coaches and mentors to train developers on their finer points, nudge projects forward, fight off resistance to change, answer basic questions, and gently correct misunderstandings. They must also identify weaknesses and set high expectations for project success. In other words, coaches and mentors must be prepared to hold the hands of developers pretty much night and day. It's a thankless and exhausting but necessary role. Search no further if you're looking for a way to succeed with agile methods.

24.2 Values-Driven Thinking

Only a small fraction of agile methods' values and principles are directly related to technical practices, such as agile planning, user stories, pair programming, and test-driven development. The majority of agile values and principles have to do with people skills. Developers are not known for their people skills and often want to be left alone to solve challenging programming problems.

Agile methods are designed to maximize business value for their customers. They accomplish this by demanding rich, high-context communication to capture customers' needs in the form of user stories. How can developers fulfill this fundamental tenet of agile methods if they refuse to interact with their customers? It's not uncommon for developers to actually dislike their customers. Agile methods also demand intensive collaboration between developers. That is, developers must actually cooperate to solve difficult computer programming problems together.

Agile methods demand obsessive adaptability to rapidly changing customer needs and market conditions. There it is, we've used the C word: change. Traditional methods are optimized to minimize if not eliminate change. That is, they are designed to lock down all requirements over a period of years at the customer's expense and then punish anyone who makes a change. Agile methods do the exact opposite. They require developers to slavishly adapt to changing market conditions. Processes and documents have to be light so as not to exhaust customers' resources. You'll be in a world of hurt if you think agile methods are all about the technical tools and practices.

24.3 Hybrid Agile Methods

There are many types and kinds of agile methods, such as Scrum, Extreme Programming, Dynamic Systems Development, Feature-Driven Development, and Crystal Methods. Although there are too many practices to mention all of them here, a few are product owners and onsite customers, sprint and release planning, backlogs and user stories, daily standups and pair programming, retrospectives, test-driven development, and continuous integration. Which agile method is best? Or, which practices are best?

All of them are effective. The answer is the right tool for the right job. There is a pervasive myth, mostly within the agile methods community, that agile methods are a set of immutable rules and practices and those who refuse to follow all of the rules and practices must be excommunicated or at least ostracized so as not to contaminate everyone's thinking. Nothing can be further from the truth. Agile methods are more like a set of tools rather than a set of rules.

Those zealous for Extreme Programming or Scrum may cling to their rules. If you find yourself zealous for the law, then we implore you to consider the values of agile methods instead. Customer collaboration, teamwork, iterative development, and adaptability to change will get you further in the long run, especially if you find yourself in a variety of challenging market conditions. Perhaps you work on a virtually distributed team or are forced to use a traditional method. Maybe you won't be doing software development but rather will be working as a systems analyst. In that case, consider the right mix of tools for the right job rather than clinging to a set of rules and practices.

24.4 Complexity and Scalability

There is a myth that agile methods are designed for small and simple problems and traditional methods for large, complex ones. To propagate this theory would be to demonstrate a complete lack of understanding of the fundamental tenets of agile methods. To further this fallacy would also be to completely reject its underlying theory. Rooted in complex adaptive systems, agile methods are based on the notion of flexibility and adaptability to change as a fundamental underlying theory. That is, agile methods are designed to tackle large and complex problems.

Agile methods are also based on the notion that the market is dynamic, constantly changing, and fundamentally unpredictable. Therefore, agile methods have been designed to manage the dynamic nature of the ever-changing marketplace. They do this by insisting upon a culture and process that are highly flexible and adaptable to change. Based on the theory that all of the customer's requirements cannot be known in advance, agile methods gather and then implement a few customer needs. After much adaptation and change, a final solution is obtained.

Traditional methods were not designed to deal with the same principles. They assume the problem space is stable and unchanging. Developers must document all requirements and develop a large upfront design without operational validation of the requirements. They spend a little time coding and a lot of time testing. All of the design ends up being created during testing, the requirements are abandoned, and documents become obsolete. The entire investment in all of the documentation that was supposed to optimize system quality is completely lost. Agile methods are designed for large and complex systems, while traditional methods have failed to scale up over the decades.

24.5 Quality and Reliability

Some people believe agile methods undermine software quality and reliability. Within traditional methods all requirements have to be documented over a period of years, and a few more years have to be spent devising the perfect architecture. Finally, a rigorous program of verification and validation must be carried out. Of course, project plans and systems engineering processes have to be created to stabilize everything and minimize change. Agile methods, on the other hand, perform all of these functions every 14 to 30 days. Are quality and reliability being sacrificed?

The truth is that agile methods haven't sacrificed the discipline associated with traditional methods but have merely streamlined the process. They have project plans, requirements, architectures, designs, verification, validation, documentation, sprint and release plans, backlogs and user stories, metaphors and simple designs, test-driven development, and continuous integration. Furthermore, customers validate the system, developers perform verification, and continuous test-driven development and continuous integration are performed numerous times every 14 to 30 days.

Agile methods constitute a system of verification and validation that the creators of traditional methods only imagine. They are more cost-efficient than traditional methods and result in higher quality and reliability at a fraction of the cost. All of this is not an automatic given with agile methods. It takes trial and error, practice, training, coaching, mentoring, and commitment. You may need to try a little harder if you are using agile methods and have not met or exceeded the quality and reliability of traditional methods at a fraction of the cost. It is not agile methods that have failed to address quality and reliability but traditional methods that have not done the same, economically speaking.

24.6 Documentation and Maintenance

Agile methods are often accused of ignoring documentation and maintenance. Traditional methods evolved from the large military standards of the last 50 years, which grew to become large catalogs of software documents. Among these were requirements, designs, tests, and even user documentation created for every major subsystem. It amounted to hundreds of documents for the largest of systems. These documents were created in the name of system and software maintenance.

The underlying theory of large software documentation standards is that 70% of the system life cycle is operation and maintenance. Thus, developers must document the assumptions they make about all requirements and designs for maintenance personnel. That is, the recipients of all of these documents, costing millions of dollars to produce, are the programmers who must perform software maintenance. Without this documentation, the systems cannot be maintained. Therefore, systems without documentation cannot be used for up to 70% of their total life cycles.

People using agile methods are accused of refusing to produce the documents necessary for maintenance. However, agile methods have right-sized, just-enough, and just-in-time documents. They have lightweight project plans, requirements, architectures, designs, tests, and other documents. Proponents of traditional methods simply cannot or will not recognize these documents. Studies show that maintainers do not use the documents produced by those using traditional methods. In fact, maintainers simply need the source code and good code comments to do their jobs. Then why do traditional methods require so many documents? Perhaps they simply failed to ask maintainers what they really needed.

24.7 Virtual Distributed Teams

Agile methods are often viewed as being opposed to the use of virtual distributed teams, because one of their values is teamwork and one of their lower-level principles is face-to-face interactions between customers and developers. This maximizes productivity, problem-solving ability, cost efficiency, and quality, while minimizing the dependency upon traditional documentation. Thus, there are many good reasons to insist upon face-to-face communication within agile methods. However, the emphasis on face-to-face communication has been taken to mean that offshoring or outsourcing is bad, and agile methods have been used to argue against the use of outsourcing to other countries. Although it is true that rich, high-context face-to-face communication is superior to most forms of human interaction, it is not always practical or preferable to use collocated teams.

Another agile tenet is to produce the highest-quality software at the lowest-possible cost. Sometimes, it is cost effective to capitalize on the labor rates of various regions of the world, which may also have the best technical talent. Among language and cultural barriers are the challenges associated with time. Even a small U.S. team will have difficulty communicating across four time zones. Eventually, someone will have to get up early, stay up late, sacrifice their personal or professional schedule, and have their personal life compromised. But it is possible to overcome these challenges to make agile methods work across virtual distributed teams to maximize business value.

24.8 Technological Flexibility

The use of agile methods and technological flexibility seem to go hand in hand. Some people ask, "Which came first: powerful and easy-to-use information technologies or agile methods?" The truth is both! Information technology has become simultaneously more powerful and inexpensive at an exponentially increasing pace. Do you remember Moore's Law? Every 18 months microprocessors double in speed and halve in size. This sort of technological flexibility has served to spur on the formation of agile methods. Modern information technologies enable trial-and-error methods.

However, some information technologies have digressed a bit. Do you remember how easy it was to program in HTML in the 1990s? Now we have Java, C#, .NET, Perl, Ruby, and a myriad of other third-generation languages living on into the 21st century. Some of these languages enable certain flexible behaviors such as late binding, which makes continuous integration easier, but some have become complex and difficult to manage using agile methods. We need a new generation of simple and powerful information technologies.

There are many powerful fourth-generation languages out there. Perhaps developers need to gravitate toward the use of fourth- vs. third-generation languages. There are also many commercial web services in the marketplace—cost-effective turnkey systems for composing e-commerce systems with little programming. Are agile methods only for use by programmers using third-generation languages? Or can programmers use fourth-generation languages or other tools to rapidly compose systems? Remember, the mantra of agile methods is to rapidly satisfy customers with high-quality software at the least possible cost. Does the use of third-generation languages make sense?

24.9 Agile Metrics and Models

The field of metrics and models for agile methods is almost completely unexplored. Examples of traditional metrics are size, productivity, effort, cost, schedule, quality, and reliability. There needs to be a greater focus on metrics for customer interaction, teamwork, iterative development, and adaptability to change. High-quality interactions with customers lead to higher quality, as do cooperation, communication, and trust. Expeditious development leads to early feedback and higher quality as well as adaptability to change.

Furthermore, use of customer collaboration, teamwork, iterative development, and adaptability can be quantified and monetized. Once this is completed, the values of these attributes can be fed into valuation measures such as return on investment, net present value, and real options. The use of metrics and models specially designed for agile methods will lessen the dependency on traditional measures such as productivity and defect density. These traditional measures are a poor proxy for software quality, whereas the attributes of agile methods work better.

One can explore the intricacies of customer collaboration, teamwork, iterative development, and adaptability. Within agile methods, there may be just a few major drivers of business value, even though there may be dozens of metrics for each major value. It's better to focus on a few key drivers of business value rather than go through the expense and trouble of collecting otherwise useless data. Isn't this true of traditional methods? Although there are many metrics within traditional methods, productivity and quality seem to have withstood the test of time. Isn't it about time we discovered the key drivers of business value among the metrics and models of agile methods?

24.10 Agile Training and Education

Training and education are critical factors when it comes to the success of using agile methods. Many teams start using agile methods with little training, or perhaps team members will simply read one of the many books or papers available on the topic. However, it is virtually impossible to be completely successful with agile methods unless there is some training and education. A lot of the books, papers, and training courses focus on the technical practices of using agile methods. However, education in the values of agile methods can be much more important.

Agile methods derive their business value from soft features such as customer collaboration, teamwork, and adaptability to change. It may be possible to learn how to create a user story, but can people be taught how to create personal relationships with customers and developers? Can the ability to cope with continuous change be taught in a two-day course? We have to at least try. This is better than not trying to teach the finer points of agile methods. Coaches and mentors should be used to provide just-in-time training and education as well.

Project management is often taught within the curricula of computer science, software engineering, and information systems. Agile methods, which have a lightweight and highly adaptable form of project management, are really a way of managing the development of innovative products. Therefore, agile methods can and should be taught as a form of project management for information systems. Computer science and software engineering degree programs are in sharp decline in the United States. However, business schools, especially those offering MBAs, often have requirements for courses in information systems. Many of these students are tomorrow's entrepreneurs.

24.11 Crossing the Chasm

Have agile methods crossed the chasm? Some people feel agile methods have not yet crossed the chasm of technology adoption as described in Geoffrey Moore's

1991 classic textbook, and few people are actually using them. Others feel agile methods have indeed crossed the chasm and are growing in widespread use. Agile methods are used by thousands of developers worldwide and a growing number of universities are offering courses on agile methods. Enrollments in agile methods training courses have dramatically increased, and many people have heard of them, even those using traditional methods.

Even the U.S. government sector is starting to advocate the use of agile methods on large, publicly funded projects. The heads of agencies have a vested interest in seeing their information systems succeed, which they often believe are strategic and represent a key to success. Only a few short years ago the strategic value of information systems was still being questioned by the academic community. Furthermore, these agencies know that a new product development approach is just what they need to get their strategic new systems started. Fortune 500 U.S. firms view agile methods as a powerful organizational transformation approach for jumpstarting the economic engines of their bureaucracies in today's sluggish economy.

A significant holdout seems to be the standards-setting bodies, especially those in the government sector. Regulatory agencies that establish the policies for creating new information systems seem to cling to traditional methods for large, publicly funded information systems. At the same time, nongovernment standards bodies are a little slow to adopt agile methods, especially those bodies responsible for project management, systems engineering, and software engineering standards that have evolved to represent the best ideas of Taylorism from the early 20th-century. Both government and nongovernment standards bodies have yet to embrace 21st-century new product development approaches such as agile methods.

24.12 Summary

Agile methods are 21st-century approaches for creating new software products. Designed to maximize business value for customers, they are cost-efficient ways to create high-quality software. Agile methods are based on the values of customer collaboration, teamwork, iterative development, and adaptability to change, and on principles such as rich, high-context communication and interpersonal relationships with customers and developers. Another soft principle is the notion of adaptability to change at the individual and organizational level.

Agile methods are challenging to grasp because they are based on soft-side principles in sociology, psychology, and behavior. Because these nontechnical factors tend to make learning, practicing, and mastering agile methods somewhat difficult, agile methods can take some time to fully penetrate even a small organization and become institutionalized and internalized. The use of coaches and mentors, whether internal or external, can help ease the challenges associated with the adoption of agile methods. The same can be said of virtual distributed teams.

Metrics should be used to quantify customer collaboration, teamwork, iterative development, and adaptability. These data can be monetized and translated into hard economic costs and benefits. Return on investment, net present value, and real options can be used to determine their business value. Models of the impact of agile methods on revenues and profits can also be constructed, which could complement the cost of quality, total cost of ownership, and total life cycle cost for quantifying benefits. Agile methods have many rich features that are not yet fully explored, which make them right-sized, just-enough, and just-in-time approaches for maximizing business value.

24.13 Further Readings

Eckstein, J. (2004). *Agile software development in the large: Diving into the deep.* New York, NY: Dorset House.

Elssamadisy, A. (2008). *Agile adoption patterns: A roadmap to organizational success.* Boston, MA: Addison-Wesley.

Ghavami, P. K. (2008). *Lean, agile, and six sigma information technology management: New stratagems to achieve perfection.* Seattle, WA: CreateSpace.

Hazzan, O., & Dubinsky, Y. (2008). *Agile software engineering.* London, England: Springer-Verlag.

Kelly, A. (2008). *Changing software development: Learning to become agile.* West Sussex, England: John Wiley & Sons.

Krebs, J. (2009). *Agile portfolio management.* Redmond, WA: Microsoft Press.

Larman, C., & Vodde, B. (2008). *Scaling lean and agile development: Thinking and organizational tools for large-scale Scrum.* Boston, MA: Addison-Wesley.

Leffingwell, D. (2007). *Scaling software agility: Best practices for large enterprises.* Boston, MA: Pearson Education.

Rico, D. F., & Sayani, H. H. (2009). Use of agile methods in software engineering education. *Proceedings of the Agile 2009 Conference, Chicago, Illinois, USA.*

Schwaber, K. (2007). *The enterprise and Scrum.* Redmond, WA: Microsoft Press.

Appendix

The appendix contains the formulas, values, and results used to measure the economic business value of agile methods. There are formulas for pair programming, test-driven development, Extreme Programming, Scrum, and agile methods. Generally speaking, each of the formulas is based on two basic inputs: (1) costs and (2) benefits. Therefore, the first formula estimates the costs of each major kind of agile method, whereas the second formula estimates the benefits.

The first formula is the cost model, which uses size, productivity, and quality as its basic inputs. An input of 10,000 lines of code (LOC) was used as a basis for a size estimate throughout this textbook and appendix. Then, an average productivity and quality value was used to estimate costs. Productivity and quality data from 29 actual, real-world projects using pair programming, test-driven development, Extreme Programming, and Scrum were used as a basis for cost estimation. We averaged the productivity and quality of all 29 studies to derive the inputs for agile methods.

We also used a conversion rate of $100 for this analysis. That is, each hour was expressed as $100 of business value. For net present value (NPV) and real options analysis (ROA), we used a five-year time span and an interest rate of 5%. Because ROA uses risk as an input, we rank ordered major types of agile methods by cost, normalized the values, and then used this as a basis for estimating risk. The most expensive agile method (Scrum) had a risk of 100%, whereas the least expensive agile method (Extreme Programming) had a risk of 21.2%. A factor of 100 was used to estimate maintenance costs (i.e., each residual defect was estimated to cost 100 hours of maintenance to repair).

A. Pair Programming Formulas

The formulas used to measure the economic business value of pair programming are illustrated in Figure A-1. A form of teamwork, pair programming involves

Metric	Excel formula	Value
Costs	(10000/33.4044 + 2.355 * 10 * 100) * 100	$265,436
Benefits	(10000/0.8507 + 33.3333 * 10 * 100) * 100 − 265436	$4,243,397
ROI	(4243397 − 265436)/265436 * 100%	1499%
NPV	NPV (5%, 4243397/5, 4243397/5, 4243397/5, 4243397/5, 4243397/5) − 265436	$3,408,902
d_1	(LN (4243397/265436) + (5% + 0.5 * 71.3%^2) * 5)/ (71.3% * SQRT (5))	2.692
d_2	2.692 − 71.3% * SQRT (5)	1.098
ROA	NORMSDIST (2.692) * 4243397 − NORMSDIST (1.098) * 265436 * EXP (−5% * 5)	$4,049,741

Figure A-1   Pair programming Excel formulas

two developers working together to solve a complex programming problem. Pair programming teams are productive, produce few defects, and are often compared to peer reviews from traditional methods. They support a major value of agile methods called individuals and interactions, also known as self-organizing teams, high-performance teams, or, simply, teamwork.

♦ Costs are expressed as: $(10{,}000 \div 33.4044 + 2.355 \times 10 \times 100) \times \$100$, or $265,436.
♦ Benefits are expressed as: $(10{,}000 \div 0.8507 + 33.3333 \times 10 \times 100) \times \$100 - \$265{,}436$, or $4,243,397.
♦ Return on investment (ROI) is expressed as: $(\$4{,}243{,}397 - \$265{,}436) \div \$265{,}436 \times 100\%$, or 1,499%.
♦ NPV is expressed as: $\Sigma\ (\$4{,}243{,}397 \div 5) \div 1.05^5 - \$265{,}436 \times \$100$, or $3,408,902.
♦ ROA is expressed as: *NORMSDIST* (2.692) $\times$ $4,243,397 − *NORMSDIST* (1.098) $\times$ $265,436 $\times$ *EXP* $(-5\% \times 5)$, or $4,049,741.

There are several key factors associated with pair programming. Is 33.4044 LOC/hour too high? This rate only represents the act of programming, whereas best-in-class traditional methods burdened with project management overhead average 25 LOC/hour, so this figure isn't that far off. Is 2.355 defects per thousand LOC (KLOC) too low? It's larger than best-in-class traditional methods, so probably not. Is a maintenance factor of 100 hours per defect too high? Some studies estimate maintenance costs at 1,000 hours per defect, so an estimate of 100 hours isn't unreasonable. A risk factor of 71.3% was used to estimate real options based on the normalized costs of pair programming relative to other agile methods.

B. Test-Driven Development Formulas

This section contains the formulas used to measure the economic business value of test-driven development (see Figure A-2). A form of software verification and validation, test-driven development involves writing all unit, component, system, and acceptance tests before a single test is run. This is often in the form of an automated process called continuous integration. Done well, it can be used to efficiently identify and eliminate defects. Test-driven development can be 100 times more efficient than traditional methods when combined with continuous integration.

◆ Costs are expressed as: $(10,000 \div 29.28 + 2.155 \times 10 \times 100) \times \$100$, or $249,653.
◆ Benefits are expressed as: $(10,000 \div 0.8507 + 33.3333 \times 10 \times 100) \times \$100 - \$249,653$, or $4,259,180.
◆ ROI is expressed as: $(\$4,259,180 - \$249,653) \div \$249,653 \times 100\%$, or 1,606%.
◆ NPV is expressed as: $\Sigma\ (\$4,259,180 \div 5) \div 1.05^5 - \$249,653 \times \$100$, or $3,438,351.
◆ ROA is expressed as: *NORMSDIST* (2.792) × $4,259,180 − *NORMSDIST* (1.274) × $249,653 × *EXP* (−5% × 5), or $4,073,296.

There are several key factors associated with test-driven development. Is 29.28 LOC/hour too high? This rate represents only the act of development testing and continuous integration, whereas best-in-class traditional methods burdened with project management overhead average 25 LOC/hour, so this figure isn't that far off. Is 2.155 defects/KLOC too low? It's larger than best-in-class traditional methods, so probably not. Is a maintenance factor of 100 hours per defect too

Metric	Excel formula	Value
Costs	(10000/29.28 + 2.155 * 10 * 100) * 100	$249,653
Benefits	(10000/0.8507 + 33.3333 * 10 * 100) * 100 − 249653	$4,259,180
ROI	(4259180 − 249653)/249653 * 100%	1606%
NPV	NPV (5%, 4259180/5, 4259180/5, 4259180/5, 4259180/5, 4259180/5) − 249653	$3,438,351
d_1	(LN (4259180/249653) + (5% + 0.5 * 67.9%^2) * 5)/ (67.9% * SQRT (5))	2.792
d_2	2.792 − 67.9% * SQRT (5)	1.274
ROA	NORMSDIST (2.792) * 4259180 − NORMSDIST (1.274) * 249653 * EXP (−5% * 5)	$4,073,296

Figure A-2   Test-driven development Excel formulas

high? Some studies estimate maintenance costs at 1,000 hours per defect, so an estimate of 100 hours isn't that unreasonable. A risk factor of 67.9% was used to estimate real options based on the normalized costs of test-driven development relative to other agile methods.

C. Extreme Programming Formulas

This section contains the formulas used to measure the economic business value of Extreme Programming (see Figure A-3). A collection of best practices, Extreme Programming was originally composed of 14 practices but has since grown to more than 28. It has many features that are key drivers of business value, including pair programming, test-driven development, continuous integration, refactoring, and many more practices. Extreme Programming is remarkably efficient, although it has many of the tenets of traditional methods.

- ◆ Costs are expressed as: $(10,000 \div 16.1575 + 0.7466 \times 10 \times 100) \times \$100$, or \$136,551.
- ◆ Benefits are expressed as: $(10,000 \div 0.8507 + 33.3333 \times 10 \times 100) \times 100 - \$136,551$, or \$4,372,282.
- ◆ ROI is expressed as: $(\$4,372,282 - \$136,551) \div \$136,551 \times 100\%$, or 3,102%.
- ◆ NPV is expressed as: $\Sigma\ (\$4,372,282 \div 5) \div 1.05^5 - \$136,551 \times \$100$, or \$3,649,388.
- ◆ ROA is expressed as: $NORMSDIST\ (8.077) \times \$4,372,282 - NORMSDIST$ $(7.603) \times \$136,551 \times EXP\ (-5\% \times 5)$, or \$4,265,936.

Metric	Excel formula	Value
Costs	(10000/16.1575 + 0.7466 * 10 * 100) * 100	\$136,551
Benefits	(10000/0.8507 + 33.3333 * 10 * 100) * 100 – 136551	\$4,372,282
ROI	(4372282 – 136551)/136551 * 100%	3102%
NPV	NPV (5%, 4372282/5, 4372282/5, 4372282/5, 4372282/5, 4372282/5) – 136551	\$3,649,388
d_1	(LN (4372282/136551) + (5% + 0.5 * 21.2%^2) * 5)/ (21.2% * SQRT (5))	8.077
d_2	8.077 – 21.2% * SQRT (5)	7.603
ROA	NORMSDIST (8.077) * 4372282 – NORMSDIST (7.603) * 136551 * EXP (–5% * 5)	\$4,265,936

Figure A-3　Extreme Programming Excel formulas

There are several key factors associated with Extreme Programming. Is 16.1575 LOC/hour too high? This rate represents the effort associated with the entire life cycle, whereas best-in-class traditional methods with a similar scope and size average 5.9347 LOC/hour, so this figure is rather impressive. Is 0.7466 defects/ KLOC too low? It's larger than best-in-class traditional methods, so probably not. Is a maintenance factor of 100 hours per defect too high? Some studies estimate maintenance costs at 1,000 hours per defect, so an estimate of 100 hours isn't unreasonable. A risk factor of 21.2% was used to estimate real options based on the normalized costs of Extreme Programming relative to other agile methods.

D. Scrum Formulas

This section contains the formulas used to measure the economic business value of Scrum (see Figure A-4). Scrum's model of customer collaboration is product owner and developer interaction, and its team model is self-organizing teams. Scrum uses 30-day sprints as its major type of iterative development and uses sprint planning or Extreme Programming's release planning methodology as its means of adaptability. Sprint planning, 30-day sprints, daily standups, and sprint retrospectives are major drivers of business value.

◆ Costs are expressed as: $(10,000 \div 5.4436 + 3.945 \times 10 \times 100) \times \$100$, or \$578,202.
◆ Benefits are expressed as: $(10,000 \div 0.8507 + 33.3333 \times 10 \times 100) \times \$100 - \$578,202$, or \$3,930,631.
◆ ROI is expressed as: $(\$3,930,631 - \$578,202) \times \$578,202 \times 100\%$, or 580%.

Metric	Excel formula	Value
Costs	(10000/5.4436 + 3.945 * 10 * 100) * 100	\$578,202
Benefits	(10000/0.8507 + 33.3333 * 10 * 100) * 100 − 578202	\$3,930,631
ROI	(3930631 − 578202)/578202 * 100%	580%
NPV	NPV (5%, 3930631/5, 3930631/5, 3930631/5, 3930631/5, 3930631/5) − 578202	\$2,825,313
d_1	(LN (3930631/578202) + (5% + 0.5 * 100%^2) * 5)/ (100% * SQRT (5))	2.087
d_2	2.087 − 100% * SQRT (5)	−0.149
ROA	NORMSDIST (2.087) * 3930631 − NORMSDIST (−0.149) * 578202 * EXP (−5% * 5)	\$3,659,651

Figure A-4 Scrum Excel formulas

- NPV is expressed as: Σ ($3,930,631 $\div$ 5) $\div$ 1.05^5 − $578,202 × $100, or $2,825,313.
- ROA is expressed as: *NORMSDIST* (2.087) × $3,930,631 − *NORMSDIST* (−0.149) × $578,202 × *EXP* (−5% × 5), or $3,659,651.

There are several key factors associated with Scrum. Is 5.4436 LOC/hour too low? This rate represents the effort associated with hard-nosed, real-world projects, whereas best-in-class traditional methods with a similar scope and size average 5.9347 LOC/hour, so this figure isn't that far off. Is 3.945 defects/KLOC too high? It's larger than best-in-class traditional methods, so it probably is a little high. Is a maintenance factor of 100 hours per defect too high? Some studies estimate maintenance costs at 1,000 hours per defect, so an estimate of 100 hours isn't that unreasonable. A risk factor of 100% was used to estimate real options based on the normalized costs of Scrum relative to other agile methods. That is, it was the most expensive in this data set.

E. Agile Methods Formulas

This section contains the formulas used to measure the economic business value of agile methods (see Figure A-5). Agile methods are a confluence of four major streams of management thought with respect to new product development: (1) customer collaboration, (2) teamwork, (3) iterative development, and (4) adaptability or flexibility. Each of these four major factors alone is a major driver of business value. However, agile methods derive business value not only from these new product development factors but from a synergistic combination of these factors.

Metric	Excel formula	Value
Costs	(10000/21.2374 + 1.7972 * 10 * 100) * 100	$226,807
Benefits	(10000/0.8507 + 33.3333 * 10 * 100) * 100 − 226807	$4,282,026
ROI	(4282026 − 226807)/226807 * 100%	1788%
NPV	NPV (5%, 4282026/5, 4282026/5, 4282026/5, 4282026/5, 4282026/5) − 226807	$3,480,979
d_1	(LN (4282026/226807) + (5% + 0.5 * 62.3%^2) * 5)/ (62.3% * SQRT (5))	2.985
d_2	2.985 − 62.3% * SQRT (5)	1.592
ROA	NORMSDIST (2.985) * 4282026 − NORMSDIST (1.592) * 226807 * EXP (−5% * 5)	$4,109,154

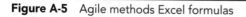

Figure A-5   Agile methods Excel formulas

- Costs are expressed as: $(10,000 \div 21.2374 + 1.7972 \times 10 \times 100) \times \$100$, or \$226,807.
- Benefits are expressed as: $(10,000 \div 0.8507 + 33.3333 \times 10 \times 100) \times \$100 - \$226,807$, or \$4,282,026.
- ROI is expressed as: $(\$4,282,026 - \$226,807) \div \$226,807 \times 100\%$, or 1,788%.
- NPV is expressed as: $\Sigma\, (\$4,282,026 \div 5) \div 1.05^5 - \$226,807 \times \$100$, or \$3,480,979.
- ROA is expressed as: *NORMSDIST* $(2.985) \times \$4,282,026 - NORMSDIST\,(1.592) \times \$226,807 \times EXP\,(-5\% \times 5)$, or \$4,109,154.

There are several key factors associated with agile methods. Is 21.2374 LOC/hour too high? This rate represents the effort associated with the entire life cycle, whereas best-in-class traditional methods with a similar scope and size average 5.9347 LOC/hour, so this figure is rather impressive. Is 1.7972 defects/KLOC too low? It's larger than best-in-class traditional methods, so probably not. Is a maintenance factor of 100 hours per defect too high? Some studies estimate maintenance costs at 1,000 hours per defect, so an estimate of 100 hours isn't that unreasonable. A risk factor of 62.3% was used to estimate real options based on the normalized average costs of agile methods relative to others. In general, agile methods are more efficient than heavyweight traditional methods.

Bibliography

Abrahamsson, P. (2007). *Speeding up embedded software development: Application of agile processes in complex systems development projects*. Eindhoven, Netherlands: Information Technology for European Advancement.

Abrahamsson, P., Moser, R., Pedrycz, W., Sillitti, A., & Succi, G. (2007). Effort prediction in iterative software development processes: Incremental versus global prediction models. *First International Symposium on Empirical Software Engineering and Measurement (ESEM 2007)*, *Madrid, Spain*, 344–353.

Abrahamsson, P., Salo, O., Ronkainen, J., & Warsta, J. (2002). *Agile software development methods: Review and analysis (478)*. Oulu, Finland: VTT Publications.

Abran, A., Moore, J. W., Bourque, P., & Dupuis, R. (2004). *Guide to the software engineering body of knowledge*. Los Alamitos, CA: IEEE Computer Society.

Agile Manifesto. (2001). *Manifesto for agile software development*. Retrieved January 1, 2009, from http://www.agilemanifesto.org.

Agrawal, M., & Chari, K. (2007). Software effort, quality, and cycle time: A study of CMM level 5 projects. *IEEE Transactions on Software Engineering, 33*(3), 145–156.

Aguanno, K. (2005). *Managing agile projects*. Lakefield, ON, Canada: Multi-Media Publications.

Allman, K. A. (2007). *Modeling structured finance cash flows with Microsoft Excel: A step-by-step guide*. Hoboken, NJ: John Wiley & Sons.

Ambler, S. W. (2007). *Agile adoption survey: March 2007*. Retrieved July 23, 2007, from http://www.ambysoft.com/downloads/surveys/AgileAdoption2007.ppt.

———. (2008). *Agile adoption survey*. Retrieved October 17, 2008, from http://www.ambysoft.com.

Argyris, C. (1976). Single-loop and double-loop models in research on decision making. *Administrative Science Quarterly, 21*(3), 363–375.

Augustine, S. (2005). *Managing agile projects*. Upper Saddle River, NJ: Prentice Hall.

Barki, H., & Hartwick, J. (1994). Measuring user participation, user involvement, and user attitude. *MIS Quarterly, 18*(1), 59–82.

Beck, K. (2001). *Extreme Programming: Embrace change*. Upper Saddle River, NJ: Addison-Wesley.

———. (2003). *Test-driven development: By example*. Boston, MA: Addison-Wesley.

Beck, K., & Fowler, M. (2001). *Planning Extreme Programming*. Upper Saddle River, NJ: Addison-Wesley.

Begel, A., & Nagappan, N. (2007). Usage and perceptions of agile software development in an industrial context: An exploratory study. *Proceedings of the First International Symposium on Empirical Software Engineering and Measurement, Madrid, Spain*, 255–264.

Behrens, P. (2006). *Agile project management (APM): Tooling survey results*. Louisville, CO: Trail Ridge Consulting.

Benaroch, M. (2002). Managing information technology investment risk: A real options perspective. *Journal of Management Information Systems, 19*(2), 43–84.

Benediktsson, O., & Dalcher, D. (2003). Effort estimation in incremental software development. *Journal of Engineering Manufacture, 150*(6), 351–357.

———. (2004). New insights into effort estimation for incremental software development projects. *Project Management Journal, 35*(2), 5–12.

———. (2005). Estimating size in incremental software development projects. *Journal of Engineering Manufacture, 152*(6), 253–259.

Berglund, E., & Priestley, M. (2001). Open-source documentation: In search of user-driven, just-in-time writing. *Proceedings of the 19th Annual International Conference on Computer Documentation, Santa Fe, New Mexico*, 132–141.

Biffl, S., Aurum, A., Boehm, B., Erdogmus, H., & Grunbacher, P. (2006). *Value-based software engineering*. Berlin, Germany: Springer-Verlag.

Bittner, K., & Spence, I. (2007). *Managing iterative software development projects*. Boston, MA: Pearson Education.

Boehm, B., & Turner, R. (2004). *Balancing agility and discipline: A guide for the perplexed*. Boston, MA: Addison-Wesley.

Boehm, B. W., Abts, C., Brown, A. W., Chulani, S., Clark, B. K., Horowitz, E., et al. (2000). *Software cost estimation with COCOMO II*. Upper Saddle River, NJ: Prentice Hall.

Bragg, S. M. (2007). *Business ratios and formulas: A comprehensive guide*. Hoboken, NJ: John Wiley & Sons.

Brown, S. L., & Eisenhardt, K. M. (1997). The art of continuous change: Linking complexity theory and time-paced evolution in relentlessly shifting organizations. *Administrative Science Quarterly, 42*(1), 1–34.

————. (1998). *Competing on the edge: Strategy as structured chaos*. Boston, MA: Harvard Business School Press.

Campanella, J. (1999). *Principles of quality costs: Principles, implementation, and use*. Milwaukee, WI: Quality Press.

Carmel, E., Whitaker, R. D., & George, J. F. (1993). PD and joint application design: A transatlantic comparison. *Communications of the ACM, 36*(4), 40–48.

Chin, G. L. (2004). *Agile project management: How to succeed in the face of changing project requirements*. New York, NY: AMACOM.

Chow, S. W. (2007). *PHP web 2.0 mashup projects: Practical PHP mashups with google maps, flickr, amazon, youtube, msn search, yahoo!* Birmingham, UK: Packt Publishing.

Cockburn, A. (2005). *Crystal clear: A human-powered methodology for small teams*. Upper Saddle River, NJ: Addison-Wesley.

Coffin, R., & Lane, D. (2006). *A practical guide to seven agile methodologies: Part 1*. Retrieved September 3, 2008, from http://www.devx.com/architect/Article/32761.

————. (2006). *A practical guide to seven agile methodologies: Part 2*. Retrieved September 3, 2008, from http://www.devx.com/architect/Article/32836.

Cohn, M. (2004). *User stories applied: For agile software development*. Boston, MA: Addison-Wesley.

————. (2006). *Agile estimating and planning*. Upper Saddle River, NJ: Pearson Education.

Conte, S. D., Dunsmore, H. E., & Shen, V. Y. (1986). *Software engineering metrics and models*. Menlo Park, CA: Benjamin Cummings.

Costanzo, L. A. (2004). Strategic foresight in a high-speed environment. *Futures, 36*(2), 219–235.

Couger, J. D. (1973). Evolution of business system analysis techniques. *ACM Computing Surveys, 5*(3), 167–198.

Crawford, C. M. (1991). The dual-drive concept of product innovation. *Business Horizons, 34*(3), 32–38.

Dalcher, D., & Benediktsson, O. (2006). Managing software development project size: Overcoming the effort-boxing constraint. *Project Management Journal, 37*(2), 51–58.

DeCarlo, D. (2004). *Extreme project management: Using leadership, principles, and tools to deliver value in the face of volatility*. San Francisco, CA: Jossey-Bass.

DeGrace, P., & Stahl, L. H. (1990). *Wicked problems, righteous solutions: A catalogue of modern software engineering paradigms*. Englewood Cliffs, NJ: Prentice Hall.

Devaraj, S., & Kohli, R. (2002). *The IT payoff: Measuring the business value of information technology investments*. Upper Saddle River, NJ: Prentice Hall.

Digital Focus. (2006). *Agile 2006 survey: Results and analysis*. Herndon, VA: Author.

DoD-STD-2167A. (1988). *Military standard: Defense system software development*. Washington, DC: Space and Naval Warfare Center.

Dunn, O. E. (1966). Information technology: A management problem. *Proceedings of the Third ACM IEEE Conference on Design Automation, New York, NY, USA*, 5.1–5.29.

Duvall, P., Matyas, S., & Glover, A. (2006). *Continuous integration: Improving software quality and reducing risk*. Boston, MA: Addison-Wesley.

Dyba, T., & Dingsoyr, T. (2008). Empirical studies of agile software development: A systematic review. *Information and Software Technology, 50*(9/10), 833–859.

Dyba, T., Arisholm, E., Sjoberg, D. I., Hannay, J. E., & Shull, F. (2007). Are two heads better than one? On the effectiveness of pair programming. *IEEE Software, 24*(6), 12–15.

Eckstein, J. (2004). *Agile software development in the large: Diving into the deep*. New York, NY: Dorset House.

El Emam, K. (2005). *The ROI from software quality*. Boca Raton, FL: Taylor and Francis.

Elssamadisy, A. (2008). *Agile adoption patterns: A roadmap to organizational success*. Boston, MA: Addison-Wesley.

Erdogmus, H. (2002). Valuation of learning options in software development under private and market risk. *The Engineering Economist, 47*(3), 308–353.

———. (2005). The economic impact of learning and flexibility on process decisions. *IEEE Software, 22*(6), 76–83.

Erdogmus, H., & Favaro, J. (2003). Keep your options open: Extreme Programming and the economics of flexibility. In M. Marchesi, G. Succi, J. D. Wells, & L. Williams (Eds.), *Extreme Programming perspectives* (pp. 503–552). New York, NY: Addison-Wesley.

Feller, J., & Fitzgerald, B. (2002). *Understanding open source software development*. London, England: Pearson Education.

Fichman, R. G. (2004). Real options and IT platform adoption: Implications for theory and practice. *Information Systems Research, 15*(2), 132–154.

Fichman, R. G., Keil, M., & Tiwana, A. (2005). Beyond valuation: Options thinking in IT project management. *California Management Review, 47*(2), 74–96.

Fishbein, M., & Ajzen, I. (1975). *Belief, attitude, intention, and behavior: An introduction to theory and research*. Reading, MA: Addison-Wesley.

Fowler, M. (1999). *Refactoring: Improving the design of existing code*. Boston, MA: Addison-Wesley.

Galin, D., & Avrahami, M. (2006). Are CMM program investments beneficial? Analyzing past studies. *IEEE Software, 23*(6), 81–87.

Galorath, D. D., & Evans, M. W. (2006). *Software sizing, estimation, and risk management*. Boca Raton, FL: Auerbach.

Gane, C. (1987). *Rapid systems development*. New York, NY: Rapid Systems Development.

Ghavami, P. K. (2008). *Lean, agile, and six sigma information technology management: New stratagems to achieve perfection*. Seattle, WA: CreateSpace.

Greenbaum, J., & Kyng, M. (1991). *Design at work: Cooperative design of computer systems*. Hillsdale, NJ: Lawrence Erlbaum.

Guckenheimer, S., & Perez, J. J. (2006). *Software engineering with Microsoft visual studio team system*. Upper Saddle River, NJ: Addison-Wesley.

Harris, D. S., Herron, D., & Iwanicki, S. (2008). *The business value of IT: Managing risks, optimizing performance, and measuring results*. Boca Raton, FL: Taylor and Francis.

Hayes, B. E. (2008). *Measuring customer satisfaction and loyalty: Survey design, use, and statistical analysis*. Milwaukee, WI: ASQ Press.

Hazzan, O., & Dubinsky, Y. (2008). *Agile software engineering*. London, England: Springer-Verlag.

Hemrajani, A. (2006). *Agile java development with spring, hibernate, and eclipse*. Indianapolis, IN: Sams Publishing.

Hericko, M., & Zivkovic, A. (2008). The size and effort estimates in iterative development. *Information and Software Technology, 50*(7/8), 772–781.

Hibbs, C., Jewett, S., & Sullivan, M. (2009). *The art of lean software development*. Sebastopol, CA: O'Reilly Media.

Highsmith, J. A. (2002). *Agile software development ecosystems*. Boston, MA: Addison-Wesley.

———. (2004). *Agile project management: Creating innovative products*. Boston, MA: Addison-Wesley.

Hightower, R., Onstine, W., Visan, P., & Payne, D. (2004). *Professional java tools for extreme programming: Ant, xdoclet, junit, cactus, and maven*. New York, NY: John Wiley & Sons.

IEEE. (1997). *IEEE standards collection: Software engineering*. New York, NY: Institute of Electrical and Electronics Engineers.

IEEE-STD-1042. (1987). *IEEE guide to software configuration management*. Piscataway, NJ: IEEE Computer Society.

IEEE-STD-1059. (1993). *IEEE guide for software verification and validation plans*. Piscataway, NJ: IEEE Computer Society.

IEEE-STD-1219. (1992). *IEEE standard for software maintenance*. Piscataway, NJ: IEEE Computer Society.

IEEE-STD-730.1. (1986). *IEEE guide for software quality assurance planning*. Piscataway, NJ: IEEE Computer Society.

In, H. P., Baik, J., Kim, S., Yang, Y., & Boehm, B. (2006). A quality-based cost estimation model for the product line life cycle. *Communications of the ACM, 49*(12), 85–88.

INCOSE. (2003). *Guide to the systems engineering body of knowledge (G2SEBOK 1.00)*. San Diego, CA: Author.

ISO-12207 (1995). *International standard for information technology: Software life cycle processes*. Geneva, Switzerland: International Organization for Standardization.

Jeffries, R., & Melnik, G. (2007). TDD: The art of fearless programming. *IEEE Software, 24*(3), 24–30.

Johnson, M. (2003). *Agile methodologies: Survey results.* Victoria, Australia: Shine Technologies.

Jones, C. (2007). *Estimating software costs: Bringing realism to estimating.* New York, NY: McGraw-Hill.

Jones, S. D., & Schilling, D. J. (2000). *Measuring team performance.* New York, NY: Jossey-Bass.

J-STD-016. (1995). *Trial use standard: Standard for information technology life cycle processes.* New York, NY: Institute of Electrical and Electronics Engineers.

Kampenes, V., Dyba, T., Hannay, J. E., & Sjoberg, D. I. (2007). A systematic review of effect size in software engineering experiments. *Information and Software Technology, 49*(11/12), 1073–1086.

———. (2009). A systematic review of quasi-experiments in software engineering. *Information and Software Technology, 51*(1), 71–82.

Kan, S. H. (2002). *Metrics and models in software quality engineering.* Reading, MA: Addison-Wesley.

Kelly, A. (2008). *Changing software development: Learning to become agile.* West Sussex, England: John Wiley & Sons.

Kinicki, A., & Kreitner, R. (2003). *Organizational behavior: Key concepts, skills, and best practices.* Boston, MA: McGraw-Hill.

Klocker, C. (2008). *Mashups: A new concept in web application programming.* Saarbrucken, Germany: VDM Verlag.

Kock, N. (2008). *E-collaboration in modern organizations: Initiating and managing distributed projects.* Hershey, PA: Information Science Reference.

Kodukula, P. (2006). *Project valuation using real options.* Fort Lauderdale, FL: J. Ross Publishing.

Krebs, J. (2009). *Agile portfolio management.* Redmond, WA: Microsoft Press.

Kruschwitz, L., & Loeffler, A. (2006). *Discounted cash flow: A theory of the valuation of firms.* West Sussex, England: John Wiley & Sons.

Larman, C. (2004). *Agile and iterative development: A manager's guide.* Boston, MA: Pearson Education.

Larman, C., & Vodde, B. (2008). *Scaling lean and agile development: Thinking and organizational tools for large-scale scrum.* Boston, MA: Addison-Wesley.

Leffingwell, D. (2007). *Scaling software agility: Best practices for large enterprises.* Boston, MA: Pearson Education.

Lui, K. M., & Chan, K. C. (2008). *Software development rhythms: Harmonizing agile practices for synergy.* Hoboken, NJ: John Wiley & Sons.

Martin, J. (1991). *Rapid application development.* New York, NY: Macmillan.

McCann, B. (2007). The relative cost of interchanging, adding, or dropping quality practices. *Crosstalk, 20*(6), 25–28.

McGibbon, T. (1997). *Modern empirical cost and schedule estimation.* Rome, NY: Air Force Research Laboratory/Information Directorate, Data and Analysis Center for Software.

McGibbon, T., Ferens, D., & Vienneau, R. L. (2007). *A business case for software process improvement: Measuring the ROI from software engineering and management.* Griffiss AFB, NY: DACS.

Mendes, E. (2008). *Cost estimation techniques for web projects.* Hershey, PA: IGI Publishing.

Middleton, P., & Sutton, J. (2005). *Lean software strategies: Proven techniques for managers and developers.* New York, NY: Productivity Press.

Millington, D., & Stapleton, J. (1995). Developing a RAD standard. *IEEE Software, 12*(5), 54–56.

MIL-STD-1521B. (1985). *Military standard: Technical reviews and audits for systems, equipments, and computer software.* Washington, DC: Air Force Systems Command.

MIL-STD-498. (1994). *Military standard: Software development and documentation.* Arlington, VA: Space and Naval Warfare Center.

Mintzberg, H. (1994). *The rise and fall of strategic planning.* New York, NY: The Free Press.

Molokken-Ostvold, K., & Jorgensen, M. (2005). A comparison of software project overruns: Flexible versus sequential development models. *IEEE Transactions on Software Engineering, 31*(5), 754–766.

Moore, J. F. (1996). *The death of competition: Leadership and strategy in the age of business ecosystems.* New York, NY: Harper Business Press.

Moore, J. W. (1997). *Software engineering standards: A user's roadmap.* Piscataway, NJ: IEEE Computer Society.

Morgan, J. N. (2005). A roadmap of financial measures for IT project ROI. *IT Professional, 7*(1), 52–57.

Muller, M. J., & Kuhn, S. (1993). Participatory design. *Communications of the ACM, 36*(6), 24–28.

Napier, R., & McDaniel, R. (2006). *Measuring what matters: Simplified tools for aligning teams and their stakeholders.* Mountain View, CA: Davies-Black.

Naur, P., & Randell, B. (1969). Software engineering. *NATO Software Engineering Conference, Garmisch, Germany,* 1–136.

Niemeyer, G., & Poteet, J. (2003). *Extreme Programming with ant: Building and deploying java applications with jsp, ejb, xslt, xdoclet, and junit.* Indianapolis, IN: Sams Publishing.

Palmer, S. R., & Felsing, J. M. (2002). *A practical guide to feature driven development.* Upper Saddle River, NJ: Prentice Hall.

Pavlicek, R. C. (2000). *Embracing insanity: Open source software development.* Indianapolis, IN: Sams Publishing.

PMBoK. (2004). *A guide to the project management body of knowledge: Third edition (PMBoK Guide).* Newtown Square, PA: Project Management Institute.

Poolton, J., & Barclay, I. (1998). New product development from past research to future applications. *Industrial Marketing Management, 27*(3), 197–212.

Poppendieck, M., & Poppendieck, T. (2003). *Lean software development: An agile toolkit for software development managers.* Boston, MA: Addison-Wesley.

————. (2007). *Implementing lean software development*. Boston, MA: Addison-Wesley.

Pow-Sang, J. A., & Jolay-Vasquez, E. (2006). An approach of a technique for effort estimation of iterations in software projects. *Proceedings of the 13th Asia Pacific Software Engineering Conference (APSEC 2006)*, Bangalore, India, 367–376.

Pressman, R. S. (2007). *Software engineering: A practitioner's approach*. New York, NY: McGraw-Hill.

Qumer, A., & Henderson-Sellers, B. (2008). An evaluation of the degree of agility in six agile methods. *Information and Software Technology, 50*(4), 280–295.

Ramsden, P. (1998). *The essentials of management ratios*. Brookfield, VT: Gower.

Reifer, D. J. (2002). *Making the software business case: Improvement by the numbers*. Upper Saddle River, NJ: Addison-Wesley.

Rico, D. F. (2000). *Using cost benefit analyses to develop software process improvement (SPI) strategies*. Rome, NY: Air Force Research Laboratory—Information Directorate (AFRL/IF), Data and Analysis Center for Software.

————. (2001). Cost and benefit analysis: Choosing a SPI method for maximum ROI. *2001 Joint Euroforum/Dutch Software Process Improvement Network Conference, Utrecht, Netherlands*.

————. (2002). How to Estimate ROI for Inspections, PSP, TSP, SW-CMM, ISO 9001, and CMMI. *Software Tech News, 5*(4), 23–31.

————. (2002). Software process improvement: Modeling return on investment (ROI). *2002 Software Engineering Institute (SEI) Software Engineering Process Group Conference (SEPG 2002), Phoenix, Arizona*.

————. (2002). The return on investment in quality. *TickIT International, 4*(4), 13–18.

————. (2004). *ROI of software process improvement: Metrics for project managers and software engineers*. Boca Raton, FL: J. Ross Publishing.

————. (2005). Practical metrics and models for return on investment. *TickIT International, 7*(2), 10–16.

————. (2008). What is the ROI of agile vs. traditional methods? An analysis of Extreme Programming, test-driven development, pair programming, and scrum (using real options). *TickIT International, 10*(4), 9–18.

————. (2008). *What is the ROI of agile vs. traditional methods? An analysis of agile methods using real options*. Retrieved June 28, 2008, from http://davidfrico.com/agile-benefits.xls.

————. (2009). *Business value of agile methods: Using return on investment*. Retrieved May 24, 2009, from http://davidfrico.com/rico09b.pdf.

Rico, D. F., & Sayani, H. H. (2009). Use of agile methods in software engineering education. *Proceedings of the Agile 2009 Conference, Chicago, Illinois, USA*.

Rico, D. F., Sayani, H. H., & Field, R. F. (2008). History of computers, electronic commerce, and agile methods. In M. V. Zelkowitz (Ed.), *Advances in computers: Emerging technologies, Vol. 73*. San Diego, CA: Elsevier.

Rico, D. F., Sayani, H. H., Stewart, J. J., & Field, R. F. (2007). A model for measuring agile methods and website quality. *TickIT International, 9*(3), 3–15.

Rogers, E. M. (1962). *Diffusion of innovation*. New York, NY: The Free Press.

Rueping, A. (2003). *Agile documentation: A pattern guide to producing lightweight documents for software projects*. West Sussex, England: John Wiley & Sons.

Salam, A. F., & Stevens, J. R. (2007). *Semantic web technologies and e-business: Toward the integrated virtual organization and business process automation*. Hershey, PA: Idea Group.

Schwaber, K. (2004). *Agile project management with scrum*. Redmond, WA: Microsoft Press.

———. (2007). *The enterprise and scrum*. Redmond, WA: Microsoft Press.

Schwaber, K., & Beedle, M. (2002). *Agile software development with scrum*. Upper Saddle River, NJ: Prentice Hall.

Senge, P. M. (1990). *The fifth discipline: The art and practice of the learning organization*. New York, NY: Doubleday.

Sfetsos, P. (2007). *Agile software development quality assurance*. Hershey, PA: Idea Group.

Shafritz, J. M., & Ott, J. S. (2001). *Classics of organization theory*. New York, NY: Wadsworth Publishing.

Shapiro, S. (1997). Splitting the difference: The historical necessity of synthesis in software engineering. *IEEE Annals of the History of Computing, 19*(1), 20–54.

Shriver, R. (2009). Measurable value with agile. *Overload, 6*(1), 4–12.

Sidky, A., Arthur, J., & Bohner, S. (2007). A disciplined approach to adopting agile practices: The agile adoption framework. *Innovations in Systems and Software Engineering, 3*(3), 203–216.

Siegel, J. G., Shim, J. K., & Hartman, S. W. (1997). *Schaum's quick guide to business formulas: 201 decision-making tools for business, finance, and accounting students*. New York, NY: McGraw-Hill.

Sikka, V. (2005). *Maximizing ROI on software development*. Boca Raton, FL: CRC Press.

Sliger, M., & Broderick, S. (2008). *The software project manager's bridge to agility*. Boston, MA: Addison-Wesley.

Sommerville, I. (2006). *Software engineering*. Reading, MA: Addison-Wesley.

Stapleton, J. (2003). *DSDM: Business focused development*. Harlow, England: Pearson Education.

Subramaniam, V., & Hunt, A. (2006). *Practices of an agile developer: Working in the real world*. Raleigh, NC: Pragmatic Bookshelf.

Subramanian, G. H., Jiang, J. J., & Klein, G. (2007). Software quality and IS project performance improvements from software development process maturity and IS implementation strategies. *Journal of Systems and Software, 80*(4), 616–627.

Takeuchi, H., & Nonaka, I. (1986). The new product development game. *Harvard Business Review, 64*(1), 137–146.

Tapscott, D., & Williams, A. D. (2006). *Wikinomics: How mass collaboration changes everything.* London, England: Penguin.

Tham, J., & Velez-Pareja, I. (2004). *Principles of cash flow valuation: An integrated market-based approach.* London, England: Elsevier.

Tockey, S. (2004). *Return on software: Maximizing the return on your software investment.* Boston, MA: Addison-Wesley.

Ton, H. (2007). A strategy for balancing business value and story size. *Proceedings of the Agile 2007 Conference, Washington, District of Columbia, USA,* 279–284.

Tushman, M. L., & O'Reilly, C. A. (1996). Ambidextrous organizations: Managing evolutionary and revolutionary change. *California Management Review, 38*(4), 8–30.

Unhelkar, B. (2005). *Verification and validation for quality of UML 2.0 models.* Hoboken, NJ: John Wiley & Sons.

Van Solingen, R. A. (2004). Measuring the ROI of software process improvement. *IEEE Software, 21*(3), 32–38.

Van Solingen, R. A., & Rico, D. F. (2006). Calculating software process improvement's return on investment. In M. V. Zelkowitz (Ed.), *Advances in computers: Quality software development,* Vol. 66 (pp. 1–41). San Diego, CA: Elsevier.

Version One. (2008). *The state of agile development: Third annual survey.* Alpharetta, GA: Author.

Von Hippel, E. (1978). Successful industrial products from customer ideas. *Journal of Marketing, 42*(1), 39–49.

Walsh, C. (2009). *Key management ratios: The clearest guide to the critical numbers that drive your business.* Indianapolis, IN: Pearson Education.

Wang, Y., & King, G. (2000). *Software engineering processes: Principles and applications.* Boca Raton, FL: CRC Press.

Williams, L., & Kessler, R. (2003). *Pair programming illuminated.* Boston, MA: Addison-Wesley.

Wolf, H., & Roock, A. (2008). Agile becomes mainstream: Results of an online survey. *Object Spektrum, 15*(3), 10–13.

Womack, J. P., & Jones, D. T. (1996). *Lean thinking.* New York, NY: Simon & Schuster.

Wood, J., & Silver, D. (1989). *Joint application design.* New York, NY: John Wiley & Sons.

Woodcock, M., & Francis, D. (2008). *Team metrics: Resources for measuring and improving team performance.* Amherst, MA: HRD Press.

Wren, D. A. (1993). *The evolution of management thought.* Indianapolis, IN: John Wiley & Sons.

Wysocki, R. K. (2007). *Effective project management: Traditional, adaptive, and extreme.* Indianapolis, IN: Wiley Publishing.

Index

A

Acceptance testing, 28, 58, 62, 64
Adaptability, 10, see also Responding to change
Adaptability, 10, 13, 96, 172, 176, 177, 189, 190, see also Responding to change; specific methods
    benefits of, 101
    comparison of agile methods, 67, 68
    Dynamic Systems Development and, 30
    Extreme Programming and, 27
    metrics and models for, 180–181
    project management and, see Project management
    release planning and, 40
    ROA and, 149–156
    Scrum and, 26
    software engineering and, see Software engineering
    surveys of agile methods, 86
Adaptable plans, 40
Adaptive organizations, 80
Adaptive software development, 25
Aggressiveness, 27
Agile Manifesto, 4, 7
Agile methods, see also specific methods; specific topics
    antecedents of, 19–24
    benefits of, 9198, 121–129
    business value of, 159–166
        formulas for, 190–191
    comparison of, 69–74
    costs of, 91–98, 113–120
    defined, 1–2
    emergence of, 2–4
    explosion of, 4–5
    future of, 175–183
    history of, 13–18

    measures of, 103–112
    metrics and models, 75–81
    net present value of, 141–148
    practices of, 35–42
    project management, 43–48
    real options analysis of, 149–158
    return on investment of, 131–139
        metrics for, 90–104
    software engineering, 49–54
    support processes, 55–60
    survey of, 83–90
    tools and technologies, 61–66
    traditional methods vs., 167–174
    types of, 25–33, see also specific methods
        Crystal Methods, 31–32
        Dynamic Systems Development, 27, 29–30
        Extreme Programming, 27, 28
        Feature Driven Development, 30–31
        Scrum, 25–27
    values of, 7–11
Agile modeling, 25
Agility, 23
Ambler, Scott, 86
AmbySoft, surveys of agile methods, 86–87
Analyst, 9
Architect, 9
Architectural spike, 28
Architecture, 50–51, 56, 170
Automated builds, 57, 64
Automated testing, 38, 56
Automated workflow tools, 57
Autonomous groups, 37
Autonomous work groups, 13

B

Backlogs, 2, 3, 178
Beck, Kent, 27

Bell Labs, 20
Benefits, 121–129, see also specific topics
    agile methods, 91–97
        formulas for, 190–191
        traditional vs., 167, 169–170, 171,
           172
    business value and, 160–161
    effort and quality measures and, 105
    Extreme Programming, 124–125, 126,
        188–189
    metric for, 99, 100–101
    NPV and, 102
    pair programming, 122–123, 185, 186
    ROA and, 102–103, 151–156
    ROI and, 101–102
    Scrum, 125, 127, 189–190
    test-driven development, 123–124, 185,
        187–189
    time value of, 141
Blitz planning, 68
Bottom-up estimation, 113
Bug fixing, 51, 63, 100, see also Defect rate
Build automation, 64
Build-in instability, 26
Burn charts, 31
Burn down charts, 62
Business study, 27, 29
Business value, 8, 159–166, see also specific
    topics
    agile vs. traditional methods, 167–173
    benefits, 160–161
    comparison of agile methods, 67–73
    costs, 159–160
    customer collaboration and, 8
    formulas for, 185–191
    individuals and interactions and, 9
    maximizing, 1
    measures of, see specific measures
    NPV, 159, 163–164
    ROA and, 149–156, 159, 164–165
    ROI, 159, 161–162
    user stories, 121
    working software and, 9–10

C
Capability Maturity Model Integration®, 16,
    169, 170, 171, 172
Certification, 57
Certification teams, 39

Change, responding to, see Responding to
    change
Chaos theory, 13
Chief architects, 31
Chief programmer teams, 14
Chrysler Corporation, 4, 27
Class owners, 31
Closing process group, 46
Coaching, 57, 100, 146, 170, 175–176, 178,
    181
Coad, Peter, 30
Cockburn, Alistair, 31
Code analysis, 64
Code branches, 56
Code comments, 51, 79, 173
Code coverage metrics, 56
Code design, 51
Code generators, 64
Code interpreters, 63
Coding standards, 52, 56, 57, 79
Collaboration, 2, see also Customer
    collaboration
Collaboration tools, 56, 61, 62–63
Collaborative groups, 37
Collective ownership, 52
Commitment, 178
Communication, 5, 19, 45, 176, 180
    agile vs. traditional, 168
    with customers, 2, 36
    between developers, 37
    Extreme Programming, 27
    improved, 85
    project management and, 45
    quality of, 77, 121
    Scrum and, 26
    team, 62, 63
Complexity, 76, 177–178
Computer-aided manufacturing, 22
Computer-aided software engineering, 14
Computer-supported collaboration, 16
Computer-supported cooperative
    development, 15
Concept testing, 13
Concurrent engineering, 1, 20
Configuration management, 10, 14, 15, 22, 27,
    30, 55, 56–57, 67, 68
    tools for, 64
Construction, 51–52
Continuous improvement, 38

Continuous integration, 56, 57, 58, 68, 84, 93, 94, 123, 144, 151, 178, 187
   product maintenance and, 58
   testing and, 52–53
   tools for, 64
Contract closure, 46
Contract negotiation, 4, 7, 8, 77
Contracts, 3, 22
Cooperation, 180
Corrective action, 46
Cost efficiency, 21, 123–129
Cost of quality, 121–129, 141, 160–165, 167
Costs, 75, 76, 113–120, see also specific topics
   agile methods
      formulas for, 190–191
      traditional, vs., 167, 168–169, 170, 171, 172
   business value and, 159–160
   effort and quality measures and, 105
   estimation, 40, 113–120
   Extreme Programming, 116–117, 188–189
   metric for, 99–100
   NPV and, 102
   pair programming, 113–115, 185, 186
   ROA and, 102–103, 151–156
   ROI and, 101–102, 131–138
   Scrum formulas for, 118, 189–190
   surveys of agile methods, 85, 86, 87, 88, 89
   test-driven development, 115–116, 185, 187–188
Cost-schedule control systems criteria, 14
Craft industry principles, 13
Critical path method, 14, 21
Crosby, Philip, 15, 41
Cross-functional teams, 1, 20, 37, 38
Cross-platform integration, 56
Crystal Methods, 2, 16, 25, 31–32, 67
   business value from, 67
   emergence of, 3, 4, 7
   flexibility of, 70
   pros and cons, 69
   risks, 71
   usage, 72
Customer, onsite, see Onsite customers
Customer active paradigm, 20
Customer collaboration, 1, 2, 3, 4, 5, 7, 8–9, 13, 16, 17, 96, 149, 176, 177, 189, 190, see also Individuals and interactions; specific topics

agile vs. traditional, 168
benefits of, 101
comparison of agile methods, 67, 68
lean thinking and, 22
metrics and models, 76–77, 180–181
new product development and, 19, 20
onsite customers and, 36, 37
project management and, see Project management
software engineering and, 22
surveys of agile methods, 86
Customer feedback, 36, 77
Customer loyalty, 77
Customer needs, 1, 2, 149, 153, 169, 176
   capturing, 8–9
   Dynamic Systems Development and, 27
   onsite customers and, 35, 36
   pair programming and, 37
   project management and, see Project management
   release planning and, 40
   responding to change, 10
   software engineering and, see Software engineering
Customer requirements, 40, 56, 79, 169, 177–178, see also User stories; specific topics
   documenting, 15
   flexible, 27
   onsite customers and, 36
   pair programming and, 37
   project management and, 44
   user stories and, 44
   validation of, 38
Customer satisfaction, 3, 57, 77, 79, 101, 121, 167
   costs and benefits of agile methods, 91–97
   surveys of agile methods, 85, 86, 87, 88, 89
Customer trust, 77
Cycle time, 99
   surveys of agile methods, 85, 86, 87, 88, 89

D

Daily meetings, 30, 68
Daily operational builds, 56
Daily standup meetings, 16, 26
Daily standups, 2, 3, 31, 35, 37, 67, 68, 95, 146, 153, 189
   project management and, 45

Debugging, 51, 63
Defect costs, 185
Defect density, see Defect rate
Defect prevention, 38, 39, 52
Defect rate, 5, 21, 76, 79, 123–129
    agile methods, 191
        traditional methods vs., 169
    business value and, 160–165
    cost of, 116–120
    Extreme Programming, 189
    measures of, 105–111
    NPV and, 143–148
    pair programming, 186
    ROA and, 151–156
    ROI and, 132–138
    Scrum, 190
    test-driven development, 187
Deliverables, 46
De Luca, Jeff, 30
Design, 51
    tools for, 63
Design and build iteration, 27, 29
Design patterns, 16, 27
Development, evaluating software throughout, 35
Development costs, 99, 100, 113–120, 121–128, 159
    NPV and, 141–148
    ROI and, 132–138
Development managers, 31
Development tasks, 44
Development team, 35
Development tools, 61, 63
Diagrams, 31
Direct numerical control, 22
Discounting benefits, 171
Discount rate, 102, 103
Distributed teams, virtual, 179–180
Documentation, 2, 5, 22, 55–56, 78, 96, 123–129, 178–179
    agile vs. traditional, 168, 169, 170
    electronic, 68
    responding to change and, 10
    ROI and, 131–138
    software engineering, 49
    traditional methods, 3
    working software vs., 7, 9
Domain experts, 31
Domain object modeling, 30, 31
Double-loop learning, 80

Dr. Dobbs Journal, 85, 86
Dynamic analysis, 38
Dynamic Systems Development, 2, 7, 16, 25, 27, 29–30, 67
    business value from, 67
    emergence of, 3, 4, 7
    flexibility of, 70
    practices, 68
    pros and cons, 69
    risks, 71
    usage, 72

E
Earned value, 5
Earned value management, 2, 14, 62, 76
Eclipse, 63
e-commerce systems, 180
e-commerce web sites, 85
Education, 181
Effort, 75, 76
    measures of, 105–111
Egoless programming, 14
Electronic help, 56
End-user involvement, 37
Enhancements, 58
Escalation management, 30
Evolutionary development, 9
Excel formulas for business value, 185–191
Executing process group, 45
Executive involvement, 36
Experimental research, 91
Experimentation, 13
Extreme Programming, 10, 2, 16, 25, 27, 28, 67, 177, see also specific topics
    benefits of, 94, 95, 124–125, 126, 161, 169
    business value and, 67, 160
        formulas for, 185, 188–189
    capturing customer needs, 8–9
    costs of, 94, 95, 116–117, 160, 161, 162
    defect rate, 160
    emergence of, 3–4, 7
    flexibility of, 70
    individuals and interactions, 9
    measurement of, 105, 108–109
    measures of, 108–109
    NPV of, 144–146, 163, 171
    practices, 68
    productivity, 160
    project management and, 45
    pros and cons, 68–69

responding to change, 10
risks, 71
ROA of, 152–153, 154, 164, 172
ROI of, 134–136, 162, 170
software engineering, 50, 51
surveys of, 84, 86, 87, 88, 89
tools and technologies and, 61
total life cycle costs, 125
usage, 72
working software, 10

F
Facilitated workshops, 30
Failed projects, 3, 5
Feasibility study, 68
Feature build, 68
Feature Driven Development, 2, 16–17, 67,
     see also specific topics
  business value from, 67
  emergence of, 3, 4, 7
  flexibility of, 70
  practices, 68
  pros and cons, 69
  risks, 71
  surveys of, 86
  usage, 67
Feature planning, 68
Features, 8, 10
Feature sets, 31
Feature teams, 68
Feedback loops, 13
15-minute standup meetings, 9
Flexibility, 13, 20, 23, 27, 29, 190
  benefits of, 101
  comparison of agile methods, 70–71
  metrics, 80
  ROA and, 149–156
  surveys of agile methods, 86
  technological, 180
Flexible manufacturing system, 22
Flowcharts, 14
Ford, 22
14-day iterations, 9, 10, 68, 94
14-day sprints, 168
Fourth-generation languages, 15, 64, 180
Fowler, Martin, 27
Functional groups, 123–124
Functional model iteration, 27, 29
Functional silos, 9
Functional tests, 35

G
Gantt charts, 13–14
Government sector, 182
Graphical interfaces, 63

H
Help menus, 56
High-performance teams, 186
Human resources, 45
Hybrid agile methods, 177

I
IBM, 15–16, 31
IEEE standards, 2, 3, 56, 57, 58
Implementation, 27, 29
Incremental compilation, 63
Incremental development, 9
Individuals and interactions, 4, 7, 8, 9, 186, see
    also Customer collaboration
  metrics and models, 77–78
  tools and technologies and, 61
Inflation, 141, 171
  ROA and, 149, 151–156
Information distribution, 45
Information sharing, 62
Information systems flexibility, 15
Initiating process group, 44, 45
Innovation, 1, 13
Inspection, 14, 31, 35, 67, 69, 71
Intangible benefits, 100–101, 121,
    167
Integrated product teams, 20
Integration, 51
Integration testing, 68
Interaction frequency, 77
Interim work product, 46, 58
Internet, 16
Internet time, 16, 25, 27, 96
ISO standards, 56, 58
Iteration planning, 10, 31
  project management and, 44–45, 46
  quality assurance and, 57
  tools for, 62
Iterations, 28, 168
  14-day, 9, 10, 68, 94
  metrics for, 78–79
  project management and, see Project
    management
  release planning and, 40
  small, 68

Iterative development, 1, 2, 3, 5, 9, 13, 16, 17,
        31, 96, 149, 159, 173, 176, 177, 189,
        190, see also specific methods; specific
        topics
    Dynamic Systems Development and, 30
    Extreme Programming and, 27
    lean thinking and, 23
    metrics and models for, 180–181
    new product development and, 19, 20
    practices, 67, 68
    project management and, see Project
        management
    refactoring and, 39
    Scrum and, 26
    software engineering and, 22
    test-driven development and, 38
    tools and technologies and, 61

J
Japan
    new product development, 26
    product development principles, 16
Jeffries, Ron, 27
Joint Application Design, 15, 87
Joint Application Development, 87–88
Judo strategy, 16, 27, 96
Just-in-time, 22
Just-in-time electronic documentation, 68
Just-in-time evolution, 27
Just-in-time training, 181

K
Kaizen, 39, 41
Key management ratios, 99
Krafcik, John, 22

L
Lead programmers, 31
Lean development, 25
Lean thinking, 19, 22–23
Life cycles, 22

M
Maintenance, 55, 56, 58–59, 178–179
Maintenance costs, 99, 100, 101, 113–120,
        128, 185
    agile methods, 191
    Extreme Programming, 189
    NPV and, 141–148

    pair programming, 186
    ROI and, 132–138
    Scrum, 189
    test-driven development, 187
Management information crisis, 22
Management information systems, 15
Manager involvement, 36
Manufacturing metrics, 3
Marketing, 13, 20
Maturity grid, 15
Mean time between failures, 76
Measures of agile methods, 105–112
Mentoring, 100, 170, 175–176, 178, 181
Message board, 62
Metaphors, 50–51, 56, 57, 68, 84, 178
Metrics and models, 75–81, 180–181
    customer collaboration, 76–77
    individuals and interactions, 77–78
    responding to change, 79, 80
    traditional measures, 75–76
    working software, 78–79
Microsoft, 16, 27, 96
    survey of agile methods, 84–85
Microsoft Excel formulas for business value,
        185–191
Military standards, 15, 56, 57, 78
Mistake proofing, 22
MIT, 20
    survey of agile methods, 84–85
Model-driven development, 27
Modeling, 30
Modeling tools, 63
Models, see Metrics and models
Monitoring process group, 45–46
Moore's Law, 180
Morale, 85, 100
Muda, 22
Multilearning, 26

N
Net present value (NPV), 76, 99, 102, 103,
        141–148, 149, 167, 185, see also
            specific methods
    agile methods
        formulas for, 190–191
        traditional methods vs., 171–172
    business value and, 159, 163–164
    Extreme Programming, 144–146, 188–189
    formulas for, 163

metric, 102
pair programming, 142, 143, 151, 185, 186
Scrum, 146, 189–190
test-driven development, 143–144, 185, 187–188
Netscape, 16, 27, 96
New product development, 1, 16, 19, 20, 79, 149, 168
ROI metrics, 99–104
Scrum and, 26
software engineering and, see Software engineering

O
Object-oriented design, 16, 31, 67, 68
Object-oriented methods, 3, 7, 22, 27
Ohno, Taiichi, 22
Online tools, 56
Onsite customers, 4, 27, 35, 37, 67–68, 134
Open source software, 2, 16, 25
Open source tools, 56
Open workspaces, 27
Operational iterations, 79
Organizational behavior, 13
Organizational teams, 26
Overhead, 159
Overlapping design, 20
Overlapping phases, 26

P
Pair programming, see also specific topics, 2, 4, 27, 35, 37–38, 67, 68, 94, 134, 144, 152
benefits of, 92, 122–123, 161, 169
business value and, 160, 185–186
costs of, 92, 113–115, 160, 161, 162
defect rate, 160
individuals and interactions and, 9
measurement of, 105, 106–107
measures of, 106–107
NPV and, 142, 143, 163, 171
productivity, 160
project management and, 45, 46
risks and, 71
ROA and, 131–132, 133, 150–151, 162, 164, 172
ROI of, 170
software engineering and, 52
total life cycle costs, 123

Participatory Design, 4, 13, 15, 16, 25, 27, 87, 88
usage of, 72
Peer review, 52, 123, 186
Performance reporting, 45, 46
People skills, 176
Plan-driven methods, 7, see also Traditional methods
Planning process group, 44–45
PMBoK, see Project management body of knowledge
Pragmatic programming, 25
Processes, 22
traditional methods, 3, 4
Processes and tools, individuals and interactions vs., 7, 9, see also Individuals and interactions
Process grid, 15
Process improvement, 15–16
Scrum and, 26
Process improvement models, 2
Process overhead, 123
Procurement planning, 45
Product backlog, 3, 8, 10, 26
onsite customers and, 36
project management and, 44
release planning and, 40
Product design, simplifying, 39
Productivity, 5, 75, 76, 79, 99, 101, 123–129, 159, 185, see also specific topics
agile methods, 191
business value and, 160–165
costs of, 113–120
costs and benefits of agile methods, 91–97
estimation, 40
Extreme Programming, 109
measures of, 105–111
NPV and, 143–148
pair programming, 186
ROA and, 151–156
ROI and, 132–138
Scrum, 170
surveys of agile methods, 85, 86, 87, 88, 89
test-driven development, 187
Product maintenance, 55, 58–59, see also Maintenance
Product owners, 3, 35, 36, 57, 136, 146, 153, 189
Profit, 121

Program evaluation and review technique, 14, 21, 40
Programmer, 9
Programming productivity, see Productivity
Programming style guides, 52
Project charters, 44, 45
Project closure, 46
Project coordination, project management and, 45
Project execution, 45
Project failure rates, 168
Project life cycle, 2
Project management, 14, 22, 30, 79, 96, 170, 181, 186, 187
    adaptive framework, 159
    agile, 43–48
    evolution of, 13–14
    tools for, 62
Project management body of knowledge (PMBoK), 14, 43–48
Project Management Institute, 14
Project management system, 31
Project managers, 9, 31, 68
Project planning, 10, 30
Project plans, 1, 2, 9, 10, 22, 26, 40, 44, 45, 56, 79, 123–129, 178
    responding to change vs., 8, 10
    Scrum, 3
Project success, 5, 79, 83, 86, 89
    agile vs. traditional methods, 3
Project teams, 46
    project management and, 45
Prototyping, 30, 67, 68
Pull methods, 20, 22, 169
Push methods, 20

Q

Qualitative research on costs and benefits, 91
Quality, 1, 31, 41, 76, 100, 178, 191
    agile vs. traditional methods, 169, 170, 172
    controlling, 15
    cost of, 121–129, 141, 160–165, 167
    costs and benefits of agile methods, 91–97
    measures of, 105–111
    ROA and, 151–156
    ROI and, 132–138
    surveys of agile methods, 85, 86, 87, 88, 89
    testing and, 52

Quality assurance, 14, 15, 22, 35, 38, 39, 46, 55, 57
    project management and, 45
Quality control, 2, 38, 69, 71
    pair programming and, 37
Quality estimation, 40
Quality management, 30
Quality of work life, 88
Quantitative research, 83, 91
Quick release, 85

R

Rally, 62
Rapid Application Development, 2, 3, 7, 15, 16, 25, 27, 30–31, 87
Rapid development methodologies, 7, 13, 22
Rapid prototyping, 15
Rational Unified Process, 25
Real options analysis (ROA), 99, 102–103, 149–157, 167, 185, see also specific methods
    agile methods
        formulas for, 190–191
        traditional methods vs., 172–173
    business value and, 159, 164–165
    Extreme Programming, 152–153, 154, 188–189
    formulas for, 164
    metric, 102–103
    pair programming, 150–151, 185, 186
    Scrum, 153, 155, 189–190
    test-driven development, 151–152, 170, 185, 187–188
Refactoring, 4, 35, 39–40, 58, 67, 68, 144
    software engineering and, 52
Reflection, 31
Regression testing, 28, 38, 68, 93
Relationship strength, 77
Release planning, 2, 4, 10, 27, 28, 35, 40, 56, 57, 67, 68, 79, 80, 94, 134, 172, 178, 189
    documentation, 56, 57
    flexibility and, 70
    project management and, 43, 44, 45, 46
    quality assurance and, 57
    software engineering, 50, 51
    tools for, 62
Release plans, 3, 10, 31
Reliability, 76, 178

Repairs, 58
Requesting seller responses, 45
Requirements, 3, 50–51
Requirements documents, 2, 9, 77
Requirements management, 170
Requirements prioritization, 30
Requirements specifications, 50, 168
Responding to change, 1, 4, 5, 7, 8, 10, 16,
        17, 65, 121, 153, 159, 176, see also
        Adaptability; specific topics
    lean thinking and, 23
    metrics and models, 79–80
    new product development and, 19,
        20
    ROA and, 149–156
    software engineering and, 22
Retrospectives, 2, 26, 38, 67
Return on investment (ROI), 76, 99–104,
        131–139, 141, 149, 167, see also
        specific topics
    agile methods
        formulas for, 190–191
        traditional methods vs., 170–171
    benefits, 91–97, 99, 100–101
    business value and, 159, 161–162
    costs, 91–97, 99–100
    Extreme Programming formulas for,
        188–189
    formulas for, 162
    metric, 101–102
    NPV, 99, 102
    pair programming, 131–132, 133, 185,
        186
    ROA, 99, 102–103
    Scrum, 136–137, 189–190
    test-driven development, 132, 134, 185,
        187–188
Reusable frameworks, 63
Reuse libraries, 63
Revenue, 121
Risk control, 45, 46
Risk factor
    agile methods, 191
    Extreme Programming, 189
    pair programming, 186
    Scrum, 190
    test-driven development, 188
Risk management, 30, 67
Risk planning, 45

Risks
    comparison of agile methods, 71–72
    estimating, 185
    ROA and, 103, 149–156, 172, 173
    spreading over time, 159
ROI, see Return on investment

S
Scalability, 87, 177–178
Schedule, 75
    costs and benefits of agile methods, 91–97
Scheduling, tools for, 62
Schwaber, Ken, 25
Scientific management, 13–14, 19
Scope statements, 44, 45
Scope verification, 46
Scrum masters, 57, 153
Scrum, 2, 10, 25–27, 67, see also specific topics
    benefits of, 95, 125, 127, 161, 169
    business value from, 67, 160, 185, 189–190
    capturing customer needs, 8
    cost, 95, 118, 160, 161, 162
    defect rate, 160
    emergence of, 4, 5
    flexibility, 70
    individuals and interactions, 9
    measurement of, 105, 109–110
    measures of, 109–110
    NPV of, 146, 163, 171
    onsite customers and, 36
    pair programming and, 37
    practices, 68
    product development and, 16
    productivity, 160
    project management and, 45
    pros and cons, 68, 69
    refactoring and, 39–40
    release planning and, 40
    responding to change
    risks, 71
    ROA of, 153, 155, 164, 172
    ROI of , 136–137, 162, 170
    software engineering, 50
    surveys of, 87, 88, 89
    test-driven development and, 38–39
    tools and technologies and, 61, 62
    total life cycle costs of, 125
    usage, 72
    working software, 10

Selecting sellers, 45
Self-chosen tasks, 27
Self-determined groups, 37
Self-organizing groups, 37
Self-organizing teams, 9, 26, 136, 146, 153, 186, 189
    project management and, 45, 46
Side-by-side programming, 31
Simple designs, 51, 84, 173, 178
Simultaneous engineering, 20
Size, 75, 76
Small releases, 28
Social networking sites, 62–63
Software architecture, 50–51
Software Capability Maturity Model(r), 2, 3, 16
Software construction, 51–52
Software crisis, 14
Software design, 51
Software engineering, 1, 14, 19, 21–22, 49–54
    architecture, 49–50
    construction, 51–52
    defined, 49
    design, 51
    requirements, 49
    testing, 52–53
Software engineering body of knowledge, 15, 22, 49, 51, 52
Software engineering standards, 2
Software life cycle, 15, 55
Software methods, 14–15
Software process improvement, 15–16
Software project management, 19, 21, see also Project management
Software requirements, 50
Software standards, 15
Software testing, 52–53, see also Testing; specific types
Source code changes, 56
Source code comments, 51
Spike, 28
Spiral development, 9
Sprint backlog, 26, 40
Sprint planning, 3, 26, 40, 57, 68, 79, 80, 95, 136, 146, 153, 172, 178, 189
    documentation and, 56, 57
    project management and, 43, 44, 45, 46
    software engineering, 50
Sprint retrospectives, 26, 95, 146, 153, 189

Sprint reviews, 3, 8, 26, 67–68, 146, 153
Sprints, 2, 3, 26, 68
    14-day, 168
    30-day, 3, 9, 10, 38, 39, 40, 95136, 146, 168, 169
Standards-setting bodies, 182
Standish Report, 83
Standup meetings, 39, 16, 26
Standups, daily, 2, 3, 31, 35, 37, 45, 67, 68, 95, 146, 153, 189
Stepwise refinement, 14
Story points, 113
Structured analysis, 14, 39
Structured design, 14, 39
Structured methods, 22
Structured programming, 14, 39
Subcontracting, 45
Subtle control, 26
Support processes, 55–60, see also specific processes
    configuration management, 55, 56–57
    documentation, 55–56
    product maintenance, 55, 58–59
    quality assurance, 55, 57
    verification and validation, 55, 57–58
Support tools, 61, 63–64
Surveys of agile methods, 83–90
Sustainability, 121
Sutherland, Jeff, 25
Sync-and-stabilize, 16, 25, 27, 84, 86, 96
System dynamics, 80
System metaphors, 50–51
System quality, 167
System testing, 68, 132
Systems analysis, 20
Systems engineering, 1, 19, 20–21, 178
Systems engineering body of knowledge, 21
Systems theory, 13, 80

T

Tangible benefits, 100–101, 121, 167
Taylor, Frederick, 14
Team coding standards, 84
Team development, project management and, 45
Teams
    metrics for, 78
    tools for managing, 62, 63

Teamwork, 1, 2, 3, 5, 13, 16, 17, 96, 121,
    149, 176, 177, 185, 186, 189, see also
    Individuals and interactions; specific
    topics
  benefits of, 101
  comparison of agile methods, 67, 68
  Dynamic Systems Development and, 30
  Extreme Programming and, 27
  lean thinking and, 23
  metrics and models for, 180–181
  new product development and, 19, 20
  pair programming and, 37
  project management and, see Project
    management
  Scrum and, 26
  software engineering and, 22
  tools and technologies and, 61
Technological flexibility, 180
Technologies, agile, 61, 64–65
Test cases, 93
Test-driven development, 4, 27, 35, 38–39, 52,
    56, 67, 68, 94, 134, 144, 152, 178, see
    also specific topics
  benefits of, 93, 123–124, 161, 169
  business value and, 160, 187–188
  costs of, 93, 115–116, 160, 161, 162
  defect rate, 160
  measurement of, 105, 107–108
  measures of, 107–108
  NPV of, 143–144, 163, 171
  productivity, 160
  risks and, 71
  ROA of, 151–152, 164, 172
  ROI of, 132, 134, 162, 170
  total life cycle costs, 124
Testing, 14, 14, 30, 52–53, 123, 170, see also
    specific types
  Dynamic Systems Development and, 27
  tools for, 62, 63, 64
Testing documentation, 123
Testing productivity, 123
Test planning, 56
Test plans, 123
Test procedures, 38
Third-generation languages, 64, 180
30-day sprints, 3, 9, 10, 38, 39, 40, 95, 136,
    146, 168, 189
Time boxing, 30, 79
Time-to-market, 88, 89

Time value of benefits, 141
Time value of money, 102, 103, 172
  ROA and, 149, 151–156
Together Soft's Control Center, 31
Tools, 22, see also Processes and tools
  collaboration, 61, 62–63
  development, 61, 63
  support, 61, 63–64
  traditional methods, 3, 4
  workflow, 61, 62
Tool support environments, 30
Top-down estimation, 113
Total cost of ownership, 121, 141, 167
Total life cycle benefits, 99, 122–128, 161
Total life cycle costs, 99, 101, 115–120,
    121–129, 168
  business value and, 159–165
  effort and quality measures and, 105
  NPV and, 141–148
  ROA and, 151–156
  ROI and, 131–138
Toyota Production System, 22
Traditional methods, see also specific topics
  benefits, 169–170
  business value of, 76, 159–165
  capturing customer needs, 8
  closing processes, 46
  costs, 168–169
  costs and benefits of agile methods vs.,
    91–97; see also Benefits; Costs
  emergence of agile methods and, 3
  measures of, 105–111
  new product development, 20
  NPV, 141–148, 171–172
  project management and, see Project
    management
  project success, 3
  project teams, 9
  refactoring and, 39
  responding to change, 10
  risks, 71
  ROA and, 151–156, 172–173
  ROI and, 131–138, 99–104, 170–171
  software engineering and, see Software
    engineering
  support processes, see Support processes
  surveys of, 83
  tools and technologies, see Technologies;
    Tools

Traditional methods (*continues*)
   total life cycle costs, 123–129, 131–138
   values, 3
   working software vs., 9–10
Training, 57, 178, 181
Trust, 2, 63, 77, 78, 180
Turnkey systems, 180
Turnkey web solutions, 64, 65

U
Unit testing, 38, 39, 51, 56, 62, 64, 93, 132
   simple design and, 51
University of Maryland University College
      survey of agile methods, 85–86
Upgrades, 58
Upper management commitment, 15
Usage, comparison of agile methods, 72–73
Usage testing, 38
U.S. Department of Defense, 20, 21, 22
   standards, 56, 57
User cooperation, 56
User involvement, 15
User stories, 2, 4, 27, 28, 56, 57, 79, 80, 151,
      168, 169, 173, 176, 178, see also
         specific topics
   business value of, 121
   cost estimation and, 113
   customer collaboration, 9
   decomposing, 44, 50
   onsite customers and, 35
   product maintenance and, 58
   project management and, 44, 45
   quality assurance and, 57
   release planning and, 40
   software engineering and, 50, 51, 52
   tools for, 62
   verification and validation and, 58
   working software, 10

V
Validated iterations, 79
Validation, see Verification and validation
Values of agile methods, 7–11, see also specific
      values

customer collaboration, 7, 8–9
individuals and interactions, 7, 8, 9
responding to change, 7, 8, 10
working software, 7, 8, 9–10
Values-driven thinking, 176–177
Verification and validation, 35, 38, 52, 53, 55,
      57–58, 169, 170, 171, 178, 187
Version control, 56, 57, 68
Version One, 62
   survey of agile methods, 88–89
Video conferencing, 62, 63
Virtual distributed teams, 179–180
Virtual software design and development, 62
Visual editors, 63
Visual Studio, 63
Voice communications, 62, 63

W
Walkthroughs, 14, 68
Waste, 22
Waterfall, 20
Web hosting services, 64
What-if scenarios, 151
Wikis, 56
Work breakdown structure, 14, 44, 45
Workflow tools, 57, 61, 62
Working software, 7, 8, 9–10, 31, 96, 168, see
      also specific topics
   comparison of agile methods, 68
   maintenance of, 58
   metrics and models, 78–79
   onsite customers and, 36
   project management and, 46
   release planning and, 40
   ROA and, 149–156
   test-driven development and, 38
   tools for, 63

Y
Yahoo, 27, 96

Z
Zero defects, 2, 41